Demand Planning with SAP® APO— Concepts and Design

Avijit Dutta
Shreekant Shiralkar

Avijit Dutta and Shreekant Shiralkar
Demand Planning with SAP® APO — Concepts and Design

ISBN:	978-1-5084-3162-6
Editor:	Alice Adams
Cover Design:	Philip Esch, Martin Munzel
Cover Photo:	fotolia
Interior Design:	Johann-Christian Hanke

All rights reserved.

1st Edition 2015, Gleichen

© 2015 by Espresso Tutorials GmbH

URL: *www.espresso-tutorials.com*

Feedback
We greatly appreciate any kind of feedback you have concerning this book. Please mail us at *info@espresso-tutorials.com*.

To my wife, Mousumi, who stands by me
and our children Rishit and Rishav,
who make our life complete with joy & happiness.

Avijit Dutta

To my children Shashank and Rohan,
who are the driving forces in my life.

Shreekant Shiralkar

Table of Contents

Preface

Demand planning is an important process for supply chain management across businesses and has a significant impact on the overall efficiency of business operations. Demand planning in SAP APO is therefore, one of the most widely used modules.

The book revolves around a business scenario that requires demand planning design through SAP APO implementation. The scenario is realized progressively in chapters along with relevant concepts, business rationale, links to demand planning process flow, and the design.

The contents have been crafted for easy reading, learning, and practical application with the help of screenshots and illustrations. We recommend that readers simulate the business scenario in their SAP APO system using step-by-step procedures in the book to maximize their learning.

The book begins with an introduction to SCM and its key concepts in Chapter 1 covering supply chain planning and execution, challenges and trends, an introduction to the major SCM solutions in the marketplace, and how they enable SCM processes.

Chapter 2 explains how SAP APO enables SCM functions. The content focuses on SAP APO after an introduction to the different SAP SCM components and their functionality. We then briefly explain the business processes and functionality for different SAP APO modules. We also explain the SAP APO technical architecture and its integration to peripheral system.

Chapter 3 explains the business scenario that elaborates on the business context, challenges, and how APO DP could be a solution.

Chapter 4 explains the overall demand planning process flow that illustrates the design and deployment aspects of demand planning, including the integration of DP with APO BW and ERP. Each of the related processes/design is put onto blocks representing a uniform concept. Each of the blocks is explained in the chapter progressively with its relevance to the business scenario.

Chapters 5–8 explain the detailed design in APO BW, ERP, and APO DP in accordance with the overall demand planning process flow and the example business scenario. We also explain the concepts and business rationale for the choice of a specific design.

In Chapter 5, we explain the APO BW design that lays the foundation for gathering and loading sales history to APO DP.

In Chapter 6, we explain the design in ERP through configuration, master data, and transactions that enable integration between SCM and ERP for APO DP.

In Chapter 7, we explain the basic and foundational design in APO DP and in Chapter 8, we explain advanced design in APO DP, i.e., forecast profile, alert profiles, and macros.

Finally, we provide a set of appendices to complement the contents in the book and application of the learning on an SAP APO system. We have also included data in the appendix relating to the business scenario for its use in developing the design in the SAP APO system.

The book contents will serve the interests of beginners, who wish to understand and apply demand planning; as well as experienced professionals who want to enhance their knowledge of demand planning in SAP APO.

The sequel to this book is called *Demand Planning with SAP APO — Execution* that builds on the contents in this book and covers the execution aspects of APO DP. We recommend that our readers refer to the sequel book to complete their APO DP knowledge.

We would like to take this opportunity to express our sincere gratitude to Mukesh Kumar, who validated and reviewed contents of the book. Mukesh is an SCM professional with extensive experience in APO and ERP and currently works for a global consulting organization.

We would also like to thank Martin Munzel, Alice Adams, Johann-Christian Hanke, and the entire Espresso Tutorials publication team for their unflinching support during development of the book from its conceptual stage.

We sincerely hope readers will have a good reading experience and the book will benefit them in applying learning into practice. Only then will our efforts prove their worth. We wish our readers happy reading.

We have added a few icons to highlight important information. These include:

Tips

Tips highlight information concerning more details about the subject being described and/or additional background information.

Examples

Examples help illustrate a topic better by relating it to real world scenarios.

Attention notices

 Attention notices draw attention to information that you should be aware of when you go through the examples from this book on your own.

Finally, a note concerning the copyright: All screenshots printed in this book are the copyright of SAP SE. All rights are reserved by SAP SE. Copyright pertains to all SAP images in this publication. For simplification, we will not mention this specifically underneath every screenshot.

1 Introduction to SCM

Demand Planning (DP) is a key supply chain planning function that integrates and interacts with other functions of supply chain management (SCM) on continuous basis. This chapter focuses on explaining SCM in general to facilitate the context of understanding DP as we progress through the chapters of this book. This chapter focuses on both the general understanding of SCM from business perspective and SCM as an IT solution.

We will begin by introducing SCM and its key aspects in terms of supply chain planning, supply chain execution, challenges, and trends. Additionally, we will briefly mention major SCM solutions that exist in the marketplace and how they benefit SCM in business.

Supply Chain Management (SCM) is a key lever for most companies because it is one of the aspects that determine competitiveness. SCM is more relevant in the current climate in which circumstances are more dynamic and have more uncertainties than ever before.

In this chapter we explain SCM, as SCM forms the context and reason for Demand Planning; in other words, proper demand planning contributes to SCM. Demand planning itself does not operate in isolation in respect to other supply chain functions as it is continuously impacted by the other functions in the supply chain. Therefore, in order to focus and understand demand planning it is essential to understand SCM; because it is in this SCM space that demand planning makes its mark (i.e., takes inputs and provides outputs back to SCM). To ensure successful demand planning, we need to be sensitive to the factors in the supply chain that can potentially impact demand planning and consequently, supply planning as companies continue to struggle to adjust supplies and production in highly volatile market dynamics. We will, therefore, dedicate this chapter to SCM for your generic understanding.

SCM is a well-researched, heavily experimented field of management and is explained by consultants, academicians, business professionals, and management experts in many ways from many different perspectives. SCM is often identified with *Logistics Management*, *Supply Network Management*, and so on. From a software applications perspective, SCM may imply only the supply chain planning aspects and not supply chain execution. For our purposes, we will view SCM in this chapter from the business perspective as articulated in the definition below. We will use the term *chain* to mean *network*. Also, we will view the business interpretation of SCM as both planning and execution unless we specifically mention a particular technical SCM solution. For example, SAP SCM will mean the SCM solution offered by SAP that does not really include all aspects of business-oriented SCM. We will explain this more in detail as we progress.

SCM is the management of the products, services, financials, and information across the entire network of business entities, processes, and partners.

Partners represent business associates

 Partners represent business associates like suppliers, customers, service providers, distributors, wholesalers, retailers, subcontractors, bankers, and transporters.

SCM strives to achieve the following:

- ▶ Increase Return on Investments (ROI)
- ▶ Lower Total Cost of Ownership (TCO)
- ▶ Increase customer satisfaction
- ▶ Increase employee satisfaction
- ▶ Increase shareholders value creation
- ▶ Achieve harmony with the extraneous stakeholders, i.e., society at large, environment, etc.
- ▶ Attain sustainable competitive advantages

In the 1980s, SCM was mostly focused on cost control and quality management. This was mainly because of corporate restructuring and foreign competition that warranted a lean supply chain.

In the 1990s, SCM focus was on the global market and customers; thanks to globalization. Quality and cost focus of the 1980s were not enough as companies had to consider service level, custom built products, and delivery.

In the 2000s, there was an unprecedented growth of the Internet and its influence impacted everything including SCM. The onslaught was so sudden and rapid that companies took to all types of experimentation to survive. The emergence of business-to-business (B2B) e-commerce and business-to-customer (B2C) e-commerce redefined SCM and spread to the arena of the Internet with a focus on automation.

E-commerce: a trade in electronic mode

 E-commerce represents the trade carried out in electronic mode. With advent of the Internet and digitization of business processes, this mode of trade has a huge influence on the marketplace today.

Today, we encounter emerging niche technologies like big data, cloud computing, internet of things, mobile applications, social media, high definition analytics, and in-memory computing. These technologies are connecting, collaborating, and digitizing the world like never before and consequently, are impacting SCM. From a business perspective, SCM is no longer looked at only from cost saving standpoint, but also from the perspective of extracting competitive advantage and increasing service level.

In essence, the supply chain is continuously evolving from a more inward and close-knit business phenomenon to a more outward, collaborative and multi-faceted revolution. SCM itself has necessitated the introduction of new technologies. Similarly, the advent of new technologies is influencing the way supply chains or networks are constructed.

Companies have to keep pace with the uncertainties and changes in SCM and adopt supply chain management as part of their overall business strategy. SCM needs to assess and improvise, keeping in mind the challenges and trends. This initiative has to be adopted as a culture in the company and that is possible only when SCM awareness is spread and buy-in is obtained across the company. To succeed and succeed vigorously, companies must embrace SCM involving all stakeholders at all levels of the company.

In the following sections, we will explain the key aspects of SCM and SCM solutions.

1.1 Key aspects of SCM

We noticed that SCM is continuously evolving due to market dynamics and internal activities. It is therefore essential to understand what constitutes SCM, what challenges SCM faces that justifies the way SCM is the way it is, what trends exist in SCM, and what trends continue to shape SCM.

Functionally, SCM implies both supply chain planning, as well as supply chain execution.

Supply chain is exposed to different challenges, e.g., business challenges, technical challenges, regulatory challenges. Just as supply chain is laden with challenges, so also is SCM.

Trends are patterns and inclinations that make a collective impact. SCM is also, not independent of trends. Numerous trends influence SCM and will potentially influence SCM in the near future. In this section, we will explain these aspects.

1.1.1 Supply chain planning

Supply chain planning is the part of SCM that deals with the planning of supply chain activities.

In a typical manufacturing supply chain planning set up, we do sales planning for the finished goods through forecasting. Based on the forecast and actual sales, we carry out supply planning at the retail centers which in turn, generates dependent demand at the supplying distribution centers. Based on the dependent and independent demand at supplying distribution centers, we carry out supply planning. Likewise, we do demand and supply planning for the entire supply chain network. Additionally, we do transportation planning for the entire network.

Eventually, dependent demand and independent demands accrue to the manufacturing plants, where we do production planning for the finished goods. Next, production planning for the finished goods at the manufacturing plant triggers demand and supply planning for the entire bill of materials including assemblies, components, raw materials, etc. At the lowest level, supply planning for raw materials or packaging materials gives rise to procurement plans for procuring the raw materials or packaging materials from suppliers. Additionally, we also carry out service planning and subcontract planning for services and subcontracting materials respectively. Furthermore, at the manufacturing plant, we carry out synchronized capacity planning as part of detailed scheduling.

Supply chain planning varies from network to network, from company to company, etc. Every company and its supply chain have unique supply chain planning. Efficient supply chain planning aligns with appropriate supply chain strategy and supply chain execution. This alignment in turn ensures interactions at all levels in order to lower total cost of ownership, increase customer service levels, and increase return on investment.

Typical supply chain planning activities

 The typical supply chain planning activities involved in a supply chain network are: demand planning, supply network planning, production planning, transportation planning, inventory planning, procurement planning, quality planning, maintenance planning, etc.

1.1.2   Supply chain execution

Supply chain execution is the part of SCM that deals with execution of supply chain activities.

In a typical manufacturing supply chain execution set up, we procure raw materials and services from suppliers and service providers respectively, carriers ship the raw materials to the manufacturer, manufacturers align with other departments and produce the assemblies and finished goods. Manufacturers interact with other market stakeholders (bankers, logistics service providers, etc.) and manufacture the finished goods.

Next, we allocate finished goods to the supply chain distributer through carriers. The distributer in turn distributes the finished goods for intermediate storage to the wholesaler. The wholesaler then distributes to the retailer and the retailer finally sells to the consumer. At times, we sell finished goods directly to the customer from manufacturing centers or distribution centers. The company also interacts with other stakeholders in the supply chain like bankers, insurance providers, government officials, etc.

Supply chain execution activities vary from network to network and from company to company. Every company and its supply chain have a unique supply chain execution process. Efficient supply chain execution devise and align with appropriate supply chain strategy and planning, and thereby, ensures interactions at all levels in order to lower the total cost of ownership, increase customer service levels, and increase return on investment.

Typical supply chain execution activities

 Typical supply chain execution activities carried out in a supply chain network are: purchasing, warehousing, manufacturing, subcontracting, transporting, selling, maintenance, and quality inspection.

1.1.3 SCM challenges

With so many uncertainties, complications, and costs involved, supply chain brings its own set of challenges to companies. We will explain some of the major supply chain challenges that companies face in the following section.

i) Dearth of supply chain visibility

With globalization, opening of new markets, increased complexities, etc. supply chain visibility is becoming increasingly difficult, rending companies with excess work in capital, inventory excess, stock outs, and miscommunication

ii) Decreased customer loyalty

Global business has become customer driven because there are so many options available to choose from in the market. This phenomenon is making it very difficult to retain continuous loyalty of customers over a period of time.

iii) Stretched supply chains with increased risk

Globalization and a quickly changing world order is stretching the supply chain and increasing its need to collaborate, innovate, and exhibit a high degree of responsiveness.

iv) Short product lifecycle

Product innovation has become the order of the day with new products appearing on the market, driven by customer demand or competition. There is no other way but to continuously research and innovate products in alignment with margins, quality, and customer expectations.

v) Improper synchronization of plan and execution

The success of any company depends on vision, i.e., foresight to see the future. We plan in a perfect world, but execute in the real world. The challenge remains that the success of any company depends to a large extent on how much we are able to reduce the gap between plan and execution. This is all the more relevant for SCM as it involves both planning and execution.

vi) Different supply chain facilities have conflicting priorities

Different departments, warehouses, centers etc. often have conflicting priorities.

Conflicting priorities amongst sales, purchasing, and manufacturing

 The sales department wants the manufacturing department to be stringent in terms of meeting delivery commitments, whereas the purchasing department wants the manufacturing department to be flexible towards delivery commitments to customers; as the supplier would like to have a buffer in making raw materials available for production supply, towards meeting uncertainties in supply lead time, etc. Similarly, the manufacturing department's objective of producing large batches to avoid stock outs and absorb capacity bottlenecks conflicts with storage departments and distribution centers objective of keeping minimal inventory.

---

vii) Ineffective capacity and asset utilization

Companies often end up with either overutilization or underutilization of capacities and assets due to improper planning and improper execution.

viii) Increased supply chain disruption

Supply chains face disruptions occasionally due to supply shortages, growing focus on greenhouse gas emissions, increased government regulations, increased product recalls, counterfeit products, quality issues, etc.

1.1.4 Trends in SCM

Multiple trends are reshaping supply chains and management of them. Some trends existed for many years, yet continue to be there and continue to influence SCM (e.g., globalization). New supply chain trends influence the way business is defined and the way companies are managed. We will explain some of the major trends that impact SCM in the following sections.

i) Opening up of protected economies

The decoupling of protected economies from government protection and widening the markets, albeit with new regulations and new culture, have brought new approaches to SCM.

ii) Globalization

The world has literally become a global village with its people as global citizens. This phenomenon has an enormous impact on supply chains in terms of availability of large networks, optimization based on multiple business options, global scope, increased complexities, and difference of culture, regulations, and language.

iii) Increased market consumption

With the advent of technology and flexibility of operations goods are being produced, distributed, and sold at a competitive quality and price. This phenomenon consequently increases market consumption. This behavior enables supply chain managers to devise new strategies for SCM.

iv) Networked and digitized world

The advent of new dimensions and emerging niche technologies like big data, cloud computing, social media, internet of things, high definition analytics, and in-memory computing are connecting, collaborating, and digitizing the world, thereby influencing the business, companies, and consequently SCM. This phenomenon warrants an SCM solution that is equipped with such technologies.

v) Increased government regulation and compliance

Increased emphasis on corporate social responsibility, environmental awareness, changing political world order, steep increase in global trade, and increased government regulation and compliance impacts supply chains with new and unknown challenges.

vi) Evolution of supply chain from linear processes to a network

Supply chains are being transformed from linear and sequential processes to global customer centric demand networks laden with uncertainties and complexities.

vii) Volatile global economy

The global economy is impacted by both real and virtual disruptions from unexpected sources. This necessitates that companies stay alert as they cannot afford to operate oblivious to global economic developments. This phenomena impacts supply chain planning and execution. Disruptions can range from natural disasters to global financial credit freezes. This type of environment makes supply chains vulnerable to unknown disruptions.

viii) Transition from linear supply chains to responsive and collaborative demand networks

Companies are transforming themselves from traditional linear and sequential supply chains, to more responsive and collaborative demand driven networks. These networks are proactively responding to shorter product lifecycles, triggers, etc. with customer centricity, agility, partner collaboration and in real time. Collaboration is both across networks, as well as across virtual communities

ix) Mobile supply chain

Using mobile phones and mobile applications has already taken a big leap and is very much in vogue. Also, the capabilities of mobile phones have massively improved. Meaning, anyone can stay connected. Mobile applications also provide a myriad of information and capabilities, e.g., data retrieval, event management, data capture and dispatch, progress tracking, host of reporting functionality. In this pursuit, SCM will not be left behind and work is already underway around making SCM mobile applications compliant. Logistics companies in particular will derive significant advantages in this development and it will drastically reduce the communication gap and thereby time and cost.

1.2   SCM solutions

In order to cope with the complexity of SCM and to get a first-hand competitive edge, it has become critical for the companies to select an Information Technology (IT) oriented SCM solution. Several of the ERP and SCM vendors have made significant investments in developing solutions that provide a wide range of SCM solutions for both planning and execution.

SCM: Not a panacea

SCM solutions are just an enabler and therefore, SCM solutions by itself should not be taken as a panacea for all supply chain challenges.

In order to tackle supply chain challenges head on, we need to ensure that we have absolute executive commitment, availability of resources, employee involvement, consulting partner's expertise and an alignment of: company vision and supply chain projects objectives. We explain below a snapshot of the major SCM solutions and their benefits.

1.2.1   Multiple SCM solutions

There are multiple SCM solutions available to choose from different SCM solution providers. Sometimes, we select a single and comprehensive SCM solution and sometimes, we select a combination of solutions. We will explain three of the major SCM solutions in the following section.

SAP SCM

The *SAP SCM* application automates customer-oriented business processes across the entire supply chain network. This application is powered by state-of-the-art NetWeaver technology and helps integrate the company functions running on SAP, as well as non-SAP technology. The SAP SCM application helps organizations realize maximum return on investment. The SAP SCM application helps companies with planning, coordination, partner collaboration, optimization, and execution. Thereby, enabling companies to stay ahead of the competition, respond to market sensitivities, stay customer-centric, and address SCM challenges head on with visibility throughout the network.

SAP is an ERP vendor that added an SCM solution to its product portfolio.

In SAP, we carry out supply chain execution activities like procurement, sales, production execution, shipment, accounting, costing, etc. in the ERP system; whereas we carry out supply chain planning activities like demand planning, supply network planning, production planning, scheduling, service parts planning, and transportation planning in the SAP SCM system. Nevertheless, the SAP SCM system also includes some execution activities like global availability checks, supply network collaboration, event management, and extended warehouse management that seamlessly integrates with the execution system (i.e. SAP ERP).

The SAP SCM solution consists of the following components:

▶ Advance Planner and Optimizer (APO) which includes the following modules: Demand Planning (DP), Supply Network Planning (SNP), Production Planning and Detailed Scheduling (PP/DS), Transportation Planning and Vehicle Scheduling (TP/VS), Global Available to Promise (GATP) and Service Parts Planning (SPP)
▶ Event Management (EM)
▶ Supplier Network Collaboration (SNC)
▶ Extended Warehouse Management (EWM)
▶ Forecasting and Replenishment (F&R)

Some of the components of SAP SCM are also available for standalone deployment, e.g., EM, SNC, EWM, F&R and APO.

SAP also offers a Sales and Operations Planning (S & OP) solution that is driven by HANA and is available on a cloud platform as one other SCM solution as part of Integrated Business Planning (IBP).

It is important to distinguish between the term *SCM* and *SAP SCM*. SCM refers to the general business term and it includes both supply chain planning and supply chain execution. SAP SCM is a product from SAP that covers the following planning and execution components:

- ▶ SCM planning components in SAP SCM are: APO (DP, SNP, PP/DS, TP/VS, SPP) and F&R
- ▶ SCM execution components in SAP SCM are: APO GATP, EM, EWM, and SNC

As for other core SCM execution areas, SAP provides an exclusive execution system, i.e., *SAP ERP system* as *SAP ECC (Enterprise Control Component)* to carry out core SCM executions, i.e., purchasing, sales, shipment, production, maintenance, inspection, inventory management, accounting, costing, etc. However, SAP SCM and SAP ECC remain tightly integrated with each other in real time.

SAP also provides other solutions like SAP Customer Relationship Management (CRM), SAP Supplier Relationship Management (SRM), and SAP Transportation Management (TM) which contribute to SCM activities and have seamless integration with SAP ERP, as well as SAP SCM.

We will cover SAP SCM and SAP APO in detail in Chapter 2.

Oracle SCM

Oracle is an ERP vendor that added an SCM solution to its product portfolio. Oracle provides its SCM solution suite either as modular deployments, or as integrated solution deployment. The *Oracle SCM* solution can help transform SCM and provides a competitive edge for the companies using it. The Oracle SCM solution is an open, integrated, and complete solution. Oracle SCM provides functionality ranging from demand to supply to product management and can deliver operational excellence to SCM.

JDA Supply Chain Planning and Optimization

The *JDA Supply Chain Planning and Optimization* solution suite provides supply chain planning and optimization for business processes spanning across the supply chain and thereby, provides a competitive edge for the companies utilizing it. The solution is available in modules and is still integrated. Because of this modularization, the implementation can be completed in phases based on business priorities.

There are numerous SCM solutions in the marketplace. Many of them provide specialized offerings, e.g., only warehouse management or only demand planning. Options are also available in terms of deployment, functionality, etc.

The decision to choose a particular SCM solution, depends on a myriad of factors, for example business requirements, budget, business objectives, process compliance, legal compliance, and most of all with buy-in from all stakeholders.

Solution choice driven by internal and external factors

The decision to choose a particular solution and particular vendor should be driven by internal factors, as well as external parameters like industry benchmarking, analysts feedback, etc. so that there is objectivity and potential competitive edge in the decision making process.

Finally, the choice of a particular SCM solution should be a business decision and not an IT decision. The decision must be in alignment with the objectives and vision of the company.

1.2.2 Benefits of supply chain solutions

i) Facilitates predictable execution

SCM solutions facilitate predictable execution to provide functionality to validate, simulate, and iterate.

ii) Demand and supply alignment

Aligns demand and supply management in a profitable way, so as to spur revenue growth and reduce total cost of ownership for the supply chain.

iii) Attains global supply chain pipeline visibility

Helps attain global supply chain pipeline visibility into risks, information, inventory, etc. thereby, helping to prevent supply chain disruptions.

iv) Decreases overall inventory and obsolescence

Proper demand and supply management optimizes inventory across the entire supply chain.

v) Increases supply chain efficiency

Increases supply chain efficiency through process automation, exceptions management, and optimized warehouse and lead time management.

vi) Improves planning accuracy

Improves planning accuracy through state-of-the-art technology, collaboration, and simulations.

vii) Reduces cycle time

Reduces cycle time through proper lead time management and by establishing supply chain visibility.

viii) Increases margins and reduces total cost of ownership

Increases the margins and reduces total cost of ownership by providing visibility, agility, and optimization.

ix) Increases customer satisfaction

Increases customer satisfaction by meeting delivery commitments, quality commitments, and by passing on benefits to the customer.

x) Improves partner collaboration

Improves partner collaboration by using web user interface and communication technologies embedded in the solution.

1.3   Summary

In this chapter, we introduced the concept of SCM both from business perspective, and from IT solution perspective in order to understand where demand planning fits into the big picture. We covered a general SCM framework in this chapter.

In this chapter, we explained the key aspects of SCM in terms of supply chain planning, supply chain execution, challenges, and trends in SCM. We also briefly explained the major SCM solutions that exist in the marketplace and the benefits that SCM solutions bring to the table.

In the next chapter, we will focus on the IT solutions for SAP SCM and SAP APO in particular before we delve into DP. We will take a closer look at APO in terms of the solution, business processes, and architecture. We will follow this approach because DP is a module that sits in the APO component of the SAP SCM solution. Hence, an understanding of APO will help us understand DP in a more structured manner.

2 APO as an SAP SCM solution

It is essential to understand and appreciate SAP APO and SAP SCM in general while learning about Demand Planning (DP). In this chapter, we will focus on the context of SAP SCM and SAP APO. DP is a module within APO wherein APO is a component of SAP SCM. DP takes its input from several other modules and components and vice-versa. The tasks and actions executed within DP have consequences on many functions of SAP APO and SAP SCM. For instance, the demand plan output from APO DP decides the supply network plan in APO SNP. Similarly, APO DP decides the production plan in APO PP/DS. The contextual knowledge of APO and SCM will essentially help understand and appreciate DP as we progress through this book.

We begin by introducing different components of SAP SCM and their functionality in brief. Next, we will focus on SAP APO, wherein we describe the different business processes that SAP APO espouses through its modules. We will explain different APO modules, their functionality, SAP APO integration to other systems, and an overview of SAP APO architecture.

SAP Supply Chain Management (SAP SCM) is the supply chain management solution from SAP that originally evolved from *SAP Advance Planning and Optimization* (APO) Version 1.1 in 1998. Thereafter, other components were also added to *SAP APO* and formed *SAP SCM*. SAP SCM exists as a combination of multiple components as shown in Figure 2.1.

Therefore, SAP SCM is a superset of SAP APO. It is important to note that SCM as a business term includes both supply chain planning, as well as supply chain execution activities. However, SAP SCM mostly centers on planning activities with SAP APO as its core component. Other select execution modules in SCM are EM, SNC, EWM, and APO GATP. The main SCM execution solution from SAP lies in the SAP ERP solution SAP ECC, which has logistics modules like sales and distribution, materials management, production execution, etc. SAP ECC also has planning components albeit with limited functionality.

SAP SCM facilitates planning, optimization, collaboration, tracing and tracking, and warehouse management for complete management of the supply chain. In the process SAP SCM helps companies improve their return on investment and total cost of ownership.

SAP APO is a state-of-the-art and sophisticated planning solution from SAP that synchronizes demand and supply planning in the entire network and carries out production planning for the entire bill of material structure. SAP APO is the planning and optimization solution in SAP.

DP is the demand planning module from SAP APO. DP integrates with other modules in APO and helps provide an integrated planning solution. Let's dive in and take a closer look at different components in SAP SCM, APO as an SAP SCM solution and different aspects of SAP APO.

2.1 SAP Supply Chain Management

The SAP SCM solution is an umbrella solution that primarily includes planning, as well as execution activities. SAP SCM seamlessly integrates with other major solutions and applications, e.g., SAP BI, SAP ERP, and non-SAP systems as shown in Figure 2.1.

In this section, we will review the different SAP SCM components and provide a brief explanation of each.

Advance Planner and Optimizer (APO)

APO is the advanced planning and optimization solution component in SAP SCM. We review it in detail in Section 2.2.

Supplier Network Collaboration (SNC)

SNC is an SAP SCM component that facilitates collaboration with internal and external partners in the supply network. With SNC, we can collaborate with suppliers, customers, and contract manufacturers. From a system integration perspective, SNC establishes seamless integration with SAP ERP, i.e., SAP core execution system through SAP Process Integration (PI) technology. Collaboration primarily uses web technology and warrants minimal investments from partners (i.e., only a web browser).

Collaboration with suppliers includes: purchase orders, advance shipping notifications, invoices, incoming shipments, release processing, Kanban, supplier managed inventories, replenishments, forecasts, etc.

Collaboration with customers includes: vendor managed inventories, forecasts, promotions, replenishments, and advance shipping notifications.

Collaboration with contract manufacturers includes: procurement, work orders, sub-contracting purchase orders, advance shipping notifications, invoices, incoming shipments, supply network, and inventories.

Extended Warehouse Management (EWM)

EWM facilitates flexible, automated, and optimized warehouse management support for multiple goods movement and inventory management activities for warehouses. EWM is particularly suitable for companies that have high volume goods movements, process-oriented storage control, complex warehousing activities, and complex goods movement networks. EWM increases warehouse management productivity and offers centralized warehouse monitoring.

EWM is primarily an execution-oriented module and includes planning activities as well. EWM seamlessly integrates with other logistics and fulfilment processes like transportation management, logistics execution, global trade management, global available to promise checks, and event management.

EWM carries out warehouse management activities for inbound processes, outbound processes, storage and operational processes. EWM also offers cross-functional warehousing activities such as resource and labor management, cross docking, yard management, material flow system, etc.

Event Management (EM)

EM facilitates visibility on processes, assets, and performances across the entire supply network through monitoring, notification, adjustment, collaboration, and analysis of business events.

EM is able to integrate and communicate across multiple technologies, architectures, and platforms and is in a position to provide seamless visibility for the entire business network for both supply chain planning and supply chain execution.

Forecasting & Replenishment (F&R)

F&R is the SAP Forecasting and Replenishment solution in the SCM space. F&R executes forecasting on a near real-time basis with the objective of maintaining an optimum inventory across distribution centers and retail stores across the entire supply network. This is coupled with automated multilevel replenishment planning and ordering capabilities of the goods to increase productivity, decrease order fulfilment costs, and increase service levels.

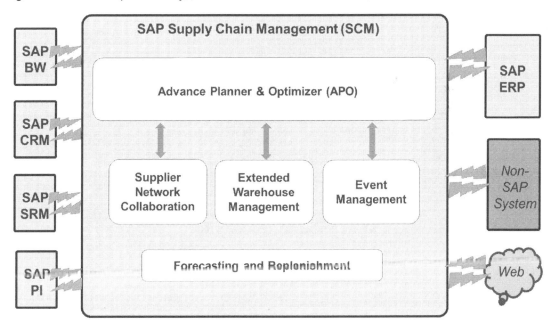

Figure 2.1: SAP SCM components and interfaces

All of the components explained above and shown in Figure 2.1 often interact with one another depending on the business requirements. Furthermore, the entire SAP SCM system integrates with the SAP ERP execution system, big time, for master and transactional data. SAP SCM also integrates with other SAP systems like SAP BW, SAP CRM, SAP

SRM, and SAP PI depending on the business need. SAP SCM can also integrate with web applications, as well as non-SAP systems.

2.2 SAP APO

SAP APO is the Advanced Planning and Optimization component of SAP SCM. The acronym APO stands for *Advance Planner and Optimizer*. SAP APO provides collaboration, planning, and optimization across the entire supply chain network.

APO: Not a standalone system

! APO cannot exist as standalone system, as it needs a backend ERP system for input data and also eventually to pass planning data back to the ERP system for execution.

SAP APO helps to address supply chain challenges by providing a robust and sophisticated planning solution.

SAP APO integrates seamlessly with other major components of SAP SCM as depicted in Figure 2.1. However, SAP APO also integrates with SAP systems, non-SAP systems, and the web as shown in Figure 2.2.

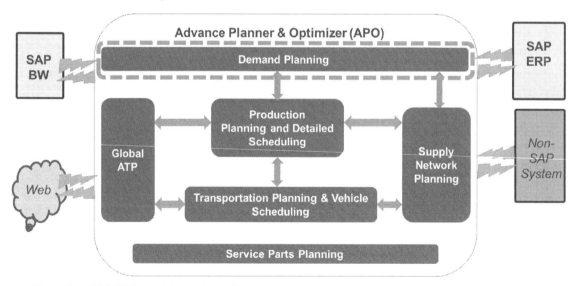

Figure 2.2: SAP APO modules and interfaces

It is important to understand that APO represents an advance planning and optimization component. This is precisely because we do get a miniature version of planning in ERP itself. The planning functionality in SAP ERP is quite generalized and is not as comprehensive as SAP APO. Needless to say, the SAP APO optimization functionality that reinforces the planning output does not exist in SAP ERP.

In this section, we will look at the different business processes and modules that pertain to SAP APO, the building blocks of SAP APO, its integration with the core execution system like SAP ERP, integration with different peripheral systems, integration with non-SAP systems, and finally SAP APO architecture.

2.2.1 Business processes and modules in SAP APO

SAP APO addresses multiple business processes through it modules, features, and functionality. Custom enhancements to SAP APO address specific business functionality needs for individual companies. In some instances, SAP APO co-exists with other technology applications that carry out very different business processes. We will look at some of the broad business processes that SAP APO handles in the following section and in Figure 2.3. This will also provide an understanding of the demand planning business process and DP module in the entire context of APO.

Let's take a closer look at Figure 2.3. At a very high level, there are five main entities in a supply chain: supplier, manufacturer, distributor, retailer, and consumer.

Please note that consumer is different from customer in the sense that the consumer is the one who finally uses or consumes the product and does not engage in moving products in the supply chain through selling or transporting. Customer in contrast is a relative term.

TV customer vs. consumer

 A TV manufacturer is a customer of the supplier of TV parts, the TV distributor is a customer of the TV manufacturer, and the TV retailer is a customer of the TV distributer. However, the person purchasing the TV in order to use it for watching at home is a consumer.

Typically, products and/or services flow from the supplier through the consumer as shown in the diagram in Figure 2.3.

Product demand comes from the consumer to the retailer and that constitutes *independent demand* of the product. That, in turn, creates *dependent demand* on the distributor. The distributor then creates dependent demand of the product to the manufacturer. However, independent demand can also come from other companies directly to the distributor or directly to manufacturer. The Demand Planning module in APO carries out the business process of planning independent demand. Using APO DP, we can carry out statistical forecasting, promotion planning, new product lifecycle planning, collaborative demand planning, etc.

Based on the planned independent demand explained above, actual independent demand in the form of sales orders and dependent demand arising in the supply network we can carry out the business process of supply planning to meet the total demand arising in the network. The *APO Supply Network Planning* (APO SNP) module handles the business process of supply planning and dependent demand generation for the network. Through APO SNP we can handle unconstrained supply network planning, constrained supply network planning, optimization, safety stock planning, deployment, transport load planning, etc.

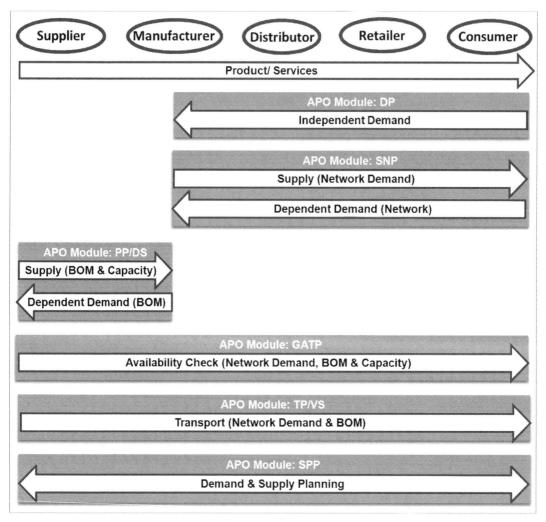

Figure 2.3: Business processes through SAP APO modules across the supply chain

Based on the product demand that accrues at the manufacturing plant out of the dependent, as well as independent demand, we can execute multi-level production planning for the *Bill of Material* (BOM) for the product. Execution of production planning for the product generates supply plans at various BOM levels. Every supply plan, in turn, creates a dependent demand for the assembly, or the raw material or packaging material. Every dependent demand in turn triggers its corresponding supply plan for the complete BOM. Supply plan can be in terms of production plan and/or capacity plan, or procurement plan, or subcontracting plan, as applicable, for the entire BOM. *APO Production Planning and Detailed Scheduling* (PP/DS) executes the business process of multi-level production planning and capacity planning for the BOM. Through APO PP/DS we can carry out constrained multi-level production planning, detailed scheduling for capacity planning, and optimization.

Based on actual demand in terms of sales order or stock transfer orders, etc. we can carry out the business process of availability check of the product from its stock or potential receipts (purchase orders, transfer orders, etc.). In a situation where demand is more than supply, we can do an availability check based on the appropriate supply allocation. In the event of product non-availability from a particular location, we can run an availability check on a substitute location or product. Also, we can do a component level stock availability check for a configurable assembly product. Similarly, we can do an availability check by triggering production planning and by doing a capacity check. Furthermore, we also have the option of carrying out back order processing based on revised business circumstances, priorities and criteria. APO Global Available to Promise (GATP) carries out the business process of availability checks for various business requirements as explained above. Through APO GATP, we can carry out standard availability checks, product allocation based checks, location substitution and product substitution based checks, multi-level component availability checks, production planning based checks, backorder processing, and forecast based checks for sales order consumption.

In the supply chain we can also do transportation planning and vehicle scheduling for shipping the product to the customer and also for obtaining raw materials and packaging materials from the vendor. We do the transportation planning and vehicle scheduling to optimize transportation loads and to optimize transportation costs. APO Transportation Planning and Vehicle Scheduling (TP/VS) carries out the business process transportation planning and vehicle scheduling in the supply chain.

Demand and supply planning for service parts warrants different planning approaches and methodology exclusive to the service parts industry. APO Service Parts Planning (SPP) carries out the business process of service parts planning for various business requirements. Through APO SPP we can carry out standard forecasting, inventory planning, distribution requirement planning, deployment, and inventory balancing.

This explains the broad business processes and solutions through the corresponding APO modules. In the next section, we will look at the building blocks of SAP APO.

2.2.2   SAP APO building blocks

The SAP APO building blocks consist of six modules: DP, SNP, PP/DS, GATP, TP/VS and SPP. In this section, we will briefly look at each of these modules and highlight the major functionality for each.

Demand Planning (DP)

Demand planning deals with process of generating and improvising the projected demand through sophisticated statistical tools and methods in APO. Major functionality includes:

▶   *Statistical forecasting*: Method of generating statistical forecast at a particular planning level based on sales history through time series method, causal method, or a combination of these two methods.

29

▶ *Product lifecycle planning*: Method of generating forecasts for a newly launched product through the product lifecycle.

▶ *Promotions planning*: Method of incorporating promotions for demand planning. Promotions could be a one-time event (e.g., a product launch offer), or a regular promotion (e.g., advertising campaigns).

▶ *Consensus planning*: Method of improvising the demand planning by consolidating inputs from various stakeholders, e.g., marketing, finance etc.

▶ *Sales and operations planning*: Method of generating constrained demand planning by taking different business constraints into account, e.g., supplier constraints, production capacity constraints, etc.

▶ *Collaborative demand planning*: Method of collaborating with stakeholders outside the organizational boundaries; e.g., collaborating with vendor or customer over web on demand plan sharing.

▶ *Characteristics-based forecasting*: Method of forecasting at the level of product characteristics. Typically applicable for configurable products.

Supply Network Planning (SNP)

Supply Network Planning deals with consistent global supply planning for the entire supply network integrating manufacturing, purchasing, distribution, and transportation. Major functionality includes:

▶ *Heuristics*: Method of unconstrained supply planning for the multi-site production, distribution, and retail network environment.

▶ *Capable to Match*: Method of constrained supply planning for the cross supply chain checks of capacity and material availability by considering predefined supply categorization and demand prioritization.

▶ *Optimization*: Method of constrained supply planning based on cost minimization through consideration of transportation cost, storage cost, production cost, handling cost, etc.

▶ *Deployment*: Method of replenishing stocking locations through a short-term solution of allocating available supply to demand when demand is more than supply.

▶ *Transport Load Builder*: Method of optimizing the transport loads by grouping transport shipments according to transport capacity.

Production Planning and Detailed Scheduling (PP/DS):

Production Planning and Detailed Scheduling deals with production and capacity planning by taking production constraints into consideration with the objective of increasing throughput and reducing inventory. Major functionality includes:

▶ *Production Planning*: Method of generating a short-term operations plan that matches overall production to demand. Generates supply elements like procurement proposals, planned orders, etc.

▶ *Detailed Scheduling*: Method of determining optimal production sequences by taking into account shop floor bottlenecks and production constraints.

▶ *Optimization*: Method of constrained production planning based on cost minimization through consideration of lead time, utilization, delay cost, set up cost, set up time, etc.

Global Available to Promise (GATP):

Global Available to Promise deals with an online availability check method to support the customer order fulfilment process by proposing a requested product at the required time, location, and desired quantity. Major functionality includes:

▶ *Product Availability Check*: Method of basic availability check for products in real time based on check rules for a customer orders, transfer orders, etc.

▶ *Forecast Check*: Method of availability check based on released forecast from demand plan.

▶ *Product Allocation Check*: Method of availability check based on the premise that products are allocated on fair share rule when demand is more than supply.

▶ *Rules Based ATP Check*: Method of availability check based on a rule that provides the option to choose alternate locations and alternate products.

▶ *Multilevel ATP Check*: Method of availability check that carries out multi-level component checks for a configurable product.

▶ *Capable to Promise Check*: Method of availability check that triggers the production planning and checks the production capacity.

▶ *Backorder Processing*: Method of re-determining availability check promise date, time, and quantity based on predefined priorities and changes in supply elements.

Transportation Planning and Vehicle Scheduling (TP/VS)

Transportation Planning and Vehicle Scheduling optimizes transportation loads and minimizes transportation costs. Major functionalities include: vehicle scheduling, transportation planning run (Heuristics), optimization run, dynamic route determination, and tender monitoring.

TP/VS made redundant by TM

 TP/VS has become somewhat redundant with the introduction of SAP Transportation Management (SAP TM).

Service Parts Planning (SPP)

Service Parts Planning deals with demand and supply planning for service parts. Major functionality includes:

▶ *Standard Forecasting*: Method of forecasting the demand using automatic selection of optimal statistical forecasting method.

▶ *Inventory Planning*: Method of stocking based on the trade-off between maximum service levels and lowest inventory cost. Carries out stock and de-stocking, safety stock calculation, and identifies economic order quantity.

▶ *Distribution Requirement Planning*: Method of supply planning based on requirements existing in the Bill of Distribution (BOD) network. BOD is the distribution location hierarchy.

▶ *Deployment*: Method of distributing materials in the BOD based on current requirements and available supply when demand is more than supply.

▶ *Inventory Balancing*: Method of transferring inventory between locations using paths other than BOD in order to balance inventories through a cost-benefit analysis.

2.2.3 Integration with the core execution system: SAP ERP

APO integrates seamlessly with ERP through the functional core interface (CIF). We execute CIF on establishment of RFC connections between SCM and ECC systems. We trigger CIF from the ECC system to APO for master data. However for transaction data, CIF triggers from both sides, i.e., from the ECC system to SCM and vice versa. CIF helps maintain consistencies between ECC and SCM.

We will cover the connectivity settings between ERP and APO in Section 6.2 and the CIF concept, settings, and execution in Sections 6.4 and 6.5.

2.2.4 Integration with the SAP peripheral system

APO integrates with the SAP peripheral system through the RFC connection between SCM and the particular SAP system as depicted in the schematic diagram in Figure 2.2.

APO integration to peripheral systems

APO can integrate with peripheral SAP BW through RFC. It can be integrated with other SAP systems like CRM, ECC, etc. in similar a mode.

2.2.5   Integration with non-SAP systems

Integration between APO and non-SAP systems can be done through custom ABAP inter-face development. This type of custom interface development is possible using *BAPIs (Business Application Programming Interface)* or *Application Link Enabling (ALE)*. Once we develop these interfaces, we can introduce data exchange between APO and non-SAP interfaces based on data mapping between the two systems.

In the next section, we will go into further detail on SAP APO architecture.

2.2.6   SAP APO architecture

APO architecture depicts the technical construct of the APO vis-à-vis other components and interfaces. The graphic depicted in Figure 2.4 provides an overview of the architecture of APO. APO carries out planning and optimization which deals with massive volumes of data and complex algorithms for processing. Therefore, APO requires a unique architecture that can handle large volumes of data, do faster processing, satisfy security demands, and cause minimal interruptions. This requirement is addressed by the LiveCache component of the architecture. Let's take a closer look at the concept of LiveCache.

LiveCache

LiveCache is a memory-oriented database that stores data either in time series or in order series primarily for transaction data in the APO and SCM systems. LiveCache makes use of plenty of database procedures. The LiveCache server is always stored on MaxDB, which is a database owned by SAP. LiveCache data is stored in Object Oriented Database Man-agement Systems (OODBMS), where data is identified as an object. This makes the navi-gation easier and faster. The LiveCache database with in-memory data storage provision and with OODBMS technology provides the ability to process: complex planning and opti-mization algorithms, voluminous data, and high runtime intensive tasks. This gives rise to a high level of performance that is unmatched when compared to a relationship-oriented da-tabase in ERP. In the case of an APO on HANA database, LiveCache can be chosen either as part of HANA database, or as part outside of HANA database, depending on the busi-ness requirement.

APO architecture

SAP APO architecture typically has three tiers with client-server-based interactions: the presentation layer, the application layer and the database layer, as depicted in Figure 2.4.

The *presentation layer* presents the SAP GUI (Graphic User Interface) to the user and al-lows users to interact with the SAP system. SAP GUI is the client for accessing SAP func-tions. SAP GUI interacts with SAP servers, extracts information, and displays it on the user interface. Similarly, it senses the data entered by the user and communicates back to the SAP servers.

The *application layer* processes the business logic received from the presentation layer and communicates it to both the database layer and the presentation layer. In APO, the application layer consists of the application server and optimization server. The application server processes the business logic pertaining to all APO planning activities. Optimization in APO is a heavy duty, performance intensive processing based on a complex algorithm of cost minimization, productivity maximization, etc. Therefore, optimization consumes a large amount of hardware resources and often relies on peak performance. Hence, this activity is carried out in a separate optimization server. The optimization server interacts with the servers in the database layer.

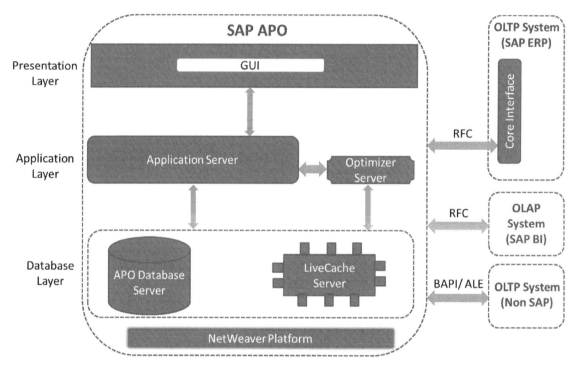

Figure 2.4: SAP APO architecture

The *database layer* stores the business data and APO application programs which are loaded to the application server and optimization server, on runtime. In APO we maintain a LiveCache server exclusive to the core APO Database server as shown in Figure 2.4. However, both the LiveCache server and APO Database server can be part of HANA database as explained earlier. The database server and the LiveCache server interact with the application layer in extracting and communicating data and information.

APO architecture is based on the SAP NetWeaver platform that supports a heterogeneous environment in both SAP and non-SAP systems. The SAP NetWeaver platform offers both a development and a runtime environment for SAP applications and it facilitates custom enhancements and integration to other SAP and non-SAP applications.

APO architecture provides a very high degree of flexibility, scalability, and performance. With the introduction of the Internet as middleware, APO architecture is often deemed a multi-tiered structure.

APO integrates with other SAP systems, e.g., OLTP (Online Transaction Processing) system SAP ERP or OLAP (Online Analytical Processing) system SAP BW through Remote Function Call (RFC). APO receives and transfers data to the core execution system like SAP ERP through a core interface. We will cover the connectivity settings between ERP and APO in Section 6.2 and the concept, settings, and execution of CIF in Section 6.4 and 6.5. APO can also be integrated with non-SAP systems through custom enhancements using BAPI (Business Application Programming Interface) or Application Link Enabling (ALE).

APO Architecture indeed has taken a leap with the advent of SAP SCM on HANA which brings in in-memory computing technology. With SAP SCM on HANA the ability to analyze and process massive quantities of data in local memory has increased multifold. Therefore, demand planning decisions on APO through APO DP has become more real time, faster, and more accurate.

2.3 Summary

In this chapter, we introduced SAP SCM with an emphasis on SAP APO, offerings, and architecture perspectives. We did this precisely because, as we proceed with introducing SAP DP with its functionality, business relevance, etc., it is essential that we understand the larger context of SAP SCM and in particular, SAP APO. This is because DP is part and parcel of SAP APO. In this chapter, we explained the different SAP SCM components and functionality in brief. Next, we focused on SAP APO, wherein we looked into the different business processes that SAP APO typically caters to with its modules. We explained the different APO modules and their corresponding functionality. Next, we will explain different integrations that happen with SAP APO and an overview of SAP APO architecture.

In the next chapter, we will introduce our business scenario, its challenges, the demand planning scenario, and how APO DP can provide a solution to the business challenges. We will use the business scenario through the remainder of the book to illustrate APO DP concepts, design, and execution.

3 Our business scenario

Demand planning is a business reality. The best way to understand demand planning concepts and design in APO is through a business example. Therefore, we will introduce a typical company with its business scenario, demand planning scenario, and challenges. Next, we will elaborate on APO DP as a demand planning solution that meets the business requirements of our typical company and addresses its challenges through its various solution elements.

We will reference the business scenario in this chapter in Chapter 4 through Chapter 8. This chapter will provide a central reference point as we demonstrate APO DP concepts and design across the following chapters.

In order to relate theory to various APO DP concepts, functions, and features, we will introduce a company called DM Consumer Appliances, Inc. with its business scenario and demand planning scenario in this chapter. We introduce the company in the form of a mini supply chain network with simple product demand and supply flow. We will incorporate the typical supply chain entities, e.g., consumers, retail stores, distribution centers, intermediate commercial customers in the form of wholesalers/ retailers and manufacturing plant. In order to explain the APO DP concepts it is essential that we follow a structured, business relevant, and a simple scenario. The emphasis on the simplicity of the business scenario is primarily to help you understand the concepts and applications of APO DP in a way that you can completely understand the ideas, approach, and methods behind the solution.

3.1 The business scenario: DM Consumer Appliances, Inc.

DM Consumer Appliances, Inc. is a consumer products company and produces medium size High Definition Television [HDTV] sets, with its head office in Atlanta, GA in the United States of America. DM Consumer Appliances, Inc. has a supply chain network with a manufacturing plant, distribution center, and retail stores as follows:

- ▶ *Atlanta Manufacturing Plant*, Atlanta, GA
- ▶ *Frankfort Distribution center*, Frankfort, KY
- ▶ *Columbus Retail Store*, Columbus, OH
- ▶ *Philadelphia Retail Store*, Philadelphia, PA

DM Consumer Appliances, Inc. has a single sales organization called DM Sales Org USA that represents its selling unit for its highest level of sales.

DM Consumer Appliances, Inc. sells its products in the unit of EA (Each) or PC (Pieces) with 1:1 relationship between EA and PC.

DM Consumer Appliances, Inc. sells its products through two distribution channels as follows:

Direct Sales:

► Direct sales to consumers through its *Columbus Retail Store*, or through its *Philadelphia Retail Store*.

► Direct sales to consumers through the web that is monitored and tracked from its Head Office in Atlanta, GA.

Indirect Sales:

► Sales through the *Frankfort Distribution Center* to its commercial customers like wholesalers or retailers, who in turn, sell to other retailers or directly to their consumers either over web or over point of sale.

► Sales through the *Atlanta Manufacturing Plant* to its commercial customers located in the vicinity of the manufacturing plant as its helps DM Consumer Appliances, Inc.'s customers' to save on logistical costs. Commercial customers like wholesalers or retailers, who in turn, sell to other retailers or directly to their consumers either over web or over point of sale.

Flow of demand from end customers, commercial customers, and their corresponding dependent demand generated in the supply chain network is illustrated in Figure 3.1.

DM Consumer Appliances, Inc. manufactures, distributes, and sells medium-sized LCD [Liquid Crystal Display] high definition televisions [HDTV] ranging in size from 32–40 inches and ranging in two resolutions, e.g., 720 pixels (abbreviated as 720p) and 1080 pixels (abbreviated as 1080p). The target market segment of DM Consumer Appliances, Inc. is household customers and sells its products under the brand name DM. DM Consumer Appliances, Inc. sells the following products that belong to the product group *LCD TVs*:

► *32" DM LCD 720p HDTV*
► *32" DM LCD 1080p HDTV*
► *39" DM LCD 1080p HDTV*

DM Consumer Appliances, Inc. is always in the leading edge of technology and therefore, decides to focus on the LED [Light Emitting Diode] TV market potential in the mid-size TV segment for household customers. *LED TVs* come with better picture quality and are lighter in weight; albeit at a higher cost. Therefore, DM Consumer Appliances, Inc. launches a 40 inch LED technology-based HDTV with a resolution of 1080 pixels under the same brand name DM for a new product group *LCD TVs as follows*:

► *40" DM LED 1080p HDTV*

The newly launched product brings additional choices to customers. DM Consumer Appliances, Inc. also sells its new product, i.e., *40" DM LED 1080p HDTV* to its household customers through the same distribution channels as those used by their LCD line of TVs. The newly launched product *40" DM LED 1080p HDTV* includes quickly changing technology, therefore, as compared to *LCD TVs* which is not evolving as fast, the *40" DM LED 1080p HDTV* product has a short lifecycle span of two years. Nevertheless, in order to keep up with the technological pace and trends, DM Consumer Appliances, Inc. will introduce different products with advance configuration in the range of *LED TVs* and plans to move ahead of its competition.

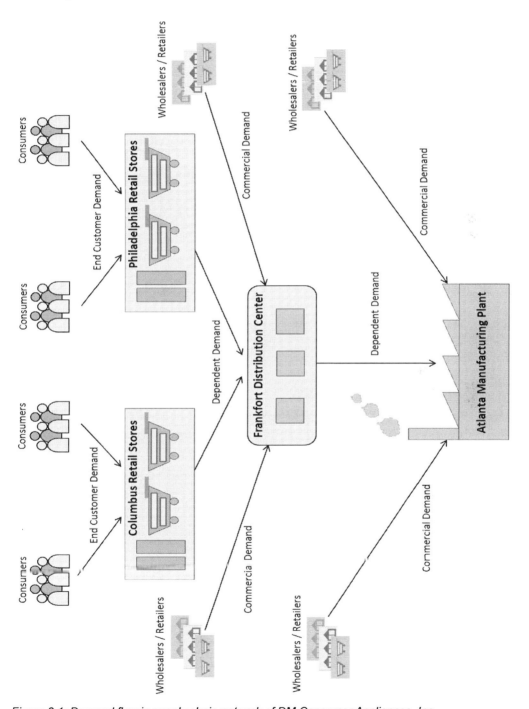

Figure 3.1: Demand flow in supply chain network of DM Consumer Appliances, Inc.

DM Consumer Appliances, Inc. promotes the new product by offering 25% off in store discounts to its customers for the initial six months of the product launch. DM Consumer Appliances, Inc. offer the discount in order to get into the LED TV market segment and would like to establish customer awareness in the short term and boost its sales and brand loyalty in the long term. Both *LCD TVs* and *LED TVs* have their respective advantages and disadvantages. However, during the promotional period the new product *40" DM LED 1080p HDTV* affects the sales of *39" DM LCD 1080p HDTV* to some extent. The impact looks insignificant when compared with the prospects that *LED TVs* bring to the table. Therefore, DM Consumer Appliances, Inc. decides to proceed with *LED TVs* despite the negative impact on one of its own products.

Presently, DM Consumer Appliances, Inc. has an SAP ERP (Enterprise Resource Planning) system for supply chain execution that forms the main logistics system. DM Consumer Appliances, Inc. likes to have seamless integration between demand planning and its ERP logistics system so that the net accumulated demand plan for all individual products of *LCD TVs* and *LED TVs* at the *Atlanta Manufacturing Plant* gets transferred to ERP for production planning. The network demand plan for all individual products of *LCD TVs* and *LED TVs* at non-manufacturing plants gets released to the supply planning system for supply planning.

Let's take a closer look at the demand planning scenario at DM Consumer Appliances, Inc.

3.2   Demand planning scenario

Figure 3.2 shows a schematic representation of the demand planning processes at DM Consumer Appliances, Inc.

The following list outlines demand planning processes at DM Consumer Appliances, Inc.:

- ▶ Use sales history data for planning purposes for the *LCD TVs*.
- ▶ Carry out forecasting for the *LCD TVs* based on its sales history.
- ▶ Analyze forecast accuracy measurement for alerts post generation of forecast.
- ▶ Carry out the forecasting with new forecasting strategy if alerts are found. Remove all alerts following the forecasting process, in iteration. The forecast model that does not throw any alerts is considered to be the best fit.
- ▶ Disaggregate forecasts from *LCD TVs* level. Analyze the disaggregation for various combinations of product, location, sales organization, regions, and distribution channel. Study the pattern and behavior thoroughly.
- ▶ Launch a new product *40" DM LED 1080p HDTV*. As a new product, it does not have any history. Hence, it refers a similar product, i.e., *39" DM LCD 1080p HDTV*.
- ▶ Carry out lifecycle planning for *40" DM LED 1080p HDTV* to replicate the demand behavior across all four phases of product lifecycle, i.e., launch, growth, maturity, and decline.
- ▶ Make customer aware of newly launched product and boost its sales through promotion of the *40" DM LED 1080p HDTV*.

► The newly launched product, similar to the *39" DM LCD 1080p HDTV,* impacts the sales of the *39" DM LCD 1080p HDTV* for the promotion period resulting in reduced sales of *39" DM LCD 1080p HDTV.*

► Verify forecast for all products for the unique combination of product and location.

► Gather inputs and buy-in on forecasting from various other stakeholders, i.e., sales (including point of sales inputs), marketing, finance, etc. and carry out manual corrections to the forecasts at product and location level for all products.

► Automate total forecast calculation.

► Takes cognizance of any significant differences between the total forecast and the corrected forecast proposed by forecasting run, in the form of alerts.

► Do manual corrections to forecasts and get rid of the alerts.

► Get total forecast as the consensus demand plan for product and location combination once all alerts are removed.

► Release the product consensus demand plan pertaining to non-manufacturing plants, i.e., *Frankfort Distribution Center, Columbus Retail Store and Philadelphia Retail Store* for supply network planning.

► Transfer the products consensus demand plan pertaining to *Atlanta Manufacturing Plant* for production planning.

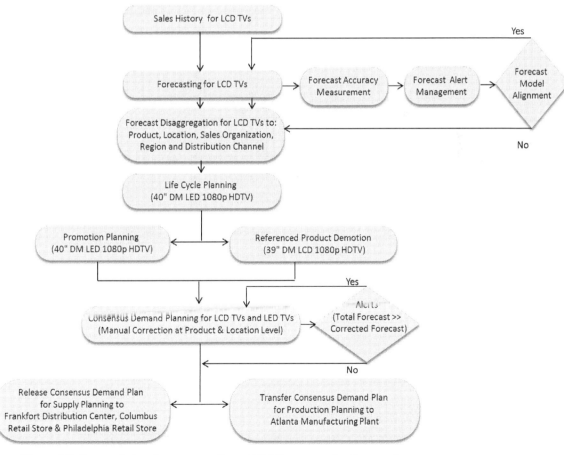

Figure 3.2: Demand planning process flow at DM Consumer Appliances, Inc.

In the following section, we will describe the different business challenges that DM Consumer Appliances, Inc. faces.

3.3 Business challenges

DM Consumer Appliances, Inc. faces multiple business challenges as depicted in Figure 3.3.

With increased globalization and the changing economic order, several players are concurrently competing with one another for the same *LCD TVs* and *LED TVs* market segment. Therefore, customers have many choices when it comes to products and are open to shifting loyalties amongst companies. This trend affects DM Consumer Appliances, Inc. in terms of reduced sales, reduced brand value, and market capitalization.

In this buyer-driven consumer's market, DM Consumer Appliances, Inc. is finding it difficult to maintain the balance between margins and retaining customers. Therefore, to maintain the margins as well as customers, DM Consumer Appliances, Inc. conducted a root cause analysis of its varied operations, to identify areas where it can control costs, enhance sales, and thereby maintain both margins and brand loyalty.

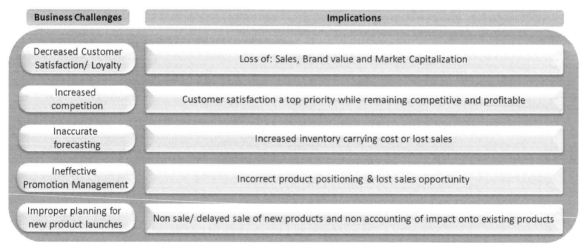

Figure 3.3: Business challenges and implications at DM Consumer Appliances, Inc.

As an outcome of this exercise, DM Consumer Appliances, Inc. identified that while in some cases there is excess inventory, in other cases there is a product shortage. Meaning there is no proper forecasting of products and consequently, there is improper supply planning. Furthermore, DM Consumer Appliances, Inc.'s *LED TVs* are not increasing sales because there is no appropriate promotion planning for *LED TVs*, as well as there is no proper demand planning for the new launches.

Therefore, DM Consumer Appliances, Inc. decides to embark on an APO DP implementation to meet its business requirements and address business challenges.

3.4 APO DP as solution to business requirements and challenges

DM Consumer Appliances, Inc. is looking for an Information Technology (IT) solution to meet its business requirements as explained through the business and demand planning scenarios and to address multiple business challenges. DM Consumer Appliances, Inc. decides to implement the SAP SCM (Supply Chain Management) solution Advance Planner and Optimizer Demand Planning (APO DP) to not only meet business requirements and address its challenges, but also expects APO DP to take its company to the next level. DM Consumer Appliances, Inc. will use the SAP ERP system for production planning and supply chain execution activities. DM Consumer Appliances, Inc. will use the Advance Planner and Optimizer Supply Network Planning (APO SNP) system for supply planning in the network.

DM Consumer Appliances, Inc. identifies several of the APO DP solution elements for its entire supply chain network to streamline its demand planning process. Solution elements of APO DP system integrate with its execution system SAP ERP and establish the necessary data exchanges and consistencies in real time. DM Consumer Appliances, Inc. anticipates several benefits of APO DP solution implementation as depicted in Figure 3.4.

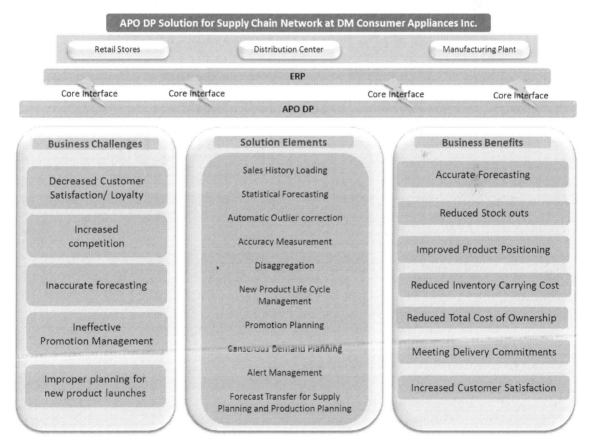

Figure 3.4: APO DP solution to business challenges at DM Consumer Appliances, Inc.

In the subsequent chapters of this book, we will demonstrate how the entire demand planning process is designed for DM Consumer Appliances, Inc. in APO DP, APO BW, and ERP system using configuration, master data, and transactions in SAP. In the process, we will connect our business scenario at DM Consumer Appliances, Inc. to APO DP processes and concepts. Henceforth, we shall refer to this chapter as 'our business scenario'.

3.5 Summary

In this chapter, we set the context for APO DP design in the form of a simple business scenario. We explained our business scenario in the form of a supply chain network with its demand flow, anticipated demand planning scenario with a schematic representation, business challenges and finally, APO DP as demand planning solution with its benefits.

The next chapter introduces the demand planning concepts through an integrated process flow diagram with APO DP and APO BW processes/ constituents.

4 Demand planning process

Looking at the process flow for APO BW and APO DP for our business scenario facilitates an end-to-end understanding of demand planning. We will combine the key learnings across the DP chapters by referencing the summarized APO BW and APO DP processes. The APO BW and APO DP process flow will also be a handy reference for applying APO DP concepts to solve business problems. In this chapter, we will describe the consolidated process flow diagram for demand planning.

In this chapter, we will look at the conceptual aspects of demand planning and associated processes. We will begin by introducing the demand planning concept. Next, we provide an integrated view of the APO BW and APO DP through the design and associated processes. While explaining the demand planning process concept we will refer to:

- ▶ Business scenario in Chapter 3 as *our business scenario*
- ▶ Integrated process flow diagram on APO BW process flow in Figure 4.1 of Section 4.2.1 as the *APO BW process flow*
- ▶ Integrated process flow diagram on APO DP process flow in Figure 4.2 of Section 4.2.2 as the *APO DP process flow*

4.1 Demand planning introduction

Demand planning has always been an integral part of business, consciously or otherwise. Quite literally, *demand* implies customer requirements in terms of sales quantity or sales revenue, etc. The word *planning* implies projections in advance.

Demand planning therefore means "customer requirement projections in advance". Demand planning is a strategic business process and impacts immediate and mid-term goals. With the advent of technology and the application of science, demand planning has matured. Today, there are software based solutions that help in increasing the effectiveness of demand planning and in increasing forecast accuracy.

APO DP is a sophisticated tool from SAP that aids the demand planning process. It brings an organized approach, agility, and accuracy to the demand planning process.

Multiple aspects of demand planning connects people and processes for example: interactive planning, exceptions management communication through alerts, consensus-based planning that takes inputs from all concerned units including sales, marketing, finance, operations, etc. Interaction between people and processes during demand planning aligns the wider organization to demand planning activities.

We carry out demand planning for a numerical figure that is typically called *key figure*, e.g., sales output or revenue. Also, demand planning is done for a particular planning level, i.e., combination of planning parameters like sales organization, region, product, product group.

These planning parameters are called *characteristics*. We do demand planning either at detailed level, or at an aggregate level based on the chosen planning level.

We carry out demand planning through statistical and analytical methods. It encompasses the following activities:

- ► Sales history data loading using the APO BW warehousing workbench.
- ► Uses history or causal factors (or both) to generate statistical forecasting using forecasting models and tools.
- ► Lifecycle planning for newly launched products.
- ► Promotions planning and cannibalization/ demotion.
- ► Aggregation and/ or disaggregation of the planned forecast.
- ► Forecast model fit assessment and measurement of accuracy.
- ► Consensus demand planning with inputs from multiple departments.
- ► Collaboration with its business partners through web/ telecommunication/ e-mail/ mobile applications/ social networks, etc.
- ► Release/ transfer of the demand plan for supply planning/ production planning,

Technically, we do demand planning in APO using LiveCache technology which mass processes the data and stores the planning results in key figures. LiveCache technology is explained in Section 2.2.6.

We often carry out back and forth integration of APO with other SAP applications, e.g., ERP, CRM, BW and non-SAP systems like MS Excel and legacy software.

APO DP is an iterative process that continually updates by incorporating new business realities, new data points, and most importantly, new ways of thinking to come up with a scientific and accurate demand plan.

In our business scenario at DM Consumer Appliances, Inc., we took into account multiple supply chain parameters for demand planning, disaggregation, aggregation, etc. Each parameter has a corresponding code as necessitated by SAP.

Code representation of sales parameters

 Sales organization DM Sales Org USA is represented by the code 5001. The distribution channel Direct Sales is represented by the code 10 and the distribution channel Indirect Sales is represented by the code 20.

The consolidated list of supply chain parameters and their demand planning code at DM Consumer Appliances, Inc. are shown in Figure 4.1.

Location	Location Code	Product Group	Product Group Code	Product	Product Code	City	Sales Organization Code	Region	Distribution Channel Code
Atlanta Manufacturing Plant	ZDM1	LCD TVs	ZDM_PG1	32" DM LCD 720p HDTV	ZDM_FG1	Atlanta, GA	5001	USA	10 & 20
Atlanta Manufacturing Plant	ZDM1	LCD TVs	ZDM_PG1	32" DM LCD 1080p HDTV	ZDM_FG2	Atlanta, GA	5001	USA	10 & 20
Atlanta Manufacturing Plant	ZDM1	LCD TVs	ZDM_PG1	39" DM LCD 1080p HDTV	ZDM_FG3	Atlanta, GA	5001	USA	10 & 20
Atlanta Manufacturing Plant	ZDM1	LED TVs	ZDM_PG2	40" DM LED 1080p HDTV	ZDM_FG4	Atlanta, GA	5001	USA	10 & 20
Frankfort Distribution Center	ZDD1	LCD TVs	ZDM_PG1	32" DM LCD 720p HDTV	ZDM_FG1	Frankfort, KY	5001	USA	10 & 20
Frankfort Distribution Center	ZDD1	LCD TVs	ZDM_PG1	32" DM LCD 1080p HDTV	ZDM_FG2	Frankfort, KY	5001	USA	10 & 20
Frankfort Distribution Center	ZDD1	LCD TVs	ZDM_PG1	39" DM LCD 1080p HDTV	ZDM_FG3	Frankfort, KY	5001	USA	10 & 20
Frankfort Distribution Center	ZDD1	LED TVs	ZDM_PG2	40" DM LED 1080p HDTV	ZDM_FG4	Frankfort, KY	5001	USA	10 & 20
Columbus Retail Store	ZDR1	LCD TVs	ZDM_PG1	32" DM LCD 720p HDTV	ZDM_FG1	Columbus, OH	5001	USA	10 & 20
Columbus Retail Store	ZDR1	LCD TVs	ZDM_PG1	32" DM LCD 1080p HDTV	ZDM_FG2	Columbus, OH	5001	USA	10 & 20
Columbus Retail Store	ZDR1	LCD TVs	ZDM_PG1	39" DM LCD 1080p HDTV	ZDM_FG3	Columbus, OH	5001	USA	10 & 20
Columbus Retail Store	ZDR1	LED TVs	ZDM_PG2	40" DM LED 1080p HDTV	ZDM_FG4	Columbus, OH	5001	USA	10 & 20
Philadelphia Retail Store	ZDR2	LCD TVs	ZDM_PG1	32" DM LCD 720p HDTV	ZDM_FG1	Philadelphia, PA	5001	USA	10 & 20
Philadelphia Retail Store	ZDR2	LCD TVs	ZDM_PG1	32" DM LCD 1080p HDTV	ZDM_FG2	Philadelphia, PA	5001	USA	10 & 20
Philadelphia Retail Store	ZDR2	LCD TVs	ZDM_PG1	39" DM LCD 1080p HDTV	ZDM_FG3	Philadelphia, PA	5001	USA	10 & 20
Philadelphia Retail Store	ZDR2	LED TVs	ZDM_PG2	40" DM LED 1080p HDTV	ZDM_FG4	Philadelphia, PA	5001	USA	10 & 20

Table 4.1: List of demand planning level entities at DM Consumer Appliances, Inc.

Aggregation and disaggregation of demand planning output depends on a select combination of the supply chain parameters mentioned in Table 4.1. Please refer to Chapter 3 for a detailed elaboration of our business scenario at DM Consumer Appliances, Inc. The following section gives an overview of the demand planning processes involved in our business scenario at DM Consumer Appliances, Inc.

4.2   Demand planning process flow

We do the demand planning at DM Consumer Appliances, Inc. through the interaction of two major areas: APO BW and APO DP.

In this section, we will provide an integrated picture of the design and processes involved in APO BW, as well as in APO DP using flow charts. Design and uniform processes are segregated and placed into exclusive blocks using dotted lines for the convenience of understanding. This method will help us to figure out what has gone into shaping any of the group of processes.

Each of the APO constituents/process steps/design steps/process groups/design groups are represented by ovals or rounded rectangles, e.g., planning area creation is a design step and it appears inside a rounded rectangle. Similarly, ERP configuration is a design group and it appears inside another rounded rectangle. Each of the APO constituents/process steps/design steps/process groups/design groups is connected to one another through an arrow that signifies the dependencies. APO constituents/process steps/design steps/process groups/design groups at the head end of the arrow are dependent on APO constituents/process steps/design steps/process groups/design groups located at the tail end of the arrow.

Therefore, we will use the following legends for Figure 4.1 and Figure 4.2:

[┌╌╌╌╌╌┐]	Blocks
▭	APO constituents/process steps/design steps/process groups/design groups
↓	Dependencies
◇	APO decision box

We briefly describe the design and processes involved in both APO BW and APO DP using process flow diagrams. We will also look at the integration touch points with ERP. We also look at the process overview of APO BW and APO DP one by one in the following sections.

4.2.1 APO BW process flow

Let's look at the design and processes involved in APO BW through a process flow diagram as illustrated in Figure 4.1.

APO BW consists of two blocks: 'Design in APO BW for Demand Planning' and 'Data Loading' as shown in Figure 4.1. The block 'Design in APO BW for Demand Planning' represents the different components that contribute to design required as prerequisite for data loading.

For DM Consumer Appliances, Inc., the source system (where original data was created) happens to be a flat file. To extract data in a particular format, we created a DataSource, based on the Source System and Application Component. The Application Component is a tree structure based logical grouping of DataSources. The DataSource is used to transfer data from a source system to a target system. We activate the DataSource which in turn creates a PSA (Persistent Staging Area).

The PSA is a transparent table that has a structure similar to a DataSource. For the same Application Component, we need to create an InfoSource that serves as a repository for InfoObjects like characteristics (qualitative parameters) and key figures (numerical parameters).

Furthermore, we need to create an InfoArea to structure and organize DSO and InfoCube in an InfoProvider. DM Consumer Appliances, Inc. wants to have an intermediate data staging area as it anticipates flat file data changes and wants the option to overwrite the data and therefore, wants a DSO. So, we create DSO based on the InfoSource and for the particular InfoArea. At the same time, DM Consumer Appliances, Inc., wants to have multidimensional reporting as it allows data aggregation. Therefore, DM Consumer Appliances, Inc. decides to stage the data in an InfoCube. We need to create the InfoCube as a data target that has multidimensional reporting capability for voluminous data.

Next, to facilitate the data transfer process between the DataSource to the DSO in accordance with the data target format, we need to create a Transformation. Similarly, we create a Transformation between the DSO and the InfoCube. You can find this entire design process illustrated in the block 'Design in APO BW for Demand Planning' in Figure 4.1.

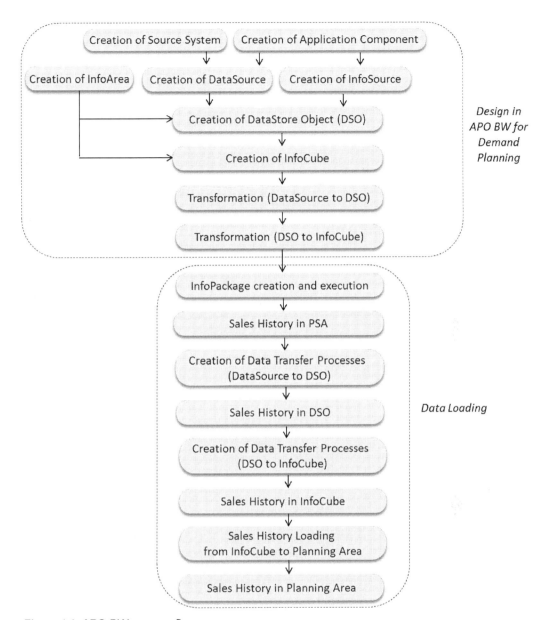

Figure 4.1: APO BW process flow

Once the APO BW design is complete, we need to carry out the data loading process as illustrated in the block titled 'Data Loading' in Figure 4.1. The data loading process starts with the flat file. The flat file maintains sales history data at the product group level (*LCD TVs*) in a particular format as the source of data, in accordance with the Source System. We create, schedule, and execute the InfoPackage to load sales history data to the PSA from a flat file. Next, we check the sales history data load onto the PSA.

We introduce the Data Transfer Process (DTP) to carry out data transfer from the data source to the data target after the data is available in PSA of APO BW. DTP, on its execution, reads, transforms, and loads data from data source to data target as per the associated Transformation. We first need to create and execute the DTP for the Transformation from the DataSource to the DSO and then verify the sales history in the DSO. Next, we create and execute the DTP for the Transformation from DSO to the InfoCube and then verify the sales history in the InfoCube.

Finally, we transfer the data from the InfoCube to the planning area and check the sales history load for *LCD TVs* for the history key figure in the APO DP LiveCache planning area. When the history data transfer is complete, we are in a position to do the demand planning executional activities like statistical forecasting and mass processing provided we have the design in ERP for demand planning and design in APO DP, in place as illustrated in Figure 4.2.

We will explain the block 'Design in APO BW for Demand Planning' of the APO BW process flow in Chapter 5. As for the APO BW execution related block 'Data Loading' of APO BW process flow, we will explain them in detail in Chapter 3 in the book *Demand Planning with SAP APO — Execution*

4.2.2   APO DP process flow

The design and processes involved in APO DP are illustrated in a process flow diagram as in Figure 4.2.

We start the design by ensuring that the necessary enterprise structure configurations for DM Consumer Appliances, Inc. are in place, in alignment with our business scenario. We also need to ensure that all of the associated IMG configurations in ERP are in place.

We ensure that all of the IMG configurations that allow for a smooth integration and connectivity between ERP and APO are in place in the ERP system. Next, we also ensure that the essential ERP master data that is the foundation for APO DP, is in place.

Based on the ERP data and the established connectivity between ERP and APO, we can generate and activate the core interface (CIF) model for transferring master data and transaction data from ERP to APO and vice versa. We can also verify the correctness of the transfer in APO DP. This briefly explains the block 'Design in ERP for Demand Planning' illustrated in Figure 4.2.

Next, we will focus on the 'Design in APO DP' represented in the block in Figure 4.2. We ensure that all IMG configurations that allow a smooth integration and connectivity between ERP and APO are in place in the APO system.

Next, based on the supply chain parameters of DM Consumer Appliances, Inc., we can determine the characteristics and use them to create the master planning object structure (MPOS). These characteristics combination constitute the planning level for DM Consumer Appliances, Inc.

Next, we determine the values of these characteristics and create and generate several characteristics value combinations to plan with. We create the storage bucket profile that determines the time horizon and periodicity for storing data. We also decide the numerical parameters for DM Consumer Appliances, Inc. and identify them as key figures for demand planning.

Based on the storage bucket profile, MPOS, CVCs and key figures we create a single planning area for DM Consumer Appliances, Inc., which constitutes the foundation for demand planning in the form of a central data structures. In order to create a network of characteristics and key figures in the LiveCache and to work with planning books, we create time series objects for the planning area. This process is also called initialization.

Based on the select key figures and characteristics we design the planning book so as to define layout and content for the interactive planning screen. We create the planning bucket profile for both the forecasting horizon and history horizon to use in the data view. Next, we define two data views based on a select set of key figures and the planning bucket profile.

We handle exceptions monitoring at DM Consumer Appliances using forecast alerts and supply & demand planning based alerts. To generate alerts, we create an alerts profile. For the planning book and one of the data view combinations, we create two macros for DM Consumer Appliances, Inc. One macro is designed to calculate the *total forecast*, i.e., consensus forecast, and other macro would generate alerts in case of exceptional entries for manual forecast adjustments.

We maintain a univariate forecast profile using *Croston's Model* as one of the initial options, along with two forecasting error calculations parameters, options for outliers, etc. However, if this model throws up exceptions, then we maintain the univariate forecast profile using *Automatic Model Selection 1* along with the two forecasting error calculations parameters, options for outliers etc., as an alternate option.

We also maintain multiple selection options for forecasting and analysis in interactive planning.

Once the design in ERP for demand planning and design in APO DP phases are complete, we can initiate the demand planning execution processes.

Let's briefly refer back to the data loading process for DM Consumer Appliances, Inc. Through data loading, we transferred the sales history for *LCD TVs* to the *history* key figure in planning book. Therefore, the history data will be available for demand planning.

We first described the interactive statistical forecasting processes as depicted in the block by the same name in Figure 4.2. Based on the history data, we calculate the proportional factors for the future horizon for three DM Consumer Appliances, Inc.'s products. We verify the proportion distribution for each of the three individual LCD TV products. Next, we do statistical forecasting through interactive demand planning at the product group *LCD TVs* level, i.e., aggregate level using Croston's model, and we find forecast alerts based on forecast accuracy measurement. This implies that Croston's model as a forecast model is not aligned and needs to be changed.

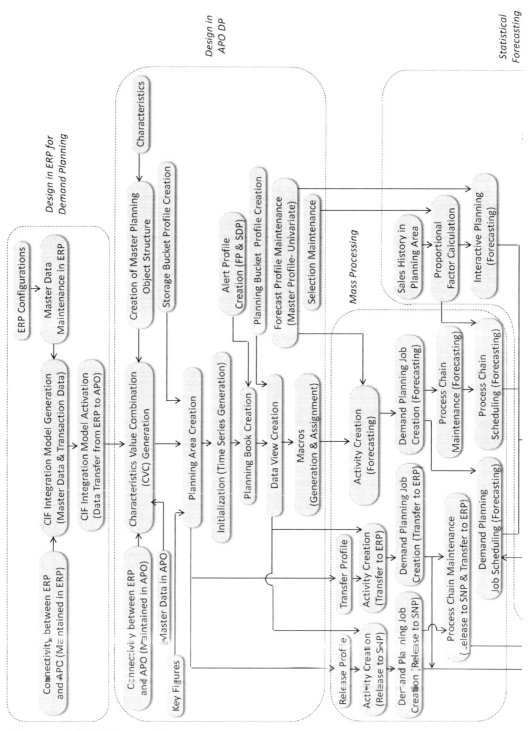

Figure 4.2: APO DP Process Flow

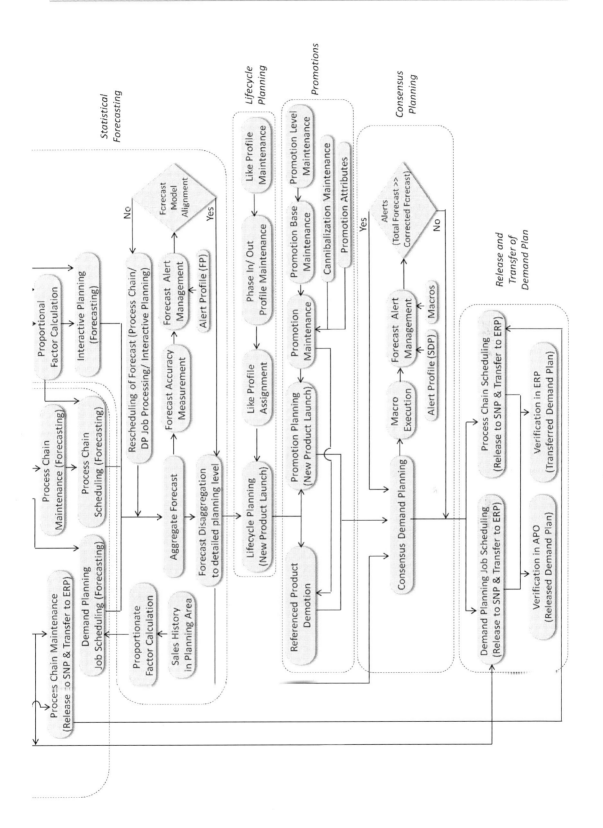

We therefore change the forecast model to *Automatic Model Selection 1* and carry out the forecast again. Alternatively, forecasting can be done either by rescheduling the background job, or by rescheduling the process chain. Once the forecast is complete, we don't find any alerts. Therefore, we consider the forecast model *Automatic Model Selection 1* and the corresponding forecast output; as it gives us a more accurate forecast. We do the statistical forecasting analysis in the planning book and also check for the forecast disaggregation for each of the individual *LCD TVs* products.

Next, let's look at mass processing. We depict mass processing in the block by the same name in Figure 4.2. Mass processing is for carrying out high volume demand planning activities. In the block diagram all the mass processing transactions and its associated design were placed together to relate to the process for our business scenario.

For DM Consumer Appliances, Inc., we use the interactive planning method to carry out statistical forecasting. We do not use the mass processing method because we want to provide exposure to the interactive planning method. This has been explained above and refers to the block 'Statistical Forecasting' in Figure 4.2. However, to demonstrate mass processing methods as well, we use the mass processing methods (through process chains) to carry out product release to SNP and product transfer to ERP and we depict that in the block 'Release and Transfer of Demand Plan' in Figure 4.2.

Nevertheless, we explain the mass processing methods and its corresponding design necessary for statistical forecasting, as mass processing can always be used as an alternative to interactive planning for DM Consumer Appliances, Inc.

In order to carry out mass processing of forecasting, first, we create the *activity* for the particular data view and forecast profile. Based on the *activity* we create the demand planning job for forecasting. Next, we either schedule the created demand planning job for forecasting directly through background processing, or maintain a process chain for forecasting and scheduling the same. The process chain is a sequence of processes that wait in the background to get triggered by an event; and processes can trigger events in turn.

As for carrying out mass processing of product release to SNP and product transfer to ERP we create corresponding profiles, activities, demand planning jobs, and process chain as the initial set up. You will find this in the block 'Mass Processing' in Figure 4.2. We execute the mass processing of product release to SNP and product transfer to ERP only after lifecycle planning, promotions, and consensus planning for DM Consumer Appliances, Inc. are complete.

At DM Consumer Appliances, Inc., we have the disaggregated forecasts for individual products of product group *LCD TVs*. DM Consumer Appliances, Inc. introduces a new product for the product group *LED TVs* whose lifecycle consists of all four phases, i.e., launch, growth, maturity, and decline phases.

Let's refer to the block 'Lifecycle Planning' in Figure 4.2 where we have depicted lifecycle planning design and execution. We maintain a *like profile* to make use of the history of one of the similar products, maintain *phase-in profile* to simulate the product's introduction phase, and maintain *phase-out profile* to simulate the product's decline phase.

Next, we assign the *like profile* to the planning area for the newly launched product *40" DM LED 1080p HDTV*. Based on this design, we can carry out lifecycle planning for the newly launched product and find the forecast in the interactive planning screen. We analyze the forecast and any alerts associated with it.

Next, DM Consumer Appliances, Inc. decides to promote the newly launched LED TV product *40" DM LED 1080p HDTV*. However, promotion of the LED TV product impacts the similar LCD TV, i.e., *39" DM LCD 1080p HDTV*. We address the requirement of promotion of one product and its impact on another product through the combination of APO promotions planning and cannibalization as depicted in the block 'Promotions' in Figure 4.2.

We maintain the initial design required for promotion planning and cannibalization. We define the promotion level for the planning area where the promotions are stored. Next, we define the promotion base with the default characteristic as the promotion level and we assign the promotion base to the promotion key figure. Furthermore, we define the promotion attribute as 'Discount' and do the set ups for cannibalization that capture the negative impact or demotion onto the sales of the product *39" DM LCD 1080p HDTV* which is not being promoted. We do the promotion maintenance based on the mentioned design.

Next, we do the promotions planning for the newly launched product *40" DM LED 1080p HDTV* by activating the maintained promotion. Promotion also results in the demotion of the referenced product, i.e., *40" DM LED 1080p HDTV*. These results are studied in interactive planning and are used as an input for the consensus demand planning.

We study the *total forecast* that gets calculated on runtime through the execution of the default macro based on disaggregated statistical forecasts for individual products, lifecycle planning, and promotions planning. Next, we gather inputs and intelligence from other stakeholders and departments like finance, marketing, strategy, etc. at DM Consumer Appliances, Inc. and include that as *manual correction* through interactive planning at the individual product level for both the product groups *LCD TVs* and *LED TVs*. In case of any alerts generated based on the default macro execution, we correct the *manual correction* entry and recalculate the *total forecast*. Finally, we take into account the refined *total forecast* at the individual product level as consensus forecast. Consensus demand planning is depicted in the block 'Consensus Planning' in Figure 4.2.

Finally, we release the disaggregated forecasts at the individual product level for *LCD TVs* and *LED TVs* to APO SNP for supply planning. We release APO SNP for the *Frankfort Distribution Center*, *Columbus Retail Store*, and *Philadelphia Retail Store* for DM Consumer Appliances, Inc. Similarly, we transfer the disaggregated forecasts at the individual product level for *LCD TVs* and *LED TVs* to the ERP system ECC for production. We transfer the forecast to ERP for the *Atlanta Manufacturing Plant* of DM Consumer Appliances, Inc.

Let's refer to the block 'Release and Transfer of Demand Plan' in Figure 4.2 that depicts the release and transfer of demand plan. We release and transfer the demand plan by scheduling the process chain pertaining to the release to SNP and transfer to ERP that was designed earlier as mentioned in block 'Mass Processing'. Once the process chain for release to SNP and transfer to ERP gets executed, we verify the release of all the products belonging to DM Consumer Appliances, Inc. in APO SNP for the *Frankfort Distribution Center*, *Columbus Retail Store* and *Philadelphia Retail Store*. Similarly, we verify the transfer of all of the products for DM Consumer Appliances, Inc. in ERP system ECC for the *Atlanta Manufacturing Plant*.

Alternatively, instead of the process chain we can schedule the demand planning job for the release to SNP and transfer to ERP that was designed earlier as mentioned in block 'Mass Processing'. Once the demand planning job is complete, we can verify the results in APO SNP and ERP system ECC in similar manner as for process chain.

We will explain the block 'Design in ERP for Demand Planning' in detail in Chapter 6 and the block 'Design in APO DP' in Chapter 7 and Chapter 8.

As for the APO DP execution related blocks, we will explain them in detail in the book *Demand Planning with SAP APO — Execution* over the chapters mentioned below corresponding to the particular blocks in Figure 4.2:

- ▶ 'Statistical Forecasting' in Chapter 4
- ▶ 'Lifecycle Planning', Promotions' and 'Consensus Planning' in Chapter 5
- ▶ 'Mass Processing' in Chapter 6
- ▶ 'Release and Transfer of Demand Plan' in Chapter 7

4.3   Summary

In this chapter, we explained the concept of demand planning in APO BW and APO DP. The entire process flow for both APO BW and APO DP were explained in brief. The process flow blocks and APO constituents/ process steps/design steps/process groups/design groups will be referred to in the following chapters. Understanding the overall process will help connect to each of the factors that influence the demand planning process.

This chapter only provides a summarized explanation of the entire APO DP flow along with its dependent flows in ERP and APO BW system. Nevertheless, we will elaborate on each of these aspects in detail in subsequent chapters.

In the next chapter, we will introduce the first set of design for demand planning, i.e., design in APO BW for demand planning.

5 Design in APO BW for demand planning

Demand planning relies heavily on historical sales data and warrants a thorough mechanism to gather sales history data. Gathering historical sales data is enabled by a well-designed data loading mechanism and process. In this chapter, we will explain the APO BW design that lays a solid foundation for gathering and loading sales history onto APO DP.

Data loading design for demand planning is done through the APO BW component of APO. APO BW forms an inherent part of the APO landscape. We will follow a step-by-step approach to building the design framework which is subsequently used for sales history data loading.

For our business scenario, at DM Consumer Appliances, Inc., we will be forecasting sales for the *LCD TVs* product group based on its sales history. Therefore, we need to load the sales history data to the planning system. However, before we can do the sales history data loading for *LCD TVs*, we need to have an APO BW design in place for DM Consumer Appliances, Inc.

In this chapter, we will describe the different APO BW design elements in sequence for our business scenario to gain an understanding of how these design elements are constructed and what purpose they serve.

You will find the reference to this section in the block 'Design in APO BW for Demand Planning' in the APO BW process flow depicted in Figure 4.1.

As we demonstrate all of the design elements that are required in APO BW, we will also explain the concept behind those designs and how that makes sense for our business scenario. We will provide a comprehensive understanding of the rationale behind the design in APO BW and how that is exemplified in our business scenario DM Consumer Appliances, Inc. We will learn how to create the following APO BW design elements: Source System, Application Component, DataSource, InfoSource, InfoArea, DSO, InfoCube, and Transformation (between the DataSource and DSO, as well as between DSO and the InfoCube).

5.1 Create the Source System

Any system from where data originates and can be extracted to APO BW is called a *Source System*. The different types of Source Systems include:

- ▶ SAP systems
- ▶ BI/ BW systems
- ▶ Flat files
- ▶ Database management systems
- ▶ Relational or multidimensional sources
- ▶ Web Services
- ▶ Non-SAP systems

For our business scenario at DM Consumer Appliances, Inc. we use a flat file as the source of raw sales history data for the product group *LCD TVs*. Therefore, in APO BW we create the flat file-based Source System.

You will find reference to this section as 'Creation of Source System' in the block 'Design in APO BW for Demand Planning' in APO BW process flow in Figure 4.1. Let's look at the process in brief.

The transaction code or menu path for the Data Warehousing Workbench in the SAP SCM system is as follows:

Transaction Code: RSA1

Menu Path: SAP MENU • INFORMATION SYSTEMS • BUSINESS INFORMATION WAREHOUSE • MODELING • DATA WAREHOUSING WORKBENCH: MODELING

Refer to Figure 5.1 on how to create a Source System. Click on SOURCE SYSTEM (❶) in the left panel under MODELING, double click on SOURCE SYSTEMS. Then right click to bring up the option CREATE and click on the CREATE option (❷). Then, choose the option FILE SYSTEM (❸) and click ENTER ✅ (❹). This brings up the screen CREATE SOURCE SYSTEM. Make the entries as shown by ❺ and then click ENTER ✅. We see the Source System created called DEMO SOURCE SYSTEM (ZDM_SS) (❻).

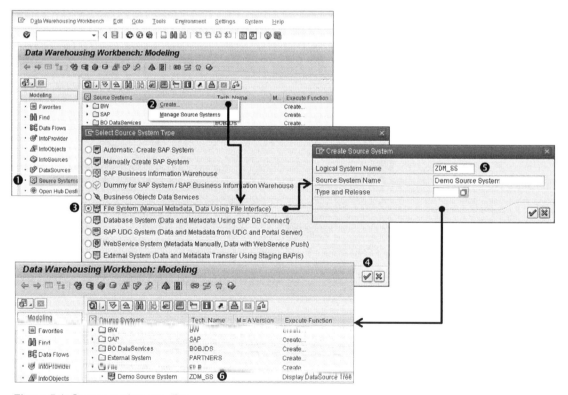

Figure 5.1: Source system creation

We will use the Source System *Demo Source System* (ZDM_SS) to create the DataSource.

5.2 Create the Application Component

The *Application Component* is a tree structure based logical grouping of DataSources.

For our business scenario at DM Consumer Appliances, Inc. we create an Application Component.

You will find the reference to this section as 'Creation of Application Component' in the block 'Design in APO BW for Demand Planning' in APO BW process flow depicted in Figure 4.1. Let's look at the process in brief.

The transaction code or menu path for the Data Warehousing Workbench in the SAP SCM system is as follows:

Transaction Code: RSA1

Menu Path: SAP MENU • INFORMATION SYSTEMS • BUSINESS INFORMATION WAREHOUSE • MODELING • DATA WAREHOUSING WORKBENCH: MODELING

See Figure 5.2 to learn how to create the Application Component. Click on INFOSOURCES (❶) in the left hand panel under MODELING, double click on INFOSOURCES. Then, right click to bring up the option CREATE APPLICATION COMPONENT and click onto it (❷). This brings up the screen CREATE APPLICATION COMPONENTS. Make entries as shown in ❸ and then click ENTER ☑ (❹). We see the Application Component called DEMO APPLN COMP (ZDM_AC) (❺).

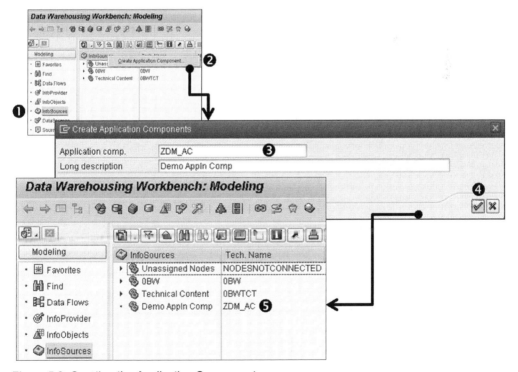

Figure 5.2: Creating the Application Component

We will use the Application Component called *Demo Appln Comp* (ZDM_AC) to create the DataSource and the InfoSource.

5.3   Create the DataSource

The *DataSource* is used to transfer data from a source system to a target system. The DataSource has a set of logically connected fields called InfoObjects that defines the sources of data. Also, the DataSource has structure, and details for transferring data to the APO BW system.

Before we get into the details of the DataSource, let's look in brief at the concepts behind InfoObjects. *InfoObjects* are the business assessment criteria and happen to be the smallest pieces in APO BW. InfoObjects are stored in *InfoObject catalogs*. There are two types of InfoObject catalogs, i.e., for characteristics and for key figures. InfoObjects include the following types:

- ▶ *Characteristics*: Represent the selection, sorting, or classifying parameters and are used as reference objects for key figures. Characteristic combination values are the level of detail at which key figure values are stored. Examples of characteristics are product group, sales organization, material numbers, etc.
- ▶ *Key figures*: Represent the parameters that have numerical transactional values, e.g., sales history, sales forecast, and revenue. Number values for key figures are called key figure values.
- ▶ *Units*: Provide meaning to the key figure values, e.g., currency units, measurement units, etc.
- ▶ *Time characteristics*: Signify time of business events, e.g., date, fiscal year, etc.
- ▶ *Technical characteristics*: Have administrative significance from a technical standpoint, e.g., unique request number in InfoCube that helps us to trace the particular data loading request in InfoCubes.

For our business scenario at DM Consumer Appliances, Inc. we create the DataSource based on the *Demo Source System* (ZDM_SS) in the Application Component *Demo Appln Comp* (ZDM_AC). Next, we continue on to design the DataSource by selecting the appropriate InfoObjects.

You will find the reference to this section as 'Creation of DataSource' in the block 'Design in APO BW for Demand Planning' in APO BW process flow depicted in Figure 4.1. Let's look at the process in brief.

The transaction code or menu path for the Data Warehousing Workbench in the SAP SCM system is as follows:

Transaction Code: RSA1

Menu Path: SAP MENU • INFORMATION SYSTEMS • BUSINESS INFORMATION WAREHOUSE • MODELING • DATA WAREHOUSING WORKBENCH: MODELING

Refer to Figure 5.3 for information on how to create the DataSource. Click on DATASOURCES in the left panel under MODELING, double click on DATASOURCES. Then, click on the icon CHOOSE SOURCE SYSTEM ⊠ and pull down the options to select FILE and ZDM_SS (DEMO SOURCE SYSTEM) (❶). On the next screen, right click on DEMO APPLN COMP (❷) and choose the option CREATE DATASOURCE (❸). Make entries as shown in ❹ and click ENTER ✔. It takes us to the screen as shown in ❺. Next, click on the EXTRACTION tab (❻) and specify the path of the source flat file and ensure the other details shown on the screen. Next, click the FIELDS tab (❼) and make entries for all of the fields as shown on the screen. Then, we click on SAVE 💾 (❽). The DataSource gets saved as ZDM_DS (DEMO DATA SOURCE) with version as IN PROCESSING SAVED (❾). Next, activate the DataSource by clicking on ACTIVATE ▮ and the version changes to green, i.e., ACTIVE (❿).

We will use *Demo Data Source* (ZDM_DS) to create the DataStore Object.

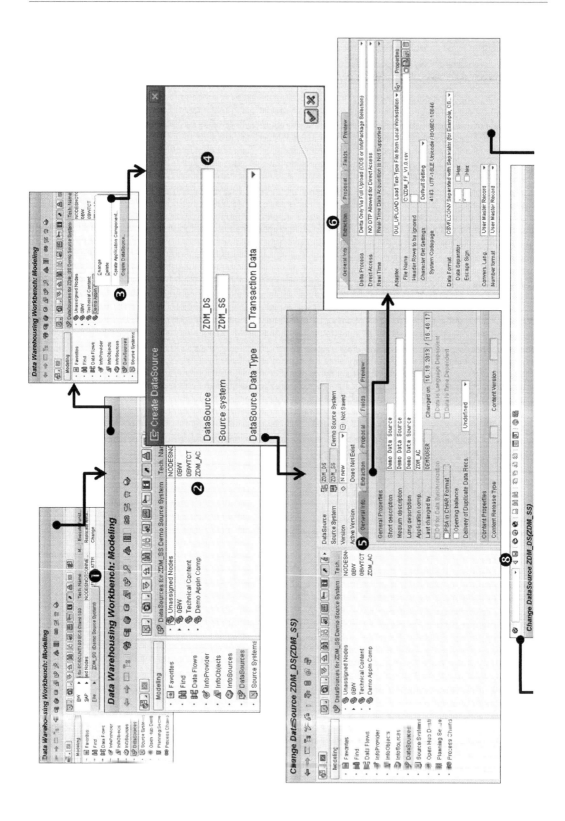

Figure 5.3: How to create the DataSource

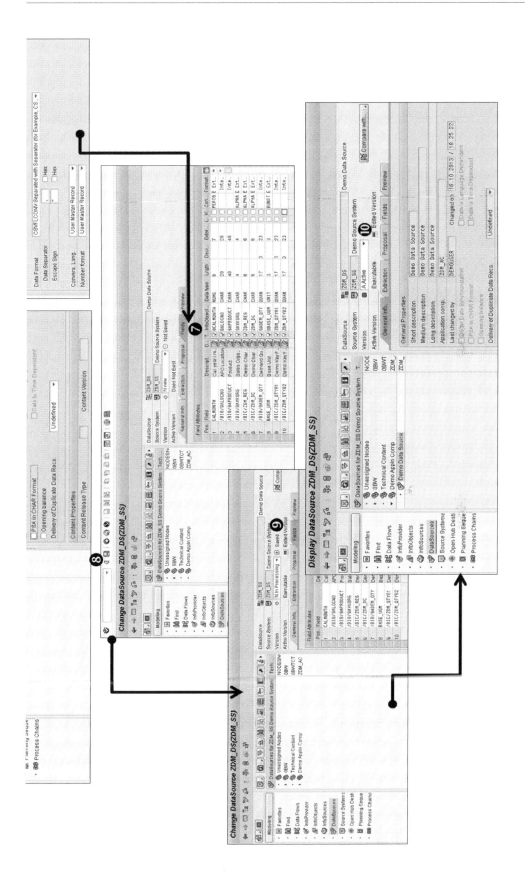

5.4   Create the InfoSource

An *InfoSource* is a quantity of summarized InfoObjects that logically go together to form a communication structure and makes itself available as data for business transactions.

For our business scenario at DM Consumer Appliances, Inc. we create an InfoSource as explained below.

You will find the reference to this section as 'Creation of InfoSource' in the block 'Design in APO BW for Demand Planning' in our APO BW process flow depicted in Figure 4.1. Let's look at the process in brief.

The transaction code or menu path for the Data Warehousing Workbench in SAP SCM system is as follows.

Transaction Code: RSA1

Menu Path: SAP MENU • INFORMATION SYSTEMS • BUSINESS INFORMATION WAREHOUSE • MODELING • DATA WAREHOUSING WORKBENCH: MODELING

Refer to Figure 5.4 for instructions on how to create an InfoSource. We click on IN-FOSOURCES (❶) in the left panel under MODELING, and double click on INFOSOURCES. Then, right click onto the DEMO APPLN COMP to bring up the option of CREATE INFOSOURCE. Click on that (❷). This brings up the screen CREATE INFOSOURCE. Make entries as shown in ❸ and then click ENTER ✅ (❹). We can see the INFOSOURCE with a list of INFOOB-JECTS (❺). Next, we activate the InfoSource by clicking on ACTIVATE 🔲 (❻). Our *Demo Infosource* (ZDM_IS) gets created and appears in DEMO APPLN COMP (ZDM_AC) (❼).

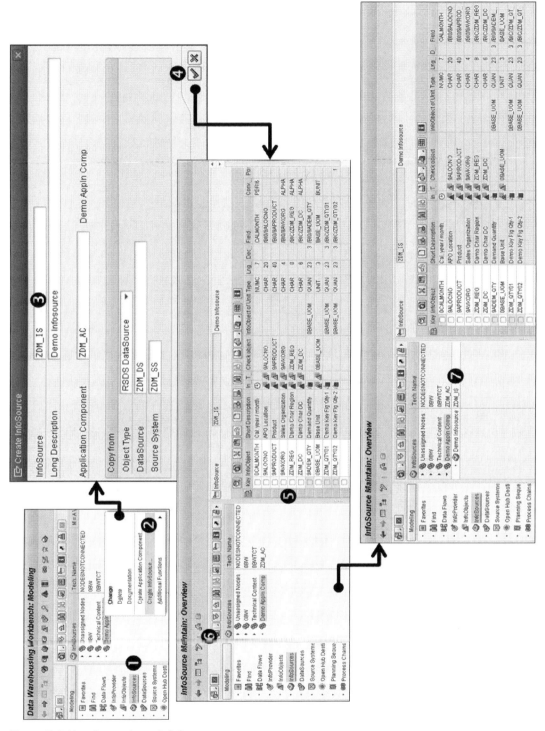

Figure 5.4: How to create an InfoSource

At DM Consumer Appliances, Inc., we refer to *Demo Infosource* (ZDM_IS) to create a DataStore Object.

5.5   Create InfoArea

In order to manage a large number of APO BW objects, it is convenient to organize them in groups. An *InfoArea* represents the highest level of grouping for a particular business function, or technical requirement. InfoArea is placed in the InfoProviders that appear in the left panel under *Modeling* in the Data Warehousing Workbench. InfoProviders constitute the objects that either contain physical data, e.g., InfoCube, DSO, and InfoObjects, or display logical views of data, e.g., MultiProviders and VirtualProviders.

For our business scenario at DM Consumer Appliances, Inc. we will group the DSO and InfoCube in a single InfoArea in InfoProvider.

You will find the reference to this section as 'Creation of InfoArea' in the block 'Design in APO BW for Demand Planning' in APO BW process flow depicted in Figure 4.1. Let's look at the process in brief.

The transaction code or menu path for the Data Warehousing Workbench in the SAP SCM system is as follows.

Transaction Code: RSA1

Menu Path: SAP MENU • INFORMATION SYSTEMS • BUSINESS INFORMATION WAREHOUSE • MODELING • DATA WAREHOUSING WORKBENCH: MODELING

Refer to Figure 5.5 for instructions on how to create an InfoArea. We click on the INFOPRO-VIDER (❶) in the left panel under MODELING, and double click on INFOPROVIDER. Then, right click and choose the option CREATE INFOAREA (❷). Make entries as shown in ❸ and click ENTER ☑ (❹). It takes us to the screen as shown in ❺.

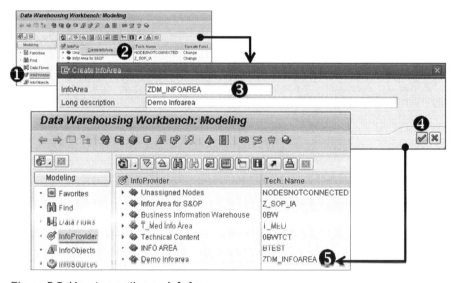

Figure 5.5: How to creation an InfoArea

We will use the *Demo Infoarea* (ZDM_INFOAREA) to create the DataStore Object and InfoCube as follows.

5.6 DSO design

The *DataStore Object (DSO)* serves as an intermediate data storage location for consolidated and cleansed transactions, or master data at a granular level. DSO is generally used for staging an enterprise data warehousing layer for cleansing purposes before it is transferred to the InfoCube for reporting. It is always best practice to have DSO in the data flow mechanism from source to target. Therefore, the data flow should ideally look like this: DataSource (original source of data) ⇨ DSO (detail level data) ⇨ InfoCube (reporting layer).

The DSO is different from the InfoCube in that data is stored in the DSO at a detailed level in fewer tables, whereas in the InfoCube data is stored at a summarized level in relational tables. Therefore, it is best to not report from DSO. In the DSO, generally, characteristics constitute the key fields for maintaining unique records and key figures constitute the data fields.

For our business scenario at DM Consumer Appliances, Inc., we anticipate flat file data changes and want the option to overwrite the data. Also, we would like to incorporate best practice in the data flow. Therefore, DM Consumer Appliances, Inc. will have a DSO in its data flow mechanism. We create the DSO based on *Demo Infosource* (ZDM_IS) for the *Demo Infoarea* (ZDM_INFOAREA) as explained below.

You will find reference to this section as 'Creation of DataStore Object (DSO)' in the block 'Design in APO BW for Demand Planning' in APO BW process flow depicted in Figure 4.1. The process is as follows.

The transaction code or menu path for the Data Warehousing Workbench in the SAP SCM system is as follows:

Transaction Code: RSA1

Menu Path: SAP MENU • INFORMATION SYSTEMS • BUSINESS INFORMATION WAREHOUSE • MODELING • DATA WAREHOUSING WORKBENCH: MODELING

Refer to Figure 5.6 for instructions on how to create a DSO. Click on the INFOPROVIDER (❶) in the left panel under MODELING, double click on INFOPROVIDER. Click on the DEMO INFOAREA. Then, right click and choose the option CREATE DATASTORE OBJECT (❷). It takes us to the EDIT DATASTORE OBJECT screen. Make entries as shown in ❸ and click CREATE 🗋 (❹). It takes us to the screen where we click on the INFOSOURCE ◈ (❺) to select the InfoSource. This takes us to the screen SELECT INFOSOURCE. Select the INFOSOURCE DEMO INFOSOURCE (ZDM_IS) (❻) and click ENTER ✓. Next, it takes us to the EDIT DATASTORE OBJECT screen where we find the list of InfoObjects defaulted from InfoSource. We can find the list of characteristics and key figures as shown by ❼ as a template. Next, we drag and drop the InfoObjects from the template to the respective KEY FIELDS and DATA FIELDS so as to find the list of InfoObjects as shown by ❽. We activate the DSO by clicking on ACTIVATE ⬆ (❾) and the DSO version changes to ACTIVE VERSION (❿). With this DEMO DSO (ZDM_DSO) gets activated and appears under DEMO INFOAREA (ZDM_INFOAREA).

We refer to *Demo DSO* (ZDM_DSO) for creating the InfoCube.

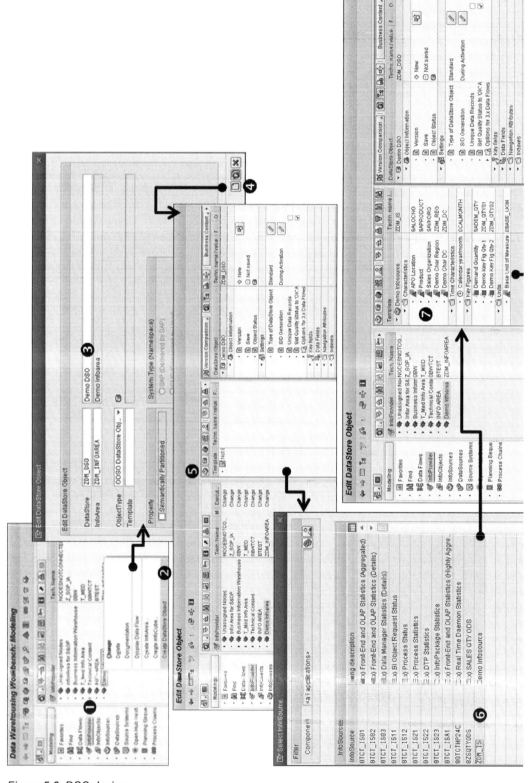

Figure 5.6: DSO design

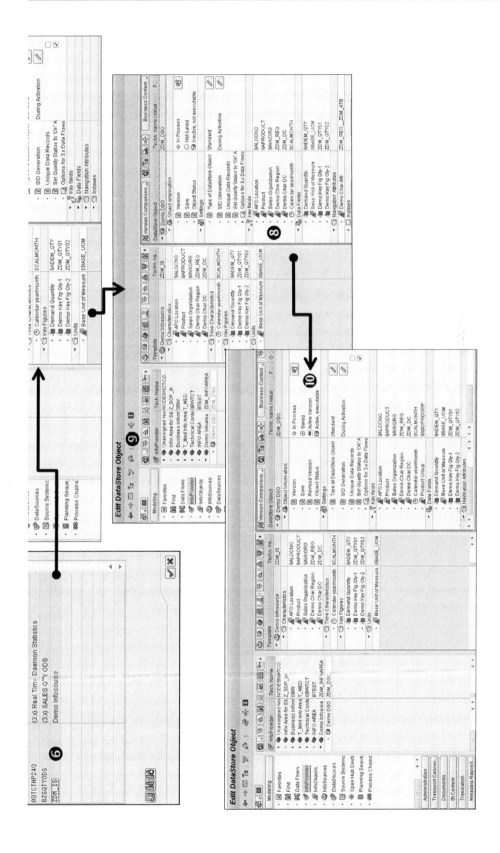

5.7   InfoCube design

We will not cover InfoCube design in detail. However, we will mention some of the key aspects of InfoCubes including data loading to the APO BW InfoCube because data loading is one of the fundamental activities required for APO demand planning.

The *InfoCube* is a multidimensional data container that is used for analysis and reporting. The InfoCube functions both as a data target and as an InfoProvider. InfoCubes have a collection of relational tables that are arranged according to a star schema. A *star schema* comes with a big fact table surrounded by multiple dimension tables. In an *APO BW star schema*, the facts in a fact table refer to key figures and dimension attributes refer to characteristics. The *fact table* and *dimension tables* are both relational database tables. InfoCubes get data from other InfoSources, or other InfoProviders. InfoCubes themselves are InfoProviders that are used for analysis and multi-dimensional reporting purposes.

A few of the key aspects of InfoCubes are as follows:

- ▶ InfoCubes are made up of numerous InfoObjects. All InfoObjects, i.e., characteristics and key figures, are independent on the InfoCube itself.
- ▶ Typically stores summarized data and are less granular compared to DSO.
- ▶ Aggregates are created for better performance of queries.
- ▶ Multi-dimensional reporting is possible in the InfoCube.
- ▶ Overwriting features are not there for data loads.

There are many types of InfoCubes, however, for our purpose we will only use the *basic InfoCube*. The basic InfoCube stores physical data through APO BW staging. Basic InfoCubes can be used both as a data target and as an InfoProvider for reporting.

For our business scenario at DM Consumer Appliances, Inc., we will create a basic InfoCube that will be used as a data target for data loading and as an InfoProvider. Therefore, the data flow for the InfoCube looks like this: DataSource (original source of data) ⇨ DSO (detail level data) ⇨ InfoCube (reporting layer).

Subsequently, we will use the data loaded onto the InfoCube for transferring data to the APO LiveCache. In this section, we explain the design of the APO BW InfoCube.

You will find reference to this section as 'Creation of InfoCube' in the block 'Design in APO BW for Demand Planning' in APO BW process flow depicted in Figure 4.1. We explain the process as follows in brief.

The transaction code or menu path for the Data Warehousing Workbench in SAP SCM system is as follows:

Transaction Code: RSA1

Menu Path: SAP MENU • INFORMATION SYSTEMS • BUSINESS INFORMATION WAREHOUSE • MODELING • DATA WAREHOUSING WORKBENCH: MODELING

Refer to Figure 5.7 for instructions on how to create an InfoCube. Click on the INFOPROVID- ER (❶) in the left panel under MODELING, double click on INFOPROVIDER. Click on the DEMO INFOAREA. Then, right click and choose the option CREATE INFOCUBE (❷). It takes us to the EDIT INFOCUBE screen. Make entries as shown in ❸ and click CREATE ▢ (❹). It takes us to the screen where we click on the DATASOURCE OBJECT ▣ (❺) to select the DSO. This takes us to the screen SELECT DATASTORE OBJECT. Select DEMO DSO (ZDM_DSO) (❻) and click ENTER ✅. Next, it takes us to the EDIT INFOCUBE screen where we find the DEMO DSO (ZDM_DSO) defaulted as template (❼). Click on SAVE ▤ (❽) and the InfoCube gets SAVED (❾) and we also find the InfoCube DEMO INFOCUBE (ZDM_IC) appearing in the DEMO INFOAREA (❿).

This completes Part 1 of 'InfoCube design'.

Let's refer to Figure 5.8 to continue with Part 2 of 'InfoCube design'. Click on DIMENSION 1 (❶) and right click. Next, click on PROPERTIES (❷). It brings up the EDIT DIMENSIONS screen. Make an entry as shown in ❸. Next, click ENTER ✅ (❹). It takes us to the screen with the modified dimension name DEMO DIMENSION (❺). We drag and drop the InfoOb- jects from the template to the respective KEY FIELDS and DATA FIELDS so as to find the list of InfoObjects as shown in ❻.

This completes the Part 2 of 'InfoCube design'.

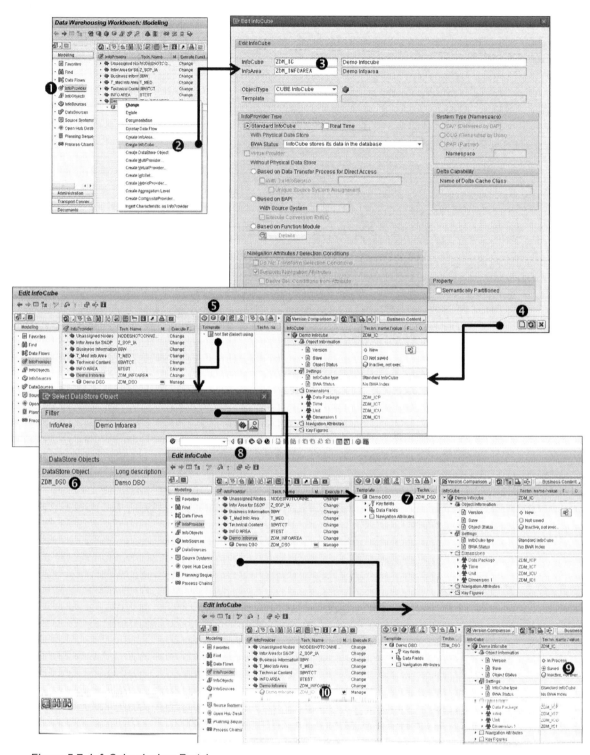

Figure 5.7: InfoCube design: Part 1

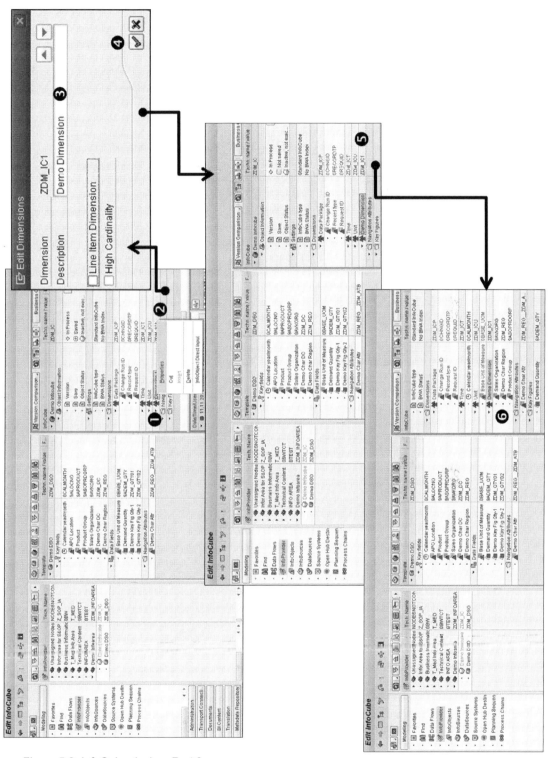

Figure 5.8: InfoCube design: Part 2

Refer to Figure 5.9 to continue with Part 3 of 'InfoCube design'. Click on DEMO DIMENSION (❶) and right click. Then click onto the InfoObject DIRECT INPUT option (❷). It brings up the screen INSERT INFOOBJECTS. Make an entry for the InfoObject 9AVERSION (❸) in order to assign an APO PLANNING VERSION while creating the Transformation between the DSO and the InfoCube. Next, click ENTER ☑ (❹). It takes us to the screen EDIT INFOCUBE with the characteristic APO PLANNING VERSION (9AVERSION) added to the DEMO DIMENSION (❺). Next, activate the InfoCube by clicking on ACTIVATE 🗈 (❻) and the InfoCube version changes to ACTIVE VERSION (❼). With this step, the DEMO INFOCUBE (ZDM_IC) is activated and appears under DEMO INFOAREA (ZDM_INFOAREA) (❽)

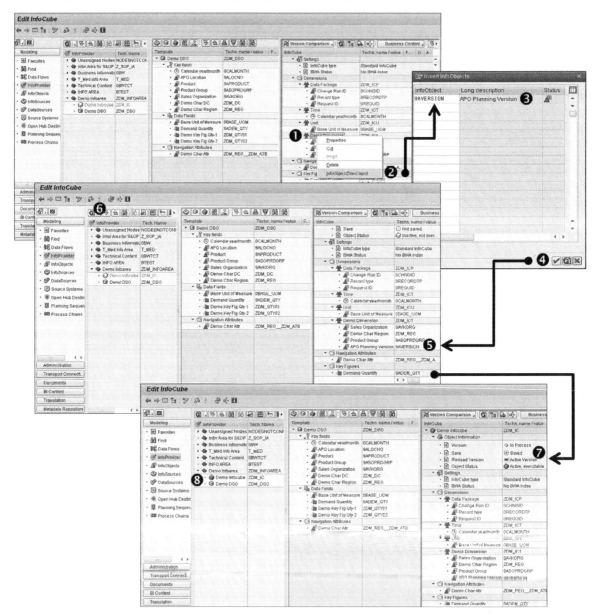

Figure 5.9: InfoCube design: Part 3

This completes the Part 3 of 'InfoCube design'. In the next section, we will make use of the DataSource, DSO, and InfoCube to design the Transformation between them to design the data flow as follows: DataSource (original source of data) ⇨ DSO (detail level data) ⇨ Info-Cube (reporting layer).

5.8 Transformation design

A *Transformation* converts the source field to the target field format based on the field mappings. When data loading is done from the source to the target system it gets converted, or transformed, as per the Transformation design between the two systems.

For our business scenario, we follow the data flow: DataSource ⇨ DSO ⇨ InfoCube. Therefore, in order to transfer *LCD TVs* sales history data from the DataSource to the DSO to the InfoCube we create two Transformations, i.e., one from the DataSource to the DSO and another one from the DSO to the InfoCube.

5.8.1 Create a Transformation between the DataSource and the DSO

A Transformation between the DataSource and the DSO will help convert the source field of the DataSource into the target format of the DSO. Accordingly, the sales history data for *LCD TVs* will get loaded to the target system during data loading process based on the conversion logic.

You will find reference to this section as 'Transformation (DataSource to DSO)' in the block 'Design in APO BW for Demand Planning' in APO BW process flow depicted in Figure 4.1. Let's take a look at the Transformation creation process in brief.

The transaction code or menu path for the Data Warehousing Workbench in the SAP SCM system is as follows:

Transaction Code: RSA1

Menu Path: SAP MENU • INFORMATION SYSTEMS • BUSINESS INFORMATION WAREHOUSE • MODELING • DATA WAREHOUSING WORKBENCH: MODELING

Refer to Figure 5.10 for instructions on how to create the Transformation between the DataSource and the DSO. Click onto the INFOPROVIDER (❶) in the left panel under MODEL-ING, double click on INFOPROVIDER. Click on DEMO DSO (❷). Then, right click and choose the option CREATE TRANSFORMATION (❸). It takes us to the CREATE TRANSFORMATION screen. Select SOURCE SYSTEM DETAILS (❹) and TARGET SYSTEM DETAILS (❺) and click ENTER ✔ (❻). It takes us to the screen CREATE TRANSFORMATION where we find the system suggested source and target field mappings (❼). Next, activate the Transformation between the DataSource and the DSO by clicking on ACTIVATE ⬚ (❽) and the Transformation version changes to ACTIVE and SAVED (❾). With this step, the Transformation between the DataSource and the DSO is activated and appears in Demo DSO and Demo Data Source as Transformation, Active ⋈ (❿).

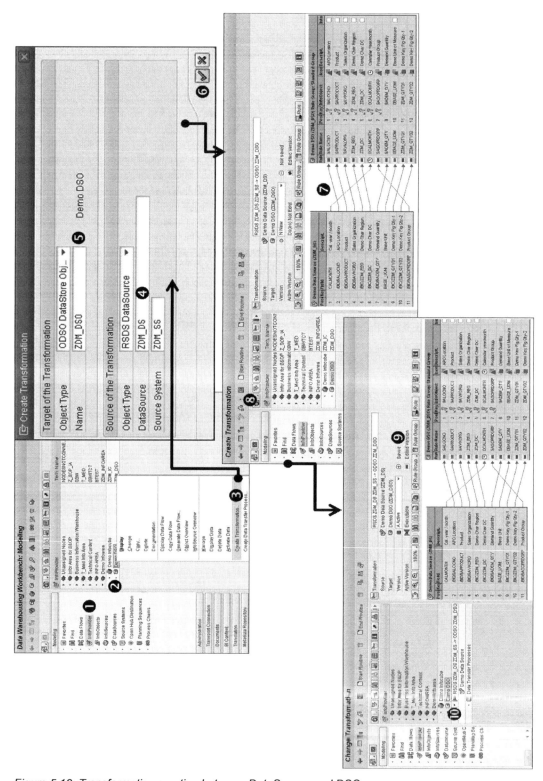

Figure 5.10: Transformation creation between DataSource and DSO

The Transformation between the DataSource and the DSO can be used for data loading from the DataSource to the DSO. Next, we explain the creation of the Transformation between the DSO and the InfoCube.

5.8.2   Create the Transformation between the DSO and the InfoCube

The Transformation between the DSO and the InfoCube will help convert the DSO source field into the target format of the InfoCube. Accordingly, the sales history data for *LCD TVs* will get loaded to the target system during data loading process based on this conversion logic.

You will find reference to this section as 'Transformation (DSO to InfoCube)' in the block 'Design in APO BW for Demand Planning' in the APO BW process flow depicted in Figure 4.1. Let's take a look at the process of creating a Transformation in brief.

The transaction code or menu path for the Data Warehousing Workbench in SAP SCM system is as follows:

Transaction Code: RSA1

Menu Path: SAP Menu • Information Systems • Business Information Warehouse • Modeling • Data Warehousing Workbench: Modeling

Refer to Figure 5.11 to create the Transformation between the DSO and the InfoCube. Click on the InfoProvider in the left panel under Modeling, double click on InfoProvider. Click on the Demo Infocube which appears under Demo Infoarea. Then, right click and choose the option Create Transformation (❶). It takes us to the Create Transformation screen. Select source system details (❷) and target system details (❸) and click Enter ☑ (❹). It takes us to the screen Create Transformation where we find the system suggested source and target field mappings (❺). Next, in the Demo Infocube (ZDM_IC) Rule Groups: Standard Group screen we find the listing of the rule names. We click on the row that corresponds to the InfoObject 9AVERSION (i.e., APO Planning Version) to select it (❻). We right click and click on the option Rule Details (❻) and it brings up the screen Rule Details. Change the description as shown in ❼. We make entries for the other details as shown in the screen rule details and click on Transfer Values (❽). It takes us to the screen Create Transformation where we find the rule name Infocube Demo Version Rule (❾) appearing in the Demo Infocube (ZDM_IC) Rule Groups: Standard Group listing. Next, we activate the Transformation between the DSO and the InfoCube by clicking on Activate ⊞ and the Transformation version changes to Active and Saved. With this step, the Transformation between the DSO and the InfoCube is activated and appears in the Demo Infocube and Demo DSO as Transformation, Active ⋈ (❿).

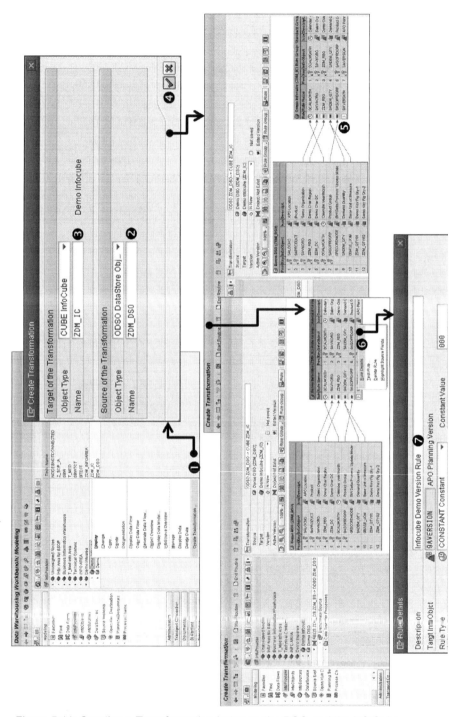

Figure 5.11: Creating a Transformation between the DSO and the InfoCube

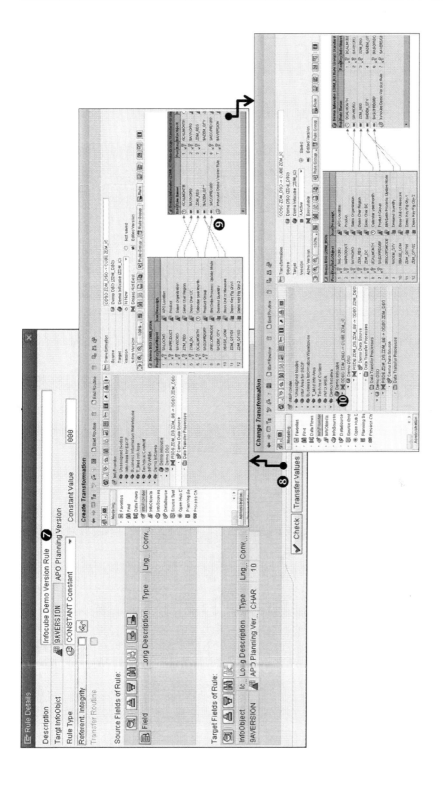

The Transformation between the DSO and the InfoCube is available for use for data loading from DSO to InfoCube.

5.9 Summary

This chapter explained the APO BW design elements that are required for demand planning in SAP APO. Designs were kept relevant to our business scenario to exemplify our understanding of APO BW concepts. Based on these designs, actual data loading to APO BW and subsequently to the APO DP planning area, will be feasible.

In the next chapter, we will look at the different designs that are required in the ERP system for us to proceed with APO DP.

6 Design in ERP for Demand Planning

APO DP supports the actual business execution in ERP system and therefore, it is necessary to have tight integration between ERP and APO DP. In this chapter, we will introduce the design in ERP including configuration, master data, and transactions that enable integration between SAP SCM and SAP ERP for APO DP.

Demand Planning in APO takes its inputs from the ERP system and the eventual output is also sent back to ERP for execution. This is because planning is for execution and hence, execution system design is a prerequisite before we can proceed with the design in APO DP and demand planning in APO. In this section, we will look at the core execution system design that is required for carrying out APO DP for our business scenario DM Consumer Appliances, Inc.

You will find the reference to this section in the block 'Design in ERP for Demand Planning' in the APO DP process flow in Figure 4.2.

The *core execution system* is an *SAP ERP* system with *ECC* as its component. As we demonstrate what designs are required in ERP, we also explain the concept behind those designs and how that is required for our business scenario. This is for us to gain a comprehensive understanding of the rationale behind the design and how it is exemplified in our business scenario DM Consumer Appliances, Inc. We maintain five design categories that are required in the core execution system, i.e., configuration in ERP, connectivity between ERP and APO, master data in ERP, core interface settings, and execution of the integration model for data transfer in the subsections that follow.

6.1 ERP configuration

ERP configuration is required in an SAP ERP ECC system and lays the foundation for any ERP activities.

You will find reference to this section as 'ERP Configurations' in the block 'Design in ERP for Demand Planning' in APO DP process flow in Figure 4.2.

In the sections below, we will look at some of the crucial and essential ERP configuration that has direct relevance for demand planning pertaining to our business scenario

6.1.1 Define plants

Demand planning is a supply chain activity that revolves around a network of logistical centers. At DM Consumer Appliances, Inc., we have a network of one distribution center, two retail stores, and one manufacturing plant.

We recognize these network locations as plants in the ERP system. Therefore, we need to ensure that we have the configuration for the definition of four locations as PLANTS as shown in Figure 6.1.

The IMG path for the configuration in the ERP system is as follows:

SAP CUSTOMIZING IMPLEMENTATION GUIDE • ENTERPRISE STRUCTURE • DEFINITION • LOGISTICS – GENERAL • DEFINE, COPY, DELETE, CHECK PLANT

Plnt	Name 1	Name 2
ZDD1	Frankfort Distribution Center	Frankfort Distribution Center
ZDM1	Atlanta Manufacturing Plant	Atlanta Manufacturing Plant
ZDR1	Columbus Retail Store	Columbus Retail Store
ZDR2	Philadelphia Retail Store	Philadelphia Retail Store

Change View "Plants": Overview — New Entries — BC Set: Change Field Values

Figure 6.1: Plants, distribution centers, and stores at DM Consumer Appliances, Inc.

6.1.2   Allocate the node types to the plants

In Section 6.1.1 we defined plants for our business scenario. Now that the plants are defined, we can recognize the type of plants as production plants (i.e., manufacturing plant), distribution center, or stores as applicable. We can do this through the configuration shown in Figure 6.2.

The IMG path for this configuration in the ERP system is as follows:

SAP CUSTOMIZING IMPLEMENTATION GUIDE • PRODUCTION • DISTRIBUTION RESOURCE PLANNING (DRP) • BASIC SETTINGS • MAINTAIN ASSIGNMENT OF NODE TYPE – PLANT • ALLOCATION OF NODE TYPE

Plant types are designated as NODE TYPES as shown in (❶) of Figure 6.2. NODE TYPES are elaborated in (❷) of Figure 6.2.

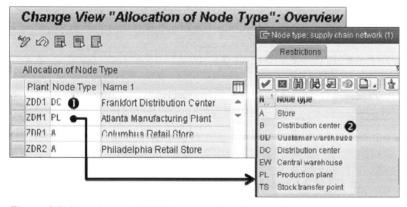

Figure 6.2: Plant types at DM Consumer Appliances, Inc.

6.1.3 Maintain storage location

For our business scenario, we make an entry for one STORAGE LOCATION as shown in Figure 6.3 for the *Atlanta manufacturing plant* where the products are stored. Similarly, storage locations could be maintained for other locations as well.

The IMG path for this configuration in the ERP system is as follows:

SAP CUSTOMIZING IMPLEMENTATION GUIDE • ENTERPRISE STRUCTURE • DEFINITION • MATERIALS MANAGEMENT • MAINTAIN STORAGE LOCATION

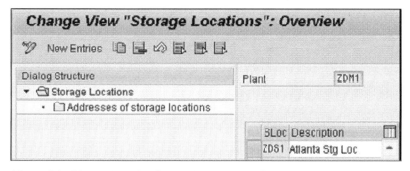

Figure 6.3: Storage location for the Atlanta manufacturing plant

6.1.4 Assign plant to company code

All the network locations for our business scenario need to be recognized in the ERP system as belonging to the company DM Consumer Appliances, Inc. Therefore, we need to ensure that the manufacturing plant, distribution center, and the retail stores are assigned to the company DM Consumer Appliances, Inc. as shown in Figure 6.4.

The IMG path for this configuration in the ERP system is as follows:

SAP CUSTOMIZING IMPLEMENTATION GUIDE • ENTERPRISE STRUCTURE • ASSIGNMENT • LOGISTICS – GENERAL • ASSIGN PLANT TO COMPANY CODE

Change View "Assignment Plant - Company Code": Overview

Assignment Plant - Company Code

CoCd	Plnt	Name of Plant	Company Name	Status
5000	ZDD1	Frankfort Distribution Center	DM Consumer Appliances Inc.	
5000	ZDM1	Atlanta Manufacturing Plant	DM Consumer Appliances Inc.	
5000	ZDR1	Columbus Retail Store	DM Consumer Appliances Inc.	
5000	ZDR2	Philadelphia Retail Store	DM Consumer Appliances Inc.	

Figure 6.4: Company code for DM Consumer Appliances, Inc.

Assignment of plant to a company

Assignment of plant to company legitimizes the plant for all accounting and transactional activities carried out in the ERP execution system post-planning activities.

6.1.5   Define MRP Controller

Any material that is required to be planned has to be assigned to a Materials Requirement Planning (MRP) controller, who monitors the planning.

We define this because *MRP Controller* field entry is mandatory for maintaining any material as master data. For our business scenario, for the sake of simplicity, we make an entry of a single MRP CONTROLLER and assign it to each of the plants as shown in Figure 6.5.

The IMG path for this configuration in the ERP system is as follows:

SAP CUSTOMIZING IMPLEMENTATION GUIDE • PRODUCTION • MATERIAL REQUIREMENTS PLANNING • MASTER DATA • DEFINE MRP CONTROLLERS

Change View "MRP Controllers": Overview

New Entries   BC Set: Change Field Values

Plnt	Name 1	MRP Cont.	MRP controller name
ZDD1	Frankfort Distribution Center	001	PERSON 1
ZDM1	Atlanta Manufacturing Plant	001	PERSON 1
ZDR1	Columbus Retail Store	001	PERSON 1
ZDR2	Philadelphia Retail Store	001	PERSON 1

Figure 6.5: MRP Controller for DM Consumer Appliances, Inc.

6.1.6   Define Floats (Scheduling Margin Key)

Floats are used to determine the basic dates in planned orders. Floats are maintained for a Scheduling Margin Key for scheduling an order. The *Scheduling Margin Key* is a mandatory field in *MRP2 view* of material master. For our business scenario, we will make an entry for the *Scheduling Margin Key* for every plant, with blank values, as we do not intend to do any ERP order execution.

The IMG path for this configuration in the ERP system is as follows:

SAP CUSTOMIZING IMPLEMENTATION GUIDE • PRODUCTION • MATERIAL REQUIREMENTS PLANNING • PLANNING • SCHEDULING AND CAPACITY PARAMETERS • DEFINE FLOATS (SCHEDULING MARGIN KEY)

Change View "Floats for Scheduling": Overview

New Entries 🗎 🗐 🗐 🖉 🗐 🗐 🗐

Plnt	Name 1	Marg.	Op. ...	Fl Bef.	Fl After	Rel. Per.
ZDD1	Frankfor Distribution Center	AAA				
ZDM1	Atlanta Manufacturing Plant	000				
ZDR1	Columbus Retail Store	000				
ZDR2	Philadelphia Retail Store	000				

Figure 6.6: Floats for scheduling

6.1.7   Maintain plant parameters

Without maintaining the plant parameters for MRP in ECC, the system will not allow the MRP run for materials chosen for planning. Hence, we maintain these configurations by copying from the SAP standard plant 1000 as shown below.

The IMG path for this configuration in ERP system is as follows:

SAP Customizing Implementation Guide • Production • Material Requirements Planning • Plant Parameters• Carry Out Overall Maintenance of Plant Parameters

To configure the plant parameters, click on CREATE (❶) as shown in Figure 6.7 and then select plant ZDM1. Then, click on CREATE (❷) and next click COPY (❸) to copy from standard SAP plant 1000 to plant ZDM1 and then finally click COPY (❹).

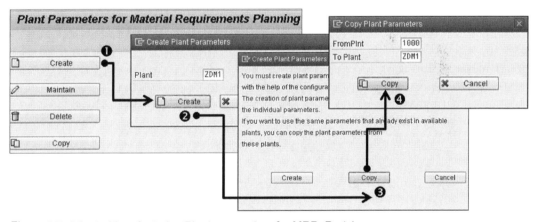

Figure 6.7: Atlanta Manufacturing Plant parameters for MRP, Part 1

Next, click MAINTAIN (❶) as shown in Figure 6.8 and select plant ZDM1 and click MAINTAIN (❷). With this, MRP the parameters of plant ZDM1 are maintained as shown in (❸). Parameters similar to plant 1000 only get maintained.

So, in this manner we maintain the PLANT PARAMETERS FOR MRP for ATLANTA MANUFACTURING PLANT (ZDM1). Likewise, we repeat the same procedures as illustrated in Figure 6.7 and Figure 6.8 for the other three plants, i.e., FRANKFORT DISTRIBUTION CENTER (ZDD1), COLUMBUS RETAIL STORE (ZDR1) and PHILADELPHIA RETAIL STORE (ZDR2).

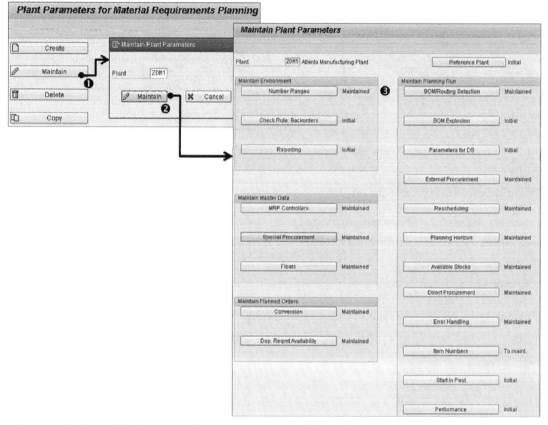

Figure 6.8: Atlanta Manufacturing Plant parameters for MRP: Part 2

6.1.8   Define the sales organization

In our business scenario, we have *DM Sales Org USA* (5001) as the sales organization, which also happens to be one of the planning levels for forecasting (see Section 3.1 and Table 4.1). The sales organization *DM Sales Org USA* (5001) is maintained as one the characteristics in the master planning object structure mentioned in Section 7.3.

Therefore, to maintain consistency we make an entry for the sales organization DM SALES ORG USA (5001) in the ERP system as well, as shown in Figure 6.9.

The IMG path for this configuration in the ERP system is as follows:

SAP CUSTOMIZING IMPLEMENTATION GUIDE • ENTERPRISE STRUCTURE • DEFINITION • SALES AND DISTRIBUTION • DEFINE, COPY, DELETE, CHECK SALES ORGANIZATION • DEFINE SALES ORGANIZATION

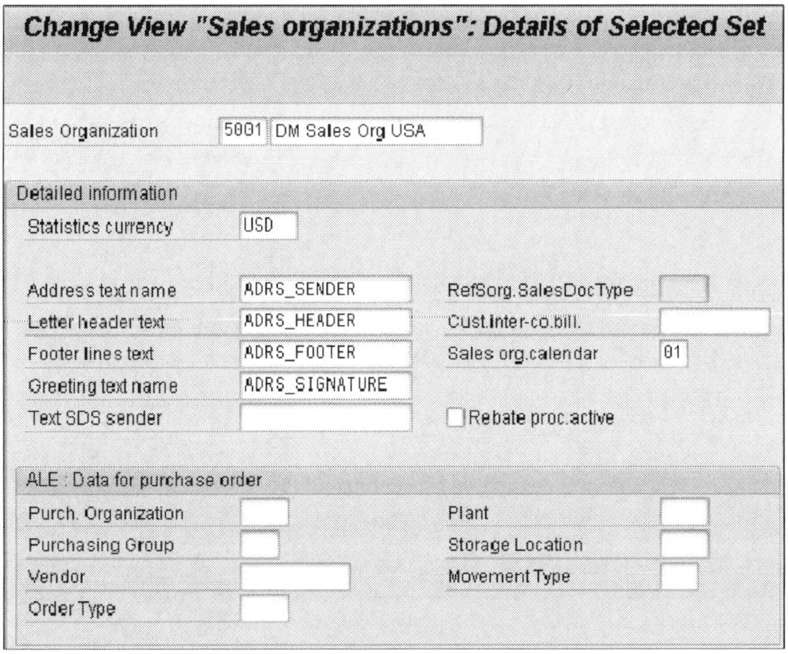

Change View "Sales organizations": Details of Selected Set

Sales Organization	5001	DM Sales Org USA

Detailed information

Statistics currency	USD		
Address text name	ADRS_SENDER	RefSorg.SalesDocType	
Letter header text	ADRS_HEADER	Cust.inter-co.bill.	
Footer lines text	ADRS_FOOTER	Sales org.calendar	01
Greeting text name	ADRS_SIGNATURE		
Text SDS sender		☐ Rebate proc.active	

ALE : Data for purchase order

Purch. Organization		Plant	
Purchasing Group		Storage Location	
Vendor		Movement Type	
Order Type			

Figure 6.9: Sales organization definition

6.1.9 Define the distribution channel

In our business scenario we have two distribution channels: *direct sales* (10) and *indirect sales* (20). The two distribution channels will be used as planning levels for forecasting. Therefore, to maintain consistency with the ERP system, we make entries of the two distribution channels in the ERP system as shown in Figure 6.10.

The IMG path for this configuration in ERP system is as follows:

SAP CUSTOMIZING IMPLEMENTATION GUIDE • ENTERPRISE STRUCTURE • DEFINITION • SALES AND DISTRIBUTION • DEFINE, COPY, DELETE, CHECK DISTRIBUTION CHANNEL • DEFINE DISTRIBUTION CHANNEL

New Entries: Overview of Added Entries

Distr. Channel	Name	
10	Direct Sales	▲
20	Indirect Sales	▼

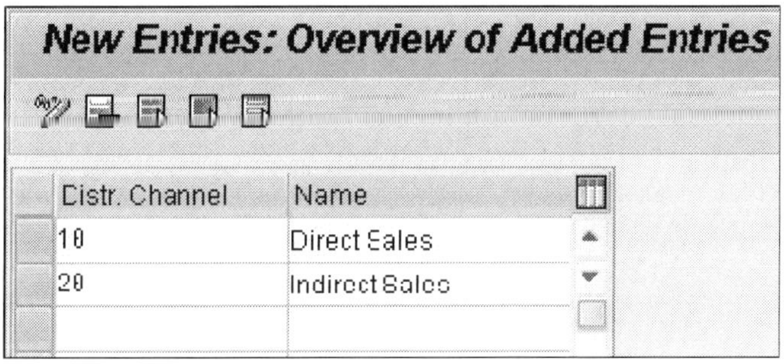

Figure 6.10: Types of distribution channels

In this section, we highlighted and explained some of the major configuration required in ERP. In the next section, we will look at the connectivity between ERP and SCM, which are required to be carried out in the ERP system itself.

6.2   Connectivity between ERP and APO

APO gathers its input from the ERP system and during planning it transfers data to ERP. Also, there are data exchanges that happen in real time between these two systems. In order to enable this interaction, we need to design connectivity between the ERP system and APO system through a series of configurations in the ERP system, as well as series of configurations in the SCM system.

You will find reference to this section as 'Connectivity between ERP and APO (Maintained in ERP)' in the block 'Design in ERP for Demand Planning' in the APO DP process flow depicted in Figure 4.2.

In the following sections, we will review the essential connectivity design in ERP for establishing a connection between the ERP and SCM systems. These designs have direct relevance for demand planning and pertain to our business scenario. These designs will establish the system infrastructure for transferring data through the *core interface* (CIF). We will explain the core interface (CIF) in detail in Section 6.4.

Typically, this type of design will be done by a Basis Administrator. Nevertheless, it's very important that we understand the connectivity and its significance. In this section, we will describe all of the connectivity that is required on the ERP side for integrating ERP to APO for our business scenario.

6.2.1   Name the logical system

The *logical system* in SAP is a unique application system that is connected to the network of multiple application systems. For our business scenario, we uniquely identify the execution system, i.e., the *ERP system ECC*, as well as the demand planning system, i.e., *SCM system*, and define them as shown in the Figure 6.11.

The IMG path for this configuration in the ERP system is as follows:

SAP CUSTOMIZING IMPLEMENTATION GUIDE • INTEGRATION WITH OTHER SAP COMPONENTS • ADVANCED PLANNING AND OPTIMIZATION • BASIC SETTINGS FOR SETTING UP THE SYSTEM LANDSCAPE • NAME LOGICAL SYSTEM

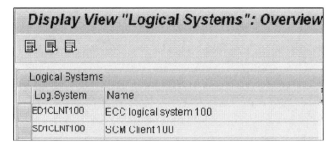

Figure 6.11: Logical systems as maintained in ERP

6.2.2   Assign the logical system to a client

The *logical system* as defined in Section 6.2.1 is connected to a *client* in the SAP land-scape so that the logical system is recognized in the system architecture. We do this as shown in Figure 6.12 for our business scenario.

The IMG path for this configuration in the ERP system is as follows:

SAP CUSTOMIZING IMPLEMENTATION GUIDE • INTEGRATION WITH OTHER SAP COMPONENTS • ADVANCED PLANNING AND OPTIMIZATION • BASIC SETTINGS FOR SETTING UP THE SYSTEM LAND-SCAPE • ASSIGN LOGICAL SYSTEM TO A CLIENT

Display View "Clients": Details

Client	100 ECC logical sys		
City	ATLANTA	Last Changed By	DEMOUSER
Logical system	ED1CLNT100	Date	15.05.2013
Std currency	USD		
Client role	C Customizing ▼		

Changes and Transports for Client-Specific Objects
- ○ Changes without automatic recording
- ● Automatic recording of changes
- ○ No changes allowed
- ○ Changes w/o automatic recording, no transports allowed

Cross-Client Object Changes
Changes to Repository and cross-client Customizing allowed ▼

Client Copy and Comparison Tool Protection
Protection level 0: No restriction ▼

CATT and eCATT Restrictions
X eCATT and CATT Allowed ▼

Figure 6.12: Logical system assignment to client in ERP

6.2.3 Specify the SAP APO release

We define the RELEASE LEVEL of the target APO planning system as shown in Figure 6.13 for our business scenario. This is a non-transportable configuration design; hence, it has to be replicated once again in the production system.

The IMG path for this configuration in the ERP system is as follows:

SAP CUSTOMIZING IMPLEMENTATION GUIDE • INTEGRATION WITH OTHER SAP COMPONENTS • ADVANCED PLANNING AND OPTIMIZATION • BASIC SETTINGS FOR SETTING UP THE SYSTEM LANDSCAPE • SPECIFY SAP APO RELEASE

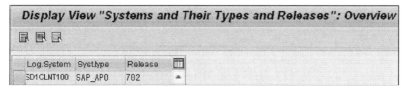

Figure 6.13: APO release for the SCM system

6.2.4 Set up the RFC destination

To set up the RFC definition, we specify the target *remote function call destination*. Ensure that the *target RFC destination* is exactly the same as the *logical system defined* in Section 6.2.1 for the *target APO planning system*. We set up the RFC DESTINATION for our business scenario as shown in Figure 6.14. In most cases, the connection type is 3 and is done in the ABAP CONNECTIONS folder. This is a non-transportable configuration; hence, this has to be replicated once again in production system.

The IMG path for this configuration in the ERP system is this:

SAP CUSTOMIZING IMPLEMENTATION GUIDE • INTEGRATION WITH OTHER SAP COMPONENTS • ADVANCED PLANNING AND OPTIMIZATION • BASIC SETTINGS FOR SETTING UP THE SYSTEM LANDSCAPE • SET UP RFC DESTINATION

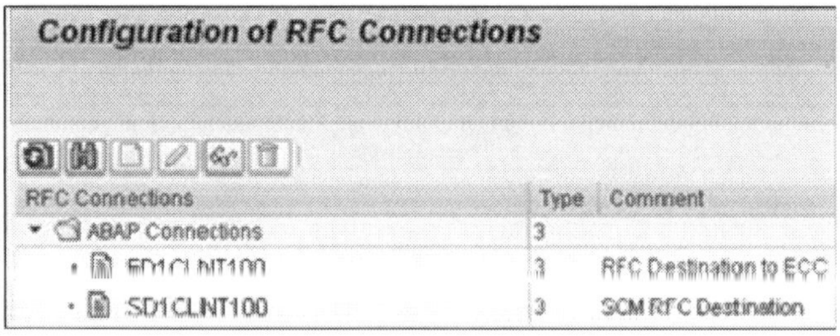

Figure 6.14: RFC definition set up in ERP

6.2.5   Set the target system and queue type

The data that is transferred to the *target system* gets temporarily stored in *queues* and the *queue type* (i.e., inbound or outbound) can be controlled either by the sending system, or receiving system. Through this configuration we can control the *queue type* for the *target system*. For our business scenario we make an entry for the queue type INBOUND as shown in Figure 6.15 as we intend to monitor data only on the receiving system side. This is a non-transportable configuration; hence, it has to be replicated once again in the production system

The IMG path for this configuration in the ERP system is as follows:

SAP CUSTOMIZING IMPLEMENTATION GUIDE • INTEGRATION WITH OTHER SAP COMPONENTS • ADVANCED PLANNING AND OPTIMIZATION • BASIC SETTINGS FOR SETTING UP THE SYSTEM LAND-SCAPE • SET TARGET SYSTEM AND QUEUE TYPE

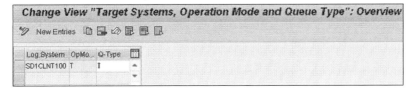

Figure 6.15: Setting up the target system and queue type

6.2.6   Set user parameters

Through this configuration, we make the user specific settings for RFC mode, i.e., activating or deactivating data transfer through CIF, configuration of the application log, and for activating/deactivating debugging. For our business scenario, we keep it the same for all users and make entries for queued RFC MODE (Q), detailed LOGGING (D), and DEBUGGING with transactional/queued RFCs for recording (R) as shown in Figure 6.16.

The IMG path for this configuration in the ERP system is as follows:

SAP CUSTOMIZING IMPLEMENTATION GUIDE • INTEGRATION WITH OTHER SAP COMPONENTS • ADVANCED PLANNING AND OPTIMIZATION • BASIC SETTINGS FOR THE DATA TRANSFER • SET USER PARAMETERS

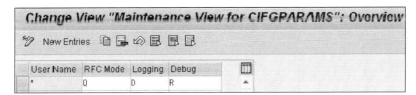

Figure 6.16: User parameters set up

In this section, we touched on the connectivity design required for establishing connectivity between ERP and SCM. In the next section, we will explain the master data that is required in ERP to carry out APO DP.

6.3   Master data in ERP

SAP *Material Master* needs to be maintained in the ERP system before it can be considered for planning in APO DP, albeit after transferring them through the core interface to APO. The master data is typically maintained in the ERP system by an ERP Functional Consultant.

You will find reference to this section as 'Master Data Maintenance in ERP' in the block 'Design in ERP for Demand Planning' in the APO DP process flow depicted in Figure 4.2.

The essential master data design in ERP that is required for planning in APO is explained below. We will explain the core interface in Section 6.4.

In this section we will show in brief, how the material *32" DM LCD 720p HDTV* (ZDM_FG1) is created in plant *Atlanta Manufacturing Plant* (ZDM1), in storage location *Atlanta Stg Loc* (ZDS1) in the ERP system, for our business scenario.

The transaction code or menu path for creating materials in the ERP system is as follows:

Transaction Code: MM01

Menu Path: SAP MENU • LOGISTICS • MATERIALS MANAGEMENT • MATERIAL MASTER • MATERIAL • CREATE (GENERAL) • IMMEDIATELY

Once we are on the transaction code screen mentioned above, we can CREATE MATERIAL (initial screen) and make entries for the material details as shown in Figure 6.17. Click on SELECT VIEWS(S) ❶ and this brings up the SELECT VIEW(S) screen where we can select the BASIC DATA1, MRP 1, MRP 2, MRP 3, MRP 4 and ACCOUNTING 1 views as shown in ❷. We choose to maintain only these views for our business scenario as it will suffice for material creation for DM Consumer Appliances, Inc.

Next, click ENTER ☑ and select plant ZDM1 and STORAGE LOCATION ZDS1 (❸) and click ENTER ☑. This takes us to the BASIC DATA1 (❹) screen. Make entries of all the necessary data in all the views: BASIC DATA1 (❹), MRP 1 (❺), MRP 2 (❼), MRP 3 (❽), MRP 4 (❾) and ACCOUNTING 1 (❿). Please note that the field MRP TYPE is entered as X0 (❻) in the MRP 1 view. MRP TYPE will qualify the material for transfer to APO through the core interface and thereby facilitate planning in APO.

Once all of the views are maintained, save the material by clicking SAVE 💾. Material ZDM_FG1 (32" DM LCD 720P HDTV) in plant ZDM1 (ATLANTA MANUFACTURING PLANT) is now created as shown in Figure 6.17.

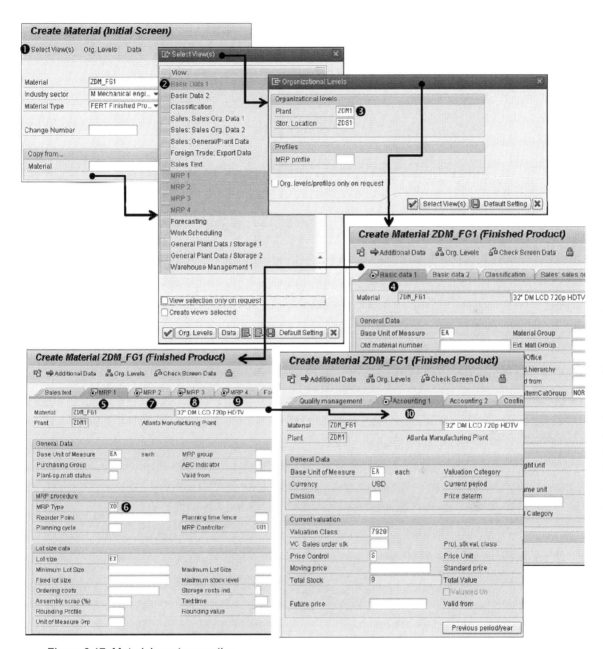

Figure 6.17: Material master creation

Similarly, we go on to create the material for the following material, plant, and storage location combinations for our business scenario at DM Consumer Appliances, Inc.:

▶ *ZDM_FG1 (32" DM LCD 720p HDTV) and ZDD1 (Frankfort Distribution Center)*
▶ *ZDM_FG1 (32" DM LCD 720p HDTV) and ZDR1 (Columbus Retail Store)*
▶ *ZDM_FG1 (32" DM LCD 720p HDTV) and ZDR2 (Philadelphia Retail Store)*
▶ *ZDM_FG2 (32" DM LCD 1080p HDTV), ZDM1 (Atlanta Manufacturing Plant) and ZDS1 (Atlanta Stg Loc)*
▶ *ZDM_FG2 (32" DM LCD 1080p HDTV) and ZDD1 (Frankfort Distribution Center)*
▶ *ZDM_FG2 (32" DM LCD 1080p HDTV) and ZDR1 (Columbus Retail Store)*
▶ *ZDM_FG2 (32" DM LCD 1080p HDTV) and ZDR2 (Philadelphia Retail Store)*
▶ *ZDM_FG3 (39" DM LCD 1080p HDTV), ZDM1 (Atlanta Manufacturing Plant) and ZDS1 (Atlanta Stg Loc)*
▶ *ZDM_FG3 (39" DM LCD 1080p HDTV) and ZDD1 (Frankfort Distribution Center)*
▶ *ZDM_FG3 (39" DM LCD 1080p HDTV) and ZDR1 (Columbus Retail Store)*
▶ *ZDM_FG3 (39" DM LCD 1080p HDTV) and ZDR2 (Philadelphia Retail Store)*
▶ *ZDM_FG4 (40" DM LED 1080p HDTV), ZDM1 (Atlanta Manufacturing Plant) and ZDS1 (Atlanta Stg Loc)*
▶ *ZDM_FG4 (40" DM LED 1080p HDTV) and ZDD1 (Frankfort Distribution Center)*
▶ *ZDM_FG4 (40" DM LED 1080p HDTV) and ZDR1 (Columbus Retail Store)*
▶ *ZDM_FG4 (40" DM LED 1080p HDTV) and ZDR2 (Philadelphia Retail Store)*

For materials in *Atlanta Manufacturing Plant* (ZDM1), we make an entry for the storage location ZDS1.

In this section, we created all the materials that are required for our business scenario. In the next section, we will create the core interface settings that will lay the foundation for integrating the master and transaction data between the ERP and APO systems.

6.4   Core interface settings

The SCM system has APO as its component. The SCM system can connect to heterogeneous systems, i.e., to another SAP system, as well as to another non-SAP system. The SCM system connects to non-SAP systems through Business Application Programming Interfaces (BAPIs). The SCM system connects to the SAP system through a standard SAP interface called a *core interface*, also called *CIF.* Transferring data between the SCM system and the ERP system is facilitated through generating and executing an *integration model*. In this section, we explain in detail how to generate an integration model for our business scenario. Generating the integration model lays the foundation for executing the integration model.

You will find reference to this section as 'CIF Integration Model Generation (Master Data & Transaction Data)' in the block 'Design in ERP for Demand Planning' in the APO DP process flow depicted in Figure 4.2.

Let's now look at the essential core interface settings in ERP that are required for planning in APO.

The *integration model* specifies the selection criteria or boundary conditions for data that will be transferred to the SCM system.

Integration model in an ERP system

 Integration models are created in the ERP system. Each model is specified by its model name, APO application, and target logical SCM system.

When we execute the integration model, we are able to transfer and interchange data between the ERP system and the SCM system. Transfer of master data is unidirectional, i.e., from ERP to SCM. In contrast, transfer of transactional data is bidirectional, i.e., from ERP to SCM and vice versa.

6.4.1 Generate integration model for location

For our business scenario, we have four locations for DM Consumer Appliances, Inc.: *Atlanta Manufacturing Plant*, *Frankfort Distribution Center*, *Columbus Retail Store* and *Philadelphia Retail Store*. We will generate an integration model that pertains to these four locations specifically as shown in Figure 6.18.

The transaction code or menu path for creating an integration model in the ERP system is as follows:

Transaction Code: CFM1

Menu Path: SAP MENU • LOGISTICS • CENTRAL FUNCTIONS • SUPPLY CHAIN PLANNING INTERFACE • CORE INTERFACE ADVANCED PLANNER AND OPTIMIZER • INTEGRATION MODEL • CREATE

For our business scenario, we make entries for the model name, target logical system and APO application as shown by ❶ as a unique combination for locations at DM Consumer Appliances, Inc. Next, select the locations for DM Consumer Appliances, Inc. by clicking onto (❷) and then enter the location details and click EXECUTE ⊕ (❸) to go back to the CREATE INTEGRATION MODEL (❹) screen. Next, save this selection as variant by clicking on the SAVE 🖫 icon (❺). Make entries of the variant details and SAVE 🖫 (❻) the variant. Go back to screen CREATE INTEGRATION MODEL.

Next, click EXECUTE ⊕ (❼) and find the number of plants selected for the integration model (❽). Next, click GENERATE IM (❾) and we get a message that the integration model was generated. Click ENTER ✔ (❿).

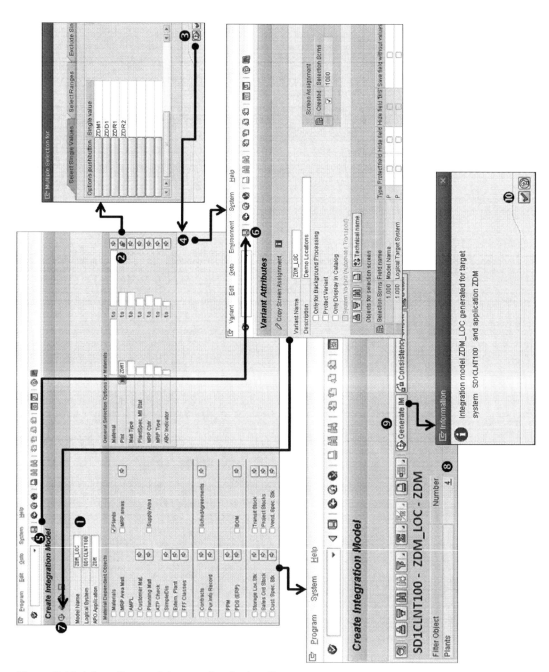

Figure 6.18: Integration model generation for locations

Following the process as explained in Figure 6.18, we are able to generate the integration model ZDM_LOC for locations in our business scenario.

6.4.2   Generate integration model for materials

For our business scenario at DM Consumer Appliances, Inc. we have four materials: ZDM_FG1, ZDM_FG2, ZDM_FG3, and ZDM_FG4 in the *Atlanta Manufacturing Plant*, *Frankfort Distribution Center*, *Columbus Retail Store* and *Philadelphia Retail Store*. We generate an integration model that pertains to the combination of these four materials and locations specifically as shown in Figure 6.19.

The transaction code or menu path for creating an integration model in the ERP system is as follows:

Transaction Code: CFM1

Menu Path: SAP MENU • LOGISTICS • CENTRAL FUNCTIONS • SUPPLY CHAIN PLANNING INTERFACE • CORE INTERFACE ADVANCED PLANNER AND OPTIMIZER • INTEGRATION MODEL • CREATE

For our business scenario, we make entries for the model name, target logical system, and APO application as shown in ❶ as a unique combination for materials and locations at DM Consumer Appliances, Inc. Next, select the materials by clicking onto (❷) and locations by clicking onto (❸) for DM Consumer Appliances, Inc. and then enter the material and location details and click EXECUTE 🔄 (❹) to go back to the CREATE INTEGRATION MODEL (❺) screen. Next, save this selection as a variant by clicking on the SAVE 💾 icon (❻). Make entries for the variant details and SAVE (❼) the variant. Go back to screen CREATE INTEGRATION MODEL.

Next, EXECUTE 🔄 (❽) the integration model and it takes us to the screen listing the number of materials. Next, we click GENERATE IM (❾) and we get a message that the integration model was generated. Click ENTER ✅ (❿).

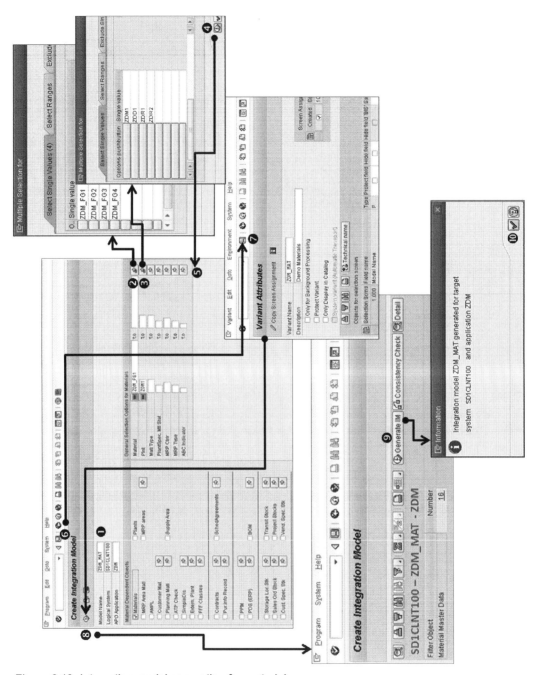

Figure 6.19: Integration model generation for materials

Following the process as explained in Figure 6.19, we are able to generate the integration model ZDM_MAT for the materials in our business scenario.

6.4.3   Generate an integration model for stocks and PIRs

In addition to generating the integration model for master data (i.e., locations and materials), we also generate an integration model for the transaction data pertaining to APO demand planning for DM Consumer Appliances, Inc.. This will facilitate the data transfer between the ERP and SCM systems.

For our business scenario, we specify the boundaries for transactions only for *stocks* and *planned independent requirements* pertaining to the four materials and four locations for DM Consumer Appliances, Inc. We generate an integration model following the process shown in Figure 6.20.

The transaction code or menu path for creating an integration model in ERP is as follows:

Transaction Code: CFM1

Menu Path: SAP MENU • LOGISTICS • CENTRAL FUNCTIONS • SUPPLY CHAIN PLANNING INTERFACE • CORE INTERFACE ADVANCED PLANNER AND OPTIMIZER • INTEGRATION MODEL • CREATE

For our business scenario, make entries for the model name, target logical system, and APO application as shown in ❶ as a unique combination of materials and locations at DM Consumer Appliances, Inc. Next, select materials by clicking onto (❷) and locations by clicking onto (❸) for DM Consumer Appliances, Inc. and then enter the material and location details and click EXECUTE � (❹) to go back to the CREATE INTEGRATION MODEL screen (❺). Next, save this selection as a variant by clicking on the SAVE 💾 icon (❻). Make entries for the variant details and SAVE 💾 (❼) the variant. Go back to screen CREATE INTEGRATION MODEL.

Next, EXECUTE 🔣 (❽) the integration model and it takes us to the screen listing the number of stocks and planned independent requirements. Next, click on GENERATE IM (❾) and we get a message that the integration model was generated. Click ENTER ✅ (❿).

Following the process as explained in Figure 6.20, we generate the integration model ZDM_TR for transactions of stocks and planned independent requirements for our business scenario.

The next section explains the execution of the integration models that we generated.

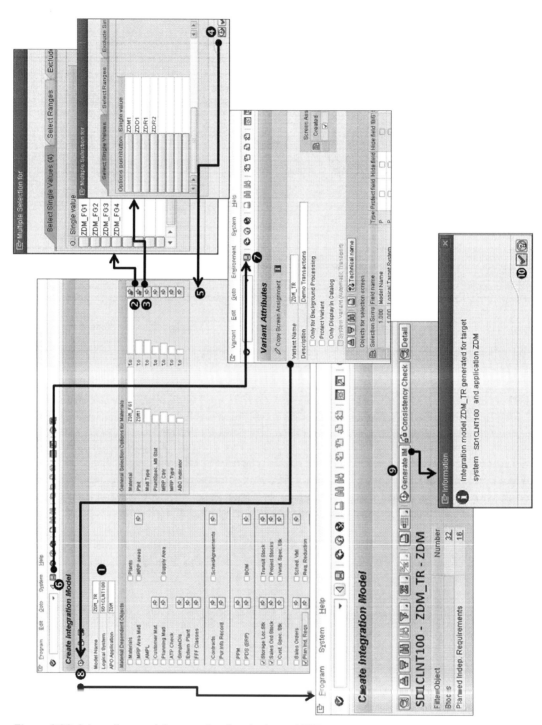

Figure 6.20: Integration model generation for stocks and PIRs

6.5 Integration model execution for data transfer

Now that we have generated the foundation for the data transfer between the ERP and SCM systems through integration model generations for our business scenario, we can execute and activate the integration model and effect the data transfer between the two connecting systems.

You will find the reference to this section as 'CIF Integration Model Activation (Data Transfer from ERP to APO)' in the block 'Design in ERP for Demand Planning' in the APO DP process flow depicted in Figure 4.2.

Next, let's look at the integration model activation mechanism in ERP that is required for planning in APO.

The execution of the integration model is done through activation, or deactivation. *Activation* leads to the initial transfer of data. However, if a new data set is transferred through a new integration model, then the data set is compared to any existing *active integration model* and only the data that does not exist in any of the active integration models will get transferred. This ensures incremental data transfer. For any data set transferred online, it must be part of an active integration model.

Retransfer data through the integration model

 If we want to retransfer data all over again, we have to deactivate the integration model and then reactivate it.

One active integration model for one data set

 We can also create multiple integration models for the same data set, however only one version can be the active one.

We can delete active, as well as inactive integration models.

Impact of integration model deletion

 Deleting an integration model will not allow data transfer between ERP and SCM unless that data exists in another active integration model. Nevertheless, deleting an integration model does not delete the data.

In this section, we will explain the activation process for the three integration models that we have generated for DM Consumer Appliances, Inc.

6.5.1   Location integration model activation

We activate the integration model ZDM_LOC that we generated earlier for DM Consumer Appliances, Inc. locations. Let's looks at the process of activation in brief (see Figure 6.21).

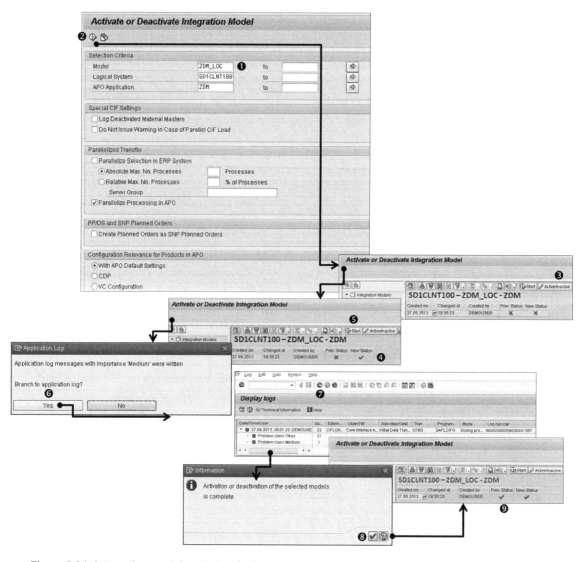

Figure 6.21: Integration model activation for locations

The transaction code or menu path for the integration model activation in the ERP system is as follows:

Transaction Code: CFM2

Menu Path: SAP MENU • LOGISTICS • CENTRAL FUNCTIONS • SUPPLY CHAIN PLANNING INTERFACE • CORE INTERFACE ADVANCED PLANNER AND OPTIMIZER • INTEGRATION MODEL • ACTIVATE

For our business scenario, we make entries for the integration model name for location, target logical system, and APO application as shown by ❶. Ensure all the other settings as shown in the figure. Next, click the EXECUTE ⊕ icon (❷) and it takes us to screen displaying the status of the integration model. Select the row and click on the ACTIVE/ INACTIVE button (❸) that changes the new status to green (❹). Next, click on the START button (❺) and the integration model activation process begins. Post integration model activation process, we get the dialogue box for branching to the APPLICATION LOG. Click YES (❻) to the dialogue and it takes us to the DISPLAY LOGS screen. After analyzing the APPLICATION LOG we go back by clicking BACK ⊙ (❼) and a window appears that informs us that the activation is complete. We click ENTER ☑ (❽) and it takes us back to the screen ACTIVATE OR DEACTIVATE INTEGRATION MODEL showing both the PREVIOUS STATUS (❾) and NEW STATUS with a green check.

We are able to activate the integration model ZDM_LOC for the locations in our business scenario by following the process as explained in Figure 6.21. Once successfully activated, these locations will be available in APO.

6.5.2 Integration model activation for materials

We activate the Integration Model ZDM_MAT that we generated earlier for DM Consumer Appliances, Inc. materials. We will review the process in brief:

The transaction code or menu path for integration model activation in the ERP system is as follows:

Transaction Code: CFM2

Menu Path: SAP MENU • LOGISTICS • CENTRAL FUNCTIONS • SUPPLY CHAIN PLANNING INTERFACE • CORE INTERFACE ADVANCED PLANNER AND OPTIMIZER • INTEGRATION MODEL • ACTIVATE

Please refer to Figure 6.22. For our business scenario, select the integration model name for material, target logical system, and APO application as shown in ❶. Ensure that all the other settings are as shown in the figure. Next, click on the EXECUTE ⊕ icon (❷) and it takes us to screen displaying the status of the integration model. Select the row and click on the ACTIVE/ INACTIVE button (❸) that changes the new status to green (❹). Next, we click on the START button (❺) and the integration model activation process begins. When the integration model activation process is complete, we get a dialogue box for branching to APPLICATION LOG. Click YES (❻) to the dialogue and it takes us to the DISPLAY LOGS screen. After analyzing the APPLICATION LOG we go back by clicking BACK ⊙ (❼) and a window appears that informs us that the activation is complete. Click ENTER ☑ (❽) and it takes us back to the screen ACTIVATE OR DEACTIVATE INTEGRATION MODEL showing both the PREVIOUS STATUS (❾) and the NEW STATUS as a green checkmark.

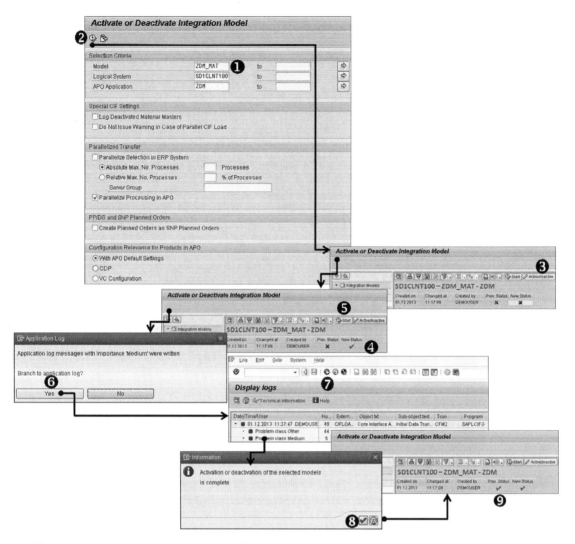

Figure 6.22: Integration model activation for materials

We are able to activate the integration model ZDM_MAT for the materials in our business scenario by following the process as explained in Figure 6.22. When they are successfully activated, these materials will be available in APO.

6.5.3 Integration model activation for stocks and PIRs

We now need to activate the integration model ZDM_TR that we generated earlier for stocks and planned independent requirements for DM Consumer Appliances, Inc. Let's look at the process in brief.

The transaction code or menu path for activating the integration model in the ERP system is as follows:

Transaction Code: CFM2

Menu Path: SAP MENU • LOGISTICS • CENTRAL FUNCTIONS • SUPPLY CHAIN PLANNING INTERFACE • CORE INTERFACE ADVANCED PLANNER AND OPTIMIZER • INTEGRATION MODEL • ACTIVATE

Please refer to Figure 6.23. For our business scenario, select the integration model name for stocks and planned independent requirements, target logical system and APO application as shown in ❶. Ensure that all the other settings are as shown in the figure. Next, click the EXECUTE ⊕ icon (❷) and it takes us to a screen displaying the status of the integration model. Select the row and click on the ACTIVE/ INACTIVE button (❸) that changes the new status to green (❹). Next, click on the START button (❺) and the integration model activation process will begin. When the integration model activation process is complete, we get the dialogue box for branching to the APPLICATION LOG. Click YES (❻) to the dialogue and it takes us to the DISPLAY LOGS screen. After analyzing the APPLICATION LOG we go back by clicking BACK ⬑ (❼) and a window appears that informs us that the activation is complete. Click ENTER ✅ (❽) and it takes us back to the screen ACTIVATE OR DEACTIVATE INTEGRATION MODEL showing both the PREVIOUS STATUS (❾) and NEW STATUS as green checkmark.

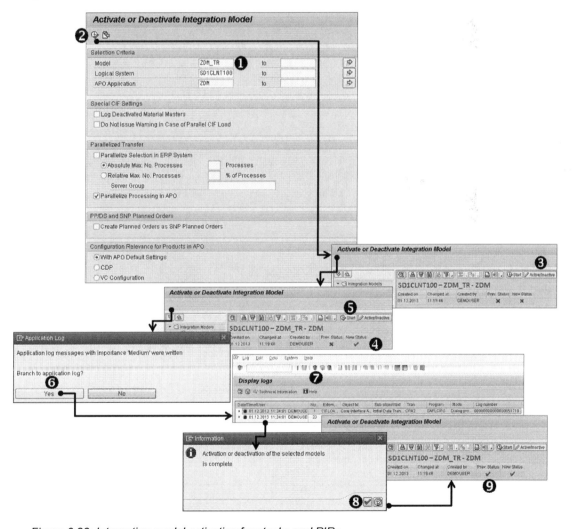

Figure 6.23: Integration model activation for stocks and PIRs

We are able to activate the integration model ZDM_TR for stocks and planned independent requirements for our business scenario by following the process as explained in Figure 6.23. Once successfully activated, the stocks and planned independent requirements, if any, becomes available in real time between the ERP and SCM systems.

6.6   Summary

In this chapter, we explained the different designs for ERP configuration and connectivity settings required to integrate ERP system and SCM system for APO demand planning for our business scenario. Furthermore, we maintained the ERP master data, core interface settings, and integration model execution to transfer and integrate the master data and transaction data between the two connected systems for our business scenario.

In the next chapter, we will introduce the basic settings for design in APO DP that needs to be carried out in the APO system itself for our business scenario.

7 Basic design in APO DP

Successful demand planning requires a robust design that considers factors like meeting business requirements, consistency and connectivity between integrated systems, and good performance. In this chapter, we will introduce the basic and foundational design in APO DP along with its concepts.

In this chapter, we will cover the basic designs that are required in SAP SCM for carrying out APO DP. These designs are prerequisites and form the foundation of APO DP. We will explain configuration in SCM for establishing connectivity between ERP and APO, master data in APO, master planning object structure, characteristics value combinations, bucket profiles, planning area, realignment and copy of data structure, planning book, data view and selections.

7.1 Establishing connectivity between ERP and APO

A demand planning system needs to source data from the primary execution system (i.e., the ERP system). Based on the design, the data from the APO DP system could flow to the ERP system to enable interaction between ERP and APO. We establish connectivity between ERP and APO through a series of configurations in the SCM system. These configurations are analogous to the ones we explained in Chapter 6.

You will find the reference to this section as 'Connectivity between ERP and APO (Maintained in APO)' in the block 'Design in APO DP' in the APO DP process flow depicted in Figure 4.2.

The connectivity configurations in SCM have direct relevance for demand planning and pertain to our business scenario described in Chapter 3. These configurations will establish the system infrastructure to transfer data through the core interface (CIF). We explained the core interface (CIF) in detail in Sections 6.4 and 6.5.

Typically, these designs are done by a Basis Administrator in consultation with an APO consultant. In this section, we will define the logical system and assign that to a client, set up an RFC destination, maintain the business system group and assign that to logical system and queue type, set up the user parameters, maintain distribution definition for demand planning results, and activate incremental data transfer.

7.1.1 Name logical system

The *logical system* in SAP is a unique application system that is connected to the network of multiple application systems. For our business scenario, we uniquely identify the execution system (i.e., ERP SYSTEM ECC), as well as the demand planning system (i.e., SCM SYSTEM) and define them as shown in the Figure 7.1. We maintain both the ERP and SCM logical system in the SCM system despite a similar configuration on the ERP.

The IMG path for this configuration in SCM system is as follows:

SAP – IMPLEMENTATION GUIDE • INTEGRATION WITH SAP COMPONENTS • INTEGRATION VIA APO CORE INTERFACE (CIF) • BASIC SETTINGS FOR CREATING THE SYSTEM LANDSCAPE • NAME LOGICAL SYSTEMS

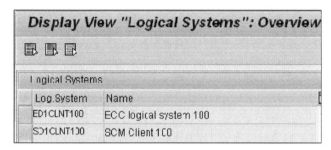

Figure 7.1: Logical systems maintained in SCM

7.1.2   Assign logical system to a client

The *logical system* as defined in Section 7.1.1 is connected to a *client* in the SAP landscape so that the *logical system* gets recognized in the system architecture. We do this as shown in Figure 7.2 for our business scenario. We maintain the client assignment of the LOGICAL SYSTEM in the SAP SCM system despite a similar configuration on the ERP side as was explained in Section 6.2.

The IMG path for this configuration in the SCM system is as follows:

SAP – IMPLEMENTATION GUIDE • INTEGRATION WITH SAP COMPONENTS • INTEGRATION VIA APO CORE INTERFACE (CIF) • BASIC SETTINGS FOR CREATING THE SYSTEM LANDSCAPE • ASSIGN LOGICAL SYSTEMS TO A CLIENT

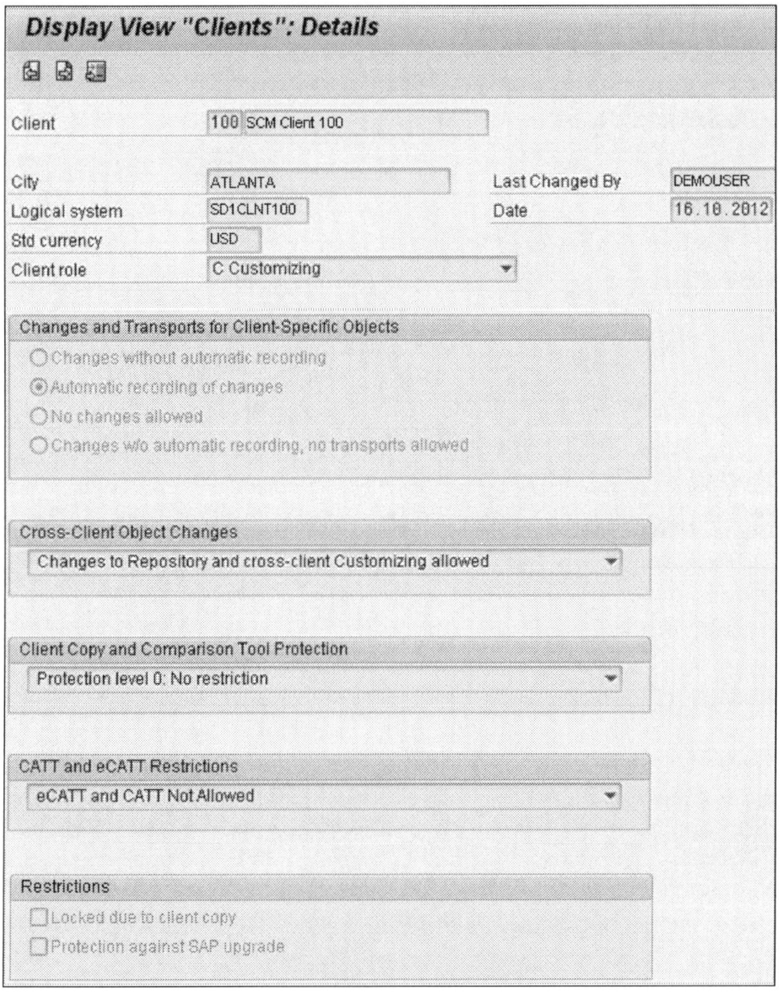

Figure 7.2: Logical system assignment to a client in SCM

7.1.3 Set up the RFC destination

In this configuration, we specify the target remote function call destination. We ensure that the target *RFC destination* is exactly the same as the *logical system* defined in Section 7.1.1 for the target *ERP execution system*. We set up the RFC DESTINATION for our business scenario as shown in Figure 7.3. In most cases, the connection type is 3 and is done in the ABAP CONNECTIONS folder. We maintain the RFC destination in the *SCM system* despite a similar configuration on the ERP side as was explained in Section 6.2.

This is a non-transportable configuration; hence, this has to be replicated once again in the production system.

The IMG path for this configuration in the SCM system is as follows:

SAP – Implementation Guide • Integration with SAP Components • Integration via APO Core Interface (CIF) • Basic Settings for Creating the System Landscape • Set Up RFC Destination

Configuration of RFC Connections

RFC Connections	Type	Comment
▼ ⌂ ABAP Connections	3	
• 📄 ED1CLNT100	3	RFC Destination to ECC
• 📄 SD1CLNT100	3	SCM RFC Destination

Figure 7.3: RFC definition set up in SCM

7.1.4 Business system group

The *business system group*, groups one or more logical systems from a business stand-point and uniquely identifies each object belonging to multiple logical systems through a unique and uniform numbering system. For our business scenario at DM Consumer Appliances, Inc., we maintain this relationship in a 1:1 ratio as explained in Section 7.1.5. In this section, we define a single BUSINESS SYSTEM GROUP common to both the ERP and SCM systems as shown in Figure 7.4.

The IMG path for this configuration in the SCM system is as follows:

SAP – Implementation Guide • Integration with SAP Components • Integration via APO Core Interface (CIF) • Basic Settings for Creating the System Landscape • Maintain Business System Group

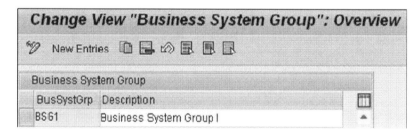

Figure 7.4: Maintenance of the business system group

7.1.5 Assign the logical system and queue type

Through this configuration we assign LOGICAL SYSTEMS, pertaining to our business scenario, to a BUSINESS SYSTEM GROUP and assign a QUEUE TYPE to the BUSINESS SYSTEM GROUP as shown in Figure 7.5. We will also assign an ERROR HANDLING TYPE to LOGICAL SYSTEMS as shown in Figure 7.5.

The data that is transferred to the target system gets temporarily stored in queues. The queue types are either *inbound queues* or *outbound queues*.

Setting queue type as inbound

 It is best practice to have the queue type set as an inbound type as it can facilitate large volumes of data transfer to the ERP system with an even load on the ERP system.

For our business scenario, we make entries for the QUEUE TYPE as INBOUND QUEUES as shown in Figure 7.5.

Queue registration

 Queues that the ERP system has to process automatically need to be registered with QIN scheduler. Ensure that requisite configurations are done for Queue-In (QIN) scheduler in the qRFC monitor on the ERP side.

The IMG path for assigning the logical system and queue type in the SCM system is as follows:

SAP – IMPLEMENTATION GUIDE • INTEGRATION WITH SAP COMPONENTS • INTEGRATION VIA APO CORE INTERFACE (CIF) • BASIC SETTINGS FOR CREATING THE SYSTEM LANDSCAPE • ASSIGN LOGICAL SYSTEM AND QUEUE TYPE

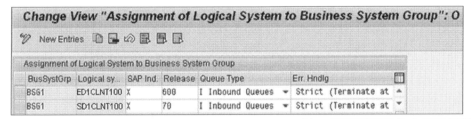

Figure 7.5: Assignment of a logical system to business system group and CIF Error Handling

7.1.6 Set user parameters

Through this configuration, we make entries for user specific settings for configuring the APPLICATION LOG, DEACTIVATING DEBUGGING, and controlling the publication of planning results through EVENT RECORDING as shown in Figure 7.6 for our business scenario.

The IMG path for this configuration in the SCM system is as follows:

SAP – IMPLEMENTATION GUIDE • INTEGRATION WITH SAP COMPONENTS • INTEGRATION VIA APO CORE INTERFACE (CIF) • BASIC SETTINGS FOR DATA TRANSFER • SET USER PARAMETERS

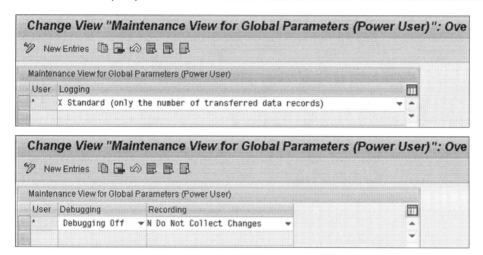

Figure 7.6: Global parameters settings for power users

7.1.7 Distribution definition

Distribution definition configuration will ensure the distribution of planning results from APO to the ERP system.

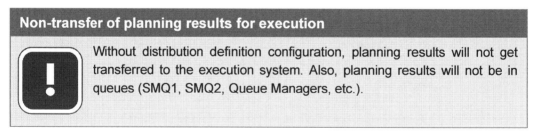

Non-transfer of planning results for execution

Without distribution definition configuration, planning results will not get transferred to the execution system. Also, planning results will not be in queues (SMQ1, SMQ2, Queue Managers, etc.).

For our business scenario at DM Consumer Appliances, Inc. we maintain the distribution definition of only PLANNED INDEPENDENT REQUIREMENTS as PUBLICATION TYPE for the ATLANTA MANUFACTURING PLANT, the FRANKFURT DISTRIBUTION CENTER, the COLUMBUS RETAIL STORE, and PHILADELPHIA RETAIL STORE as shown in Figure 7.7. We do this as we will only be carrying out demand planning. Other publication types have to be defined separately as appropriate for supply planning.

The IMG path for this configuration in the SCM system is as follows:

SAP – IMPLEMENTATION GUIDE • INTEGRATION WITH SAP COMPONENTS • INTEGRATION VIA APO CORE INTERFACE (CIF) • BASIC SETTINGS FOR DATA TRANSFER • PUBLICATION • MAINTAIN DISTRIBUTION DEFINITION

Change View "Maintenance View for Distribution Definitions": Overview

New Entries

Maintenance View for Distribution Definitions

Publ. Type	Locatn no.	LogSystem	SAP Rel.	
51 Planned Independent Requirements ▼ ZDD1		ED1CLNT100	600	▲
51 Planned Independent Requirements ▼ ZDM1		ED1CLNT100	600	▼
51 Planned Independent Requirements ▼ ZDR1		ED1CLNT100	600	
51 Planned Independent Requirements ▼ ZDR2		ED1CLNT100	600	

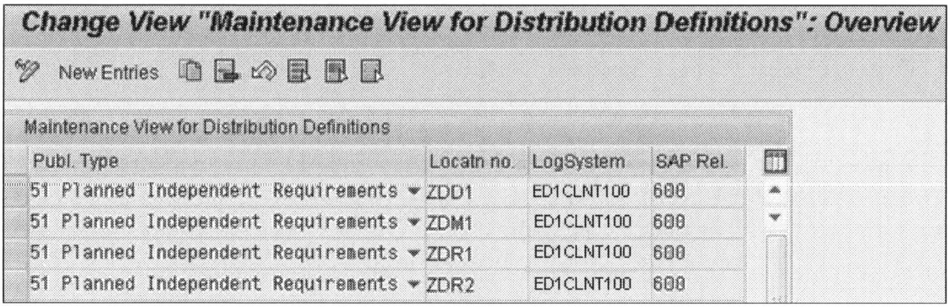

Figure 7.7: Distribution definition maintenance

7.1.8 Activate incremental data transfer

Incremental data transfer is valid only for product master data, location product master data, and the production data structure. For our business scenario, the production data structure is not relevant. Incremental data transfer configuration will allow transfer of all the correct master data out of CIF queues in one go. It will allow retransfer of master data after error correction. With every retransfer the volume of master data objects in CIF queues reduces and therefore, the retransfer mechanism becomes more effective.

However, if the incremental data transfer is not active then on correction of CIF errors for master data, all master data including the corrected ones need to be retransferred all over again. For our business scenario, we will activate the INCREMENTAL DATA TRANSFER to ensure effectiveness as shown in Figure 7.8.

The IMG path for this configuration in the SCM system is as follows:

SAP – IMPLEMENTATION GUIDE • INTEGRATION WITH SAP COMPONENTS • INTEGRATION VIA APO CORE INTERFACE (CIF) • BASIC SETTINGS FOR DATA TRANSFER • CIF ERROR HANDLING • ACTIVATE INCREMENTAL DATA TRANSFER

Change View "CIF Incremental Data Transfer Maintenance": Overview

New Entries

CIF Incremental Data Transfer Maintenance

BusSystGrp	Logical system	SAP System	SAP Rel.		Increm. DT		
BS61	ED1CLNT100	X	600 SAP ERP 2005	▼	✓		▲
BS61	SD1CLNT100	X	70 SAP SCM 7.0	▼	✓		▼

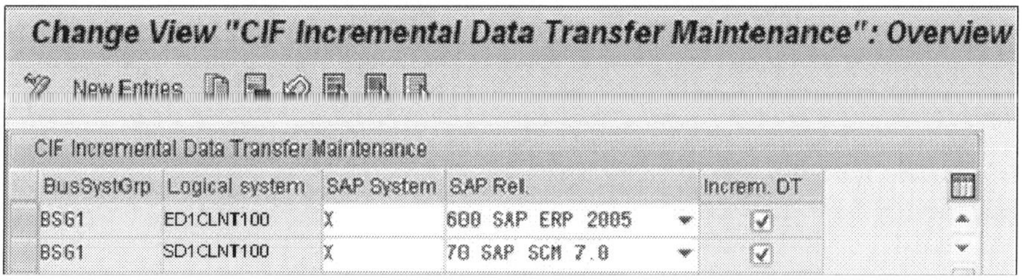

Figure 7.8: Activation of incremental data transfer

In the next section, we will explain master data in APO that we maintain for additional inputs despite transfer of the master data from the ERP system through CIF.

7.2 Master data in APO

Apart from the master data that we maintained in ERP, we have to maintain master data in the SAP SCM system as well. Unlike the ERP master data that is maintained by an ERP Consultant, the APO master data needs to be maintained by an APO Consultant. You will find the ERP master data maintained in Section 6.3.

APO master data is a prerequisite for APO Demand Planning. While some master data needs to be directly maintained in APO itself (e.g., model and version management), there are some that get transferred through the core interface from the ERP system and only needs to be modified or added with additional details in APO. It does not need to be maintained from scratch, e.g., location and product master data.

You will find the reference to this section as 'Master Data in APO' in the block 'Design in APO DP' in the APO DP process flow depicted in Figure 4.2.

In the next section, we will briefly review the master data for model and version management, locations, and products that needs to be maintained in APO for our business scenario.

7.2.1 Model and version management

Models in the supply chain form the basis of planning in APO and we can assign multiple *planning versions* to a model. We can maintain multiple models and multiple versions for simulation purposes. However, only the *active model (model 000)* and *active planning version (version 000)* are taken into account for actual planning.

We can assign models and versions to master data either in the supply chain engineer, or in the master data. You can conduct model consistency checks to verify the sanity of the model. When master data gets generated in APO through core interface, it gets automatically assigned to the active model and the active version.

For our business scenario we make an entry for the ACTIVE MODEL 000 and ACTIVE VERSION 000 as shown in Figure 7.9 and Figure 7.10.

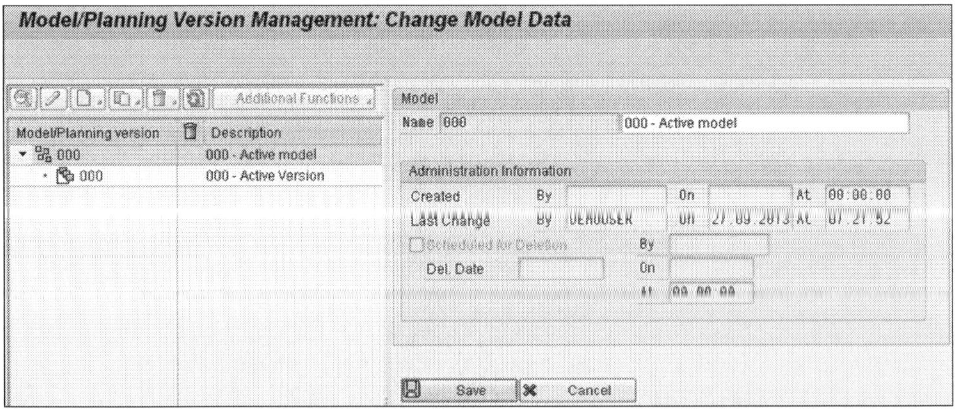

Figure 7.9: Maintenance of the model in APO

The transaction code or menu path for model and version management in the SCM system is as follows:

Transaction Code: /SAPAPO/MVM

Menu Path: SAP MENU • ADVANCED PLANNING AND OPTIMIZATION • MASTER DATA • PLANNING VERSION MANAGEMENT • MODEL AND VERSION MANAGEMENT

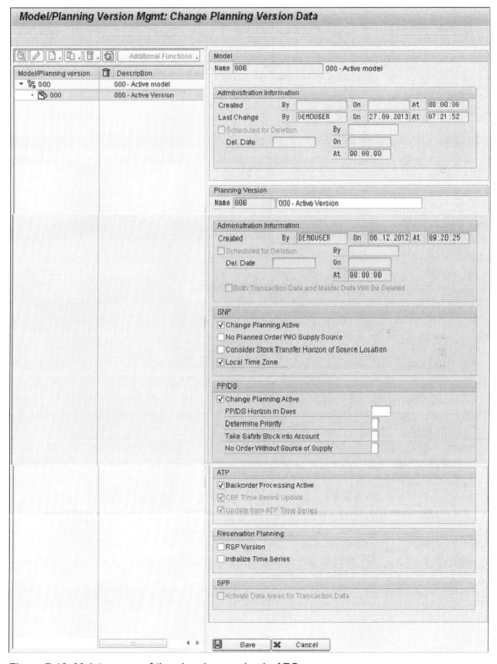

Figure 7.10: Maintenance of the planning version in APO

Once the model and planning versions are defined, they will be available for assignment to the location master and product location master in the location maintenance and product maintenance transaction in APO itself. We will explain location maintenance in the next section.

7.2.2 Location

Location in APO implies a physical or logical place where products or resources are managed. Locations are identified as *plants* in ERP. These locations typically correspond to manufacturing plants, distribution centers, stores, customers, and suppliers in ERP and they get transferred through the core interface. There are different types of locations in APO based on whether they are a manufacturing plant, distribution center, store, customer, or supplier.

For our business scenario at DM Consumer Appliances, Inc. we will only consider these locations: *Atlanta Manufacturing Plant*, *Frankfort Distribution Center*, *Columbus Retail Store* and *Philadelphia Retail Store*. We maintain locations in the ERP system as plants as explained in Section 6.1.1 and maintain their types in Section 6.1.2. Next, we transfer them through the core interface as explained in Sections 6.4 and 6.5. Once transferred through CIF these locations get automatically assigned to *active model 000* and *active planning version 000* along with their types. These locations can be seen or modified in the following transactions.

The transaction code or menu path for location maintenance in the SCM system is as follows:

Transaction Code: /SAPAPO/LOC3

Menu Path: SAP MENU • ADVANCED PLANNING AND OPTIMIZATION • MASTER DATA • LOCATION

We have four locations for DM Consumer Appliances, Inc. using the transactions mentioned above as shown in the Figures 7.11 and 7.12. For example, in Figure 7.11 the location ATLANTA MANUFACTURING PLANT (❶) as PRODUCTION PLANT TYPE (❷) is assigned to planning version 000 (❸). We also verify the details around the location by verifying the particulars in every tab (❹). We can modify these details as appropriate by going to the change mode and saving it.

Similarly, details for the FRANKFORT DISTRIBUTION CENTER, the COLUMBUS RETAIL STORE and the PHILADELPHIA RETAIL STORE details will appear as shown in Figure 7.12.

The next section explains the maintenance of products in APO.

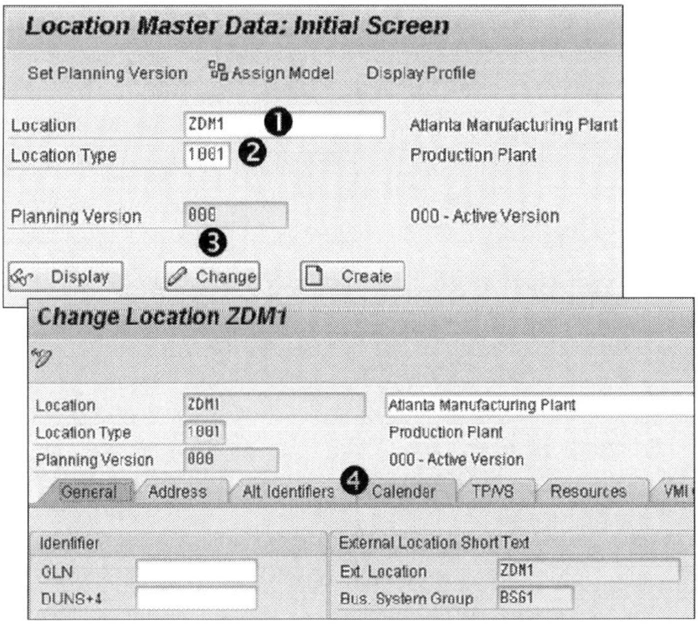

Location Master Data: Initial Screen

Set Planning Version   Assign Model   Display Profile

Location	ZDM1 ❶		Atlanta Manufacturing Plant
Location Type	1001 ❷		Production Plant
Planning Version	000		000 - Active Version

❸

Display   Change   Create

Change Location ZDM1

Location	ZDM1		Atlanta Manufacturing Plant
Location Type	1001		Production Plant
Planning Version	000		000 - Active Version

General   Address   Alt. Identifiers   ❹ Calendar   TP/VS   Resources   VMI

Identifier		External Location Short Text	
GLN		Ext. Location	ZDM1
DUNS+4		Bus. System Group	BS61

Figure 7.11: Atlanta Manufacturing Plant as location in APO

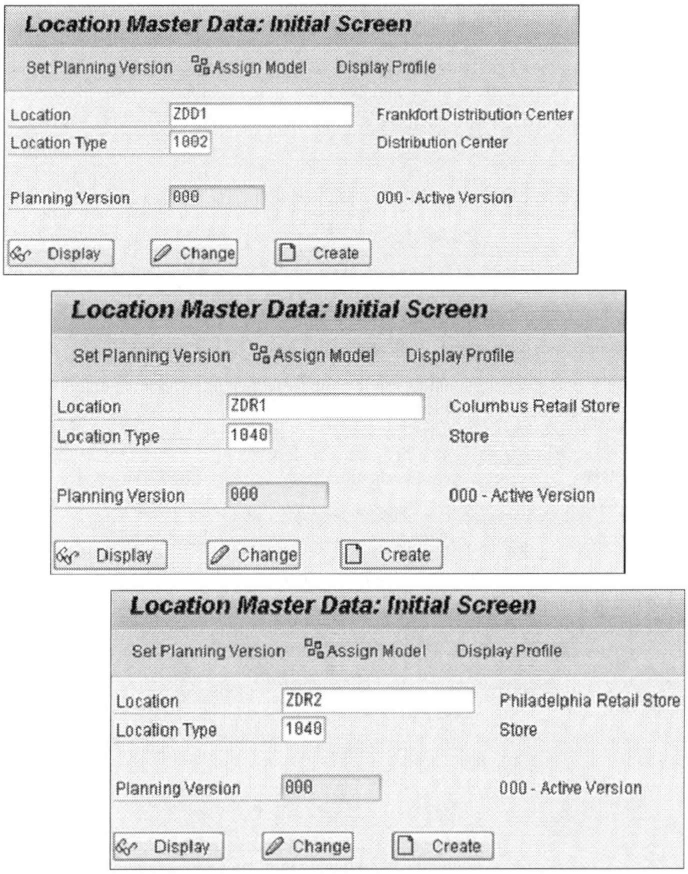

Location Master Data: Initial Screen

Set Planning Version   Assign Model   Display Profile

Location	ZDD1	Frankfort Distribution Center
Location Type	1002	Distribution Center
Planning Version	000	000 - Active Version

Display   Change   Create

Location Master Data: Initial Screen

Set Planning Version   Assign Model   Display Profile

Location	ZDR1	Columbus Retail Store
Location Type	1040	Store
Planning Version	000	000 - Active Version

Display   Change   Create

Location Master Data: Initial Screen

Set Planning Version   Assign Model   Display Profile

Location	ZDR2	Philadelphia Retail Store
Location Type	1040	Store
Planning Version	000	000 - Active Version

Display   Change   Create

Figure 7.12: DCs and stores as locations in APO

7.2.3   Product

Products are the outcome of any supply chain activity and are manufactured, distributed, and stored in the supply chain. They are identified as a *material* in ERP and are maintained in the *material master* as explained in Section 6.3. These materials get transferred to SCM through the core interface execution and appear as *Location Product* along with automatic supply chain *active model 000* and *active planning version 000* assignment.

For our business scenario at DM Consumer Appliances, Inc. we maintain the following products:

- ▶ *32" DM LCD 720p HDTV* (Product code: ZDM_FG1)
- ▶ *32" DM LCD 1080p HDTV* (Product code: ZDM_FG2)
- ▶ *39" DM LCD 1080p HDTV* (Product code: ZDM_FG3)
- ▶ *40" DM LED 1080p HDTV* (Product code: ZDM_FG4)

Each of these products is maintained in all four of the DM Consumer Appliances, Inc. locations. We maintain these products in the ERP system as *material plant* combination as explained in Section 6.3. Next, we transfer them through the core interface as explained in Section 6.4 and 6.5. Once these material plant combinations get transferred through the CIF, they are available in the SCM system as *product location* combination and get automatically assigned to *active model 000* and *active planning version 000*. These product location combinations can be seen or modified using the following transactions.

The transaction code or menu path for product master data in the SCM system is as follows:

Transaction Code: /SAPAPO/MAT1

Menu Path: SAP MENU • ADVANCED PLANNING AND OPTIMIZATION • MASTER DATA • PRODUCT

We find the product 32" DM LCD 720P HDTV (Product code: ZDM_FG1) for DM Consumer Appliances, Inc., using the transactions mentioned above, as shown in Figure 7.13 for the product's four locations.

We can also verify the details around the product location combination by verifying the particulars in every tab. We can modify these details as appropriate by going to the change mode and saving it. For example, we can make entries for multiple units and the conversion between them.

Similarly, we verify and modify the other products as appropriate: 32" DM LCD 1080P HDTV (Product code: ZDM_FG2), 39" DM LCD 1080P HDTV (Product code: ZDM_FG3) and 40" DM LED 1080P HDTV (Product code: ZDM_FG4) across all four locations for DM Consumer Appliances, Inc.

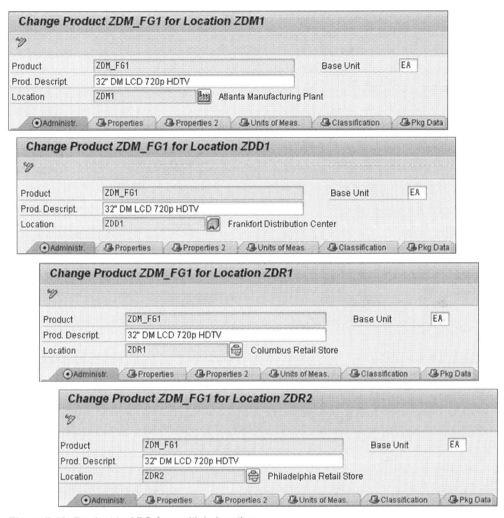

Figure 7.13: Product in APO for multiple locations

7.3 Master planning object structure design

Master planning object structure (MPOS) is the structure containing the list of characteristics that determines the level at which demand planning is created, modified, saved, aggregated, and disaggregated.

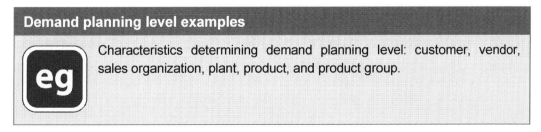

Demand planning level examples

Characteristics determining demand planning level: customer, vendor, sales organization, plant, product, and product group.

Technically, the master planning object structure is an APO InfoCube that resides in the APO Administrative Workbench. The master planning object structure is a prerequisite to creating the planning area. The master planning object structure can contain either SAP standard characteristics, or custom characteristics or a combination of both.

Master planning object structure is critical

 Master planning object structure has to be designed with utmost care, as it forms the basis of the planning area and that in turn forms the basis of APO. Characteristics in the master planning object structure cannot be changed when it is in use.

You will find the reference to this section as 'Creation of Master Planning Object Structure' in the block 'Design in APO DP' in APO DP process flow depicted in Figure 4.2.

For our business scenario we maintain one master planning object structure DEMO PLANNING OBJECT STRUCTURE as shown in Figures 7.14 and 7.15. We maintain the following planning levels for DM Consumer Appliances, Inc.: location, product, product group, sales organization, distribution channel, and region. We capture these planning levels as characteristics in the master planning object structure. We create the master planning object structure *Demo Planning Object Structure* for DM Consumer Appliances, Inc. as explained below.

The transaction code or menu path for creating master planning object structure in the SCM system is as follows:

Transaction Code: /SAPAPO/MSDP_ADMIN

Menu Path: SAP MENU • ADVANCED PLANNING AND OPTIMIZATION • DEMAND PLANNING • ENVIRONMENT • ADMINISTRATION OF DEMAND PLANNING AND SUPPLY NETWORK PLANNING

The IMG path for this configuration in the SCM system is this:

SAP – IMPLEMENTATION GUIDE • ADVANCED PLANNING AND OPTIMIZATION • SUPPLY CHAIN PLANNING • DEMAND PLANNING (DP) • BASIC SETTINGS • S&DP ADMINISTRATION

Refer to Figure 7.14 for instructions on how to create the master planning object structure for DM Consumer Appliances, Inc. Once we are on the transaction mentioned above, we click to pull down the option of PLNG OBJECT STRUCTURE as shown in ❶ and click on that. It takes us to the screen listing the existing planning object structures. Right click on the standard planning object structure 9ADPBAS and click Copy (❷). Next, it takes us to the screen COPY PLANNING OBJECT STRUCTURE and make entries as shown in ❸. Click ENTER ☑ (❹) and it creates master planning object structure ZDM_MPOS (❺). Double click on *master planning object structure ZDM_MPOS* and it takes us to the screen listing the copied characteristics (❻). This explains Part 1 of the 'Master planning object structure design'.

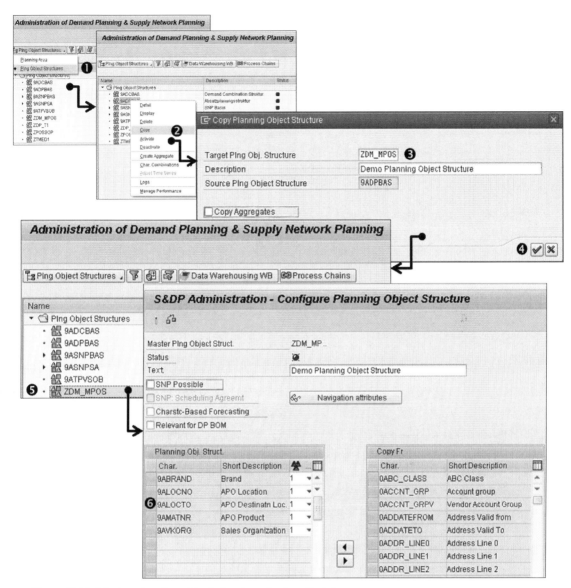

Figure 7.14: Master planning object structure design: Part 1

Let's continue with Part 2 of 'Master planning object structure design' as shown in Figure 7.15. We select the characteristics (❶) that are not required for design and click on RE-MOVE CHARACTERISTICS ▶ (❷). Similarly, select characteristics that are required for design and click on ADD CHARACTERISTICS ◀ (❸). We find the list of all of the characteristics (❹). Next, we click on ACTIVATE ⏵ (❺) to activate *Demo Planning Object Structure*. This can be found in the DISPLAY LOGS. We click ENTER ✓ (❻) and it takes us to the screen listing the DEMO PLANNING OBJECT STRUCTURE (ZDM_MPOS) with ACTIVE ▣ (❼). This step completes the design for master planning object structure for DM Consumer Appliances, Inc.

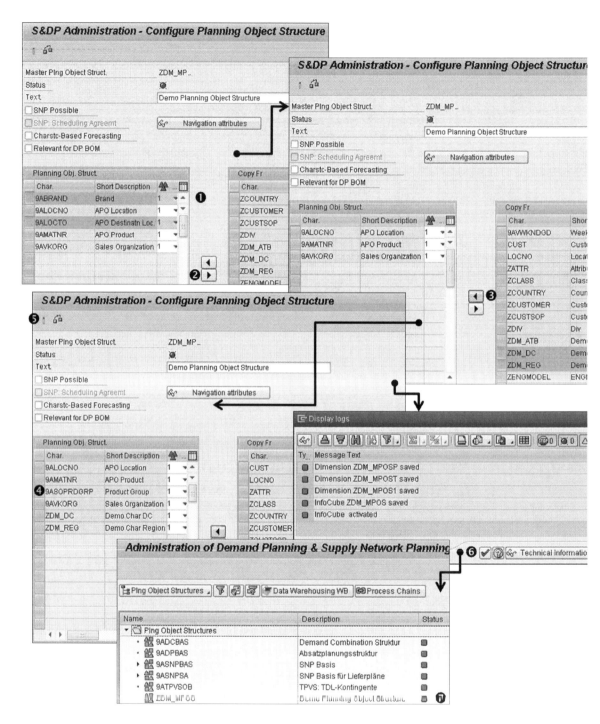

Figure 7.15: Master planning object structure design: Part 2

Changing characteristics in master planning object structure

 To change the characteristics deactivate the master planning object structure and change the status to NOT ACTIVE ⊙ . Once deactivated, the existing characteristic value combinations are deleted and the time series becomes inconsistent. After modifying or adding the new set of characteristics, reactivate the master planning object structure and change the status back to ACTIVE ⊙ . We can also run a consistency check for the master planning object structure to check the correctness.

In the next section, we will describe how characteristics values are combined and maintained in APO.

7.4 Characteristic value combinations

Characteristic value combination is the combination of the values of characteristics, based on which we can carry out the demand planning. These are specific names for the characteristics.

Characteristics vs. characteristics values

 While *Location* is a characteristic, the actual location names such as *Atlanta*, *Rome*, etc. are characteristics values.

Characteristic value combinations constitute the master data for APO DP and are planning objects in APO DP.

Master data transferred through the core interface is not sufficient to enable APO DP. Therefore, for those combinations of master data values, characteristic value combination needs to be generated to proceed with APO Demand Planning. For example, when we transfer master data like *Atlanta Manufacturing Plant* and Product *32" DM LCD 720p HDTV* through the core interface, it will not allow APO to carry out demand planning for the transferred products. Demand planning is only possible when we generate the characteristic value combinations for such master data, provided we created the master planning object structure to store the characteristic value combinations.

Characteristic value combinations define the relationship between multiple master data and form the basis for carrying out aggregation and disaggregation of key figures values. *Key figures* represent the numerical or quantitative figures for planning.

You will find the reference to this section as 'Characteristics Value Combination (CVC) Generation' in the block 'Design in APO DP' in the APO DP process flow depicted in Figure 4.2.

For our business scenario at DM Consumer Appliances we maintain characteristic value combinations for all of the planning levels listed in Table 4.1. We follow both the manual creation method, as well as mass creation method to generate the characteristic value combination as explained in the following two sections. This is to show two possibilities.

Characteristics value combination: methods

For a small number of characteristic value combinations follow manual method of CVCs creation and for large number of characteristic value combinations, follow the mass creation method of CVCs creation.

The transaction code or menu path for maintaining characteristic values in the SCM system is as follows:

Transaction Code: /SAPAPO/MC62

Menu Path: SAP MENU • ADVANCED PLANNING AND OPTIMIZATION • MASTER DATA • APPLICATION-SPECIFIC MASTER DATA • DEMAND PLANNING • MAINTAIN CHARACTERISTIC VALUES

7.4.1 Manual creation of CVCs

Ideally, we manually create CVCs when we want to create a small number of characteristic value combinations. For our business scenario we follow this method for the following two products that are part of the *LCD TVs* product group:

▶ *32" DM LCD 720p HDTV* (ZDM_FG1)
▶ *32" DM LCD 1080p HDTV* (ZDM_FG2)

Refer to Figure 7.16 to create characteristic combinations manually. Once we executed the above mentioned transaction we come to the screen MAINTAIN PLANNING-RELEVANT CHARACTERISTIC COMBINATIONS. Make an entry for the master planning object structure for DM Consumer Appliances, Inc., i.e., ZDM_MPOS (❶) and click on CREATE CHARACTERISTIC COMBINATIONS (❷). It takes us to the CREATE CHARACTERISTIC COMBINATIONS screen. Choose the option to CREATE MANUALLY (❸) and click EXECUTE ⊕ (❹). It takes us to the next screen TARGET PLANNING OBJECT STRUCTURE: ZDM_MPOS. Click INSERT ROW 📇 (❺) and it gives us the option to make entries for the data for all of the planning level details in each of the worklist characteristics. We make entries of characteristics values as shown in ❻.

The setting ADJUST TIME SERIES OBJECTS is for updating the time series objects for new and deleted CVCs. We do not flag this setting as it impacts performance. Also, we do not flag the checks in the CHECK SELECTION section as that would also impact performance. This constitutes Part 1 of 'Manual creation of CVCs'.

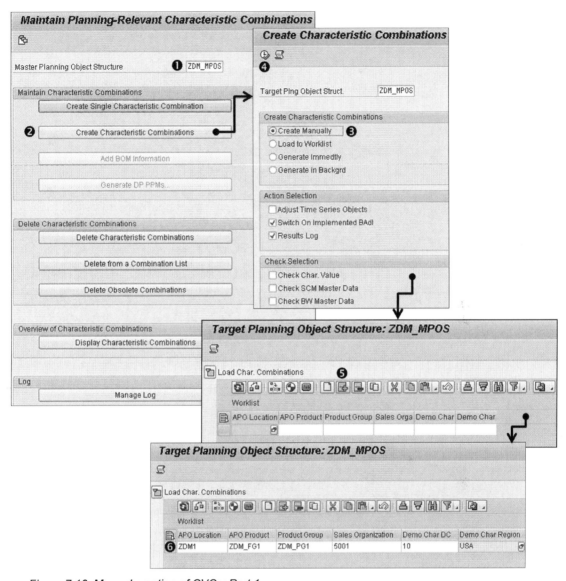

Figure 7.16: Manual creation of CVCs: Part 1

Let us refer to Figure: 7.17, as we continue the design for Part 2 of 'Manual creation of CVCs'.

After getting the planning details from Part 1, we continue to insert additional characteristic combinations using the COPY FUNCTION 🔲 (❶) and modify the entries to suit the requirements of DM Consumer Appliances, Inc. Once done, we verify all the planning level details in terms of CHARACTERISTIC VALUES (❷). Next, we SELECT ALL 🔳 (❸) values and click on GENERATE COMBINATIONS 🔲 (❹). The system displays all the generated CHARACTERISTIC COMBINATIONS (❺) for the products *32" DM LCD 720p HDTV* (ZDM_FG1) and *32" DM LCD 1080p HDTV (ZDM_FG2)*.

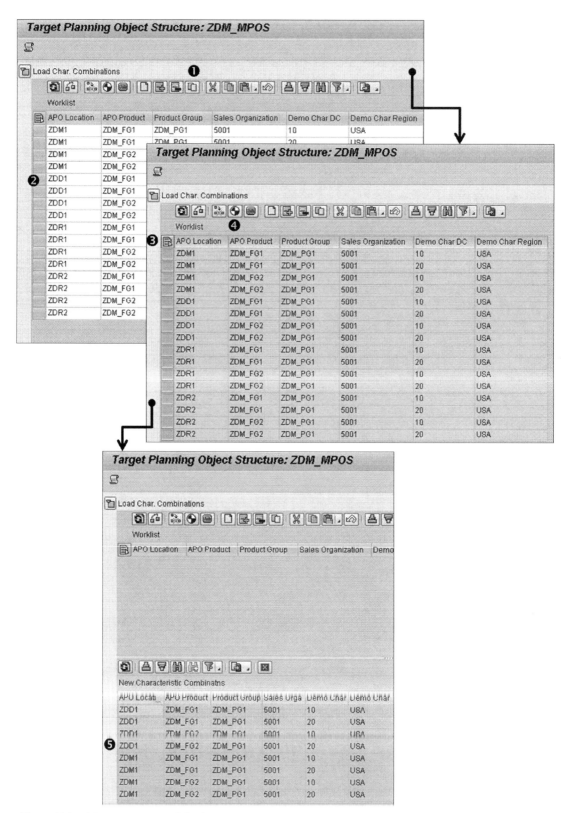

Figure 7.17: Manual creation of CVCs: Part 2

With this step, we have completed CVCs generation for two of our products manually. The next section, shows similar CVC generations through worklist loading.

7.4.2 Mass creation of CVCs through worklist loading

We create CVCs in mass through worklist loading when we want to create large numbers of characteristic value combinations. For our business scenario, we will follow this method for the following two products:

▶ *39" DM LCD 1080p HDTV* (ZDM_FG3) belonging to *LCD TVs*
▶ *40" DM LED 1080p HDTV* (ZDM_FG4) belonging to *LED TVs*

Refer to Figure 7.18 for instructions on how to create characteristic combinations through mass creation method, i.e., through worklist loading. Once we execute the transaction for *maintain characteristic values* we come to the screen MAINTAIN PLANNING-RELEVANT CHARACTERISTIC COMBINATIONS. Select the master planning object structure for DM Consumer Appliances, Inc., i.e., ZDM_MPOS (❶) and click on CREATE CHARACTERISTIC COMBINATIONS (❷). It takes us to the CREATE CHARACTERISTIC COMBINATIONS screen. Choose the option to LOAD TO WORKLIST (❸).

For our business scenario, we maintain the raw characteristic combination values in a flat file on a local computer and make an entry of the path of this file as shown in ❹.

Flat file format extraction

 The format for the flat file upload can be downloaded from the transaction pertaining to mass creation of CVCs' itself by clicking onto EXPORT 🖼 . and downloading a dummy file.

Next, we click EXECUTE 🕐 (❺). This constitutes Part 1 of 'Mass creation of CVCs through worklist loading'

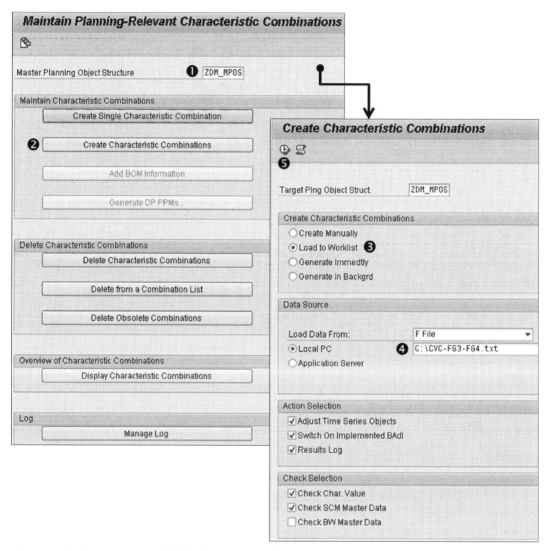

Figure 7.18: Mass creation of CVCs through worklist loading: Part 1

Let's refer to Figure: 7.19 as we continue the design for Part 2 of 'Mass creation of CVCs through worklist loading'. Once the execution is complete we verify all of the planning level details in terms of CHARACTERISTIC VALUES (❶). Next, we SELECT ALL 🗒 (❷) such values and click on GENERATE COMBINATIONS 🔲 (❸). The system displays all of the generated CHARACTERISTIC COMBINATIONS (❹) for the products *39" DM LCD 1080p HDTV* (ZDM_FG3) and *40" DM LED 1080p HDTV* (ZDM_FG4).

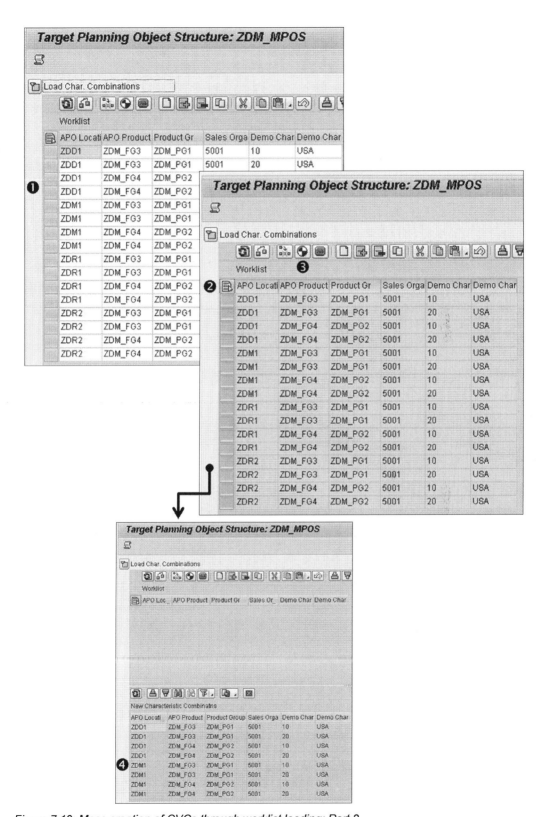

Figure 7.19: Mass creation of CVCs through worklist loading: Part 2

> ## Maintaining an optimum number of CVCs
>
> Delete the CVCs that are not required or incorrectly generated by specifying appropriate selections options available in the transaction mentioned above. Similarly, display CVCs based on appropriate filtering/selections. Note that redundant CVCs impact system performance. Therefore, we should do an assessment to ensure that we have only the optimum number of CVCs.

With this step, we have completed CVC generation for all products. In the next section, we will elaborate on the time related bucket profile design.

7.5   Storage bucket profile and planning bucket profile

There are two types of time related bucket profiles: the storage bucket profile that decides on the period for storing data and the planning bucket profile that decides on the period for planning data. In this section, we will describe these two profiles and how we can use them in our business scenario.

7.5.1   Storage bucket profile

The *storage bucket profile* determines the time bucket during which data can be saved for a planning area. It specifies the multiple periodicities and time horizon for which we can save data as shown in Figure 7.20. We can also maintain a time stream to incorporate calendars where we can define working days and holidays. The time horizon for the storage bucket profile should not be longer than the time stream duration. The storage bucket profile is essential for creating a planning area and only when you initialize the planning area, will the time series get created for the horizon. We described planning area in detail in Section 7.6.

You will find the reference to this section as 'Storage Bucket Profile Creation' in the block 'Design in APO DP' in the APO DP process flow depicted in Figure 4.2.

For our business scenario at DM Consumer Appliances we will make an entry of *Demo Storage Bucket Profile* (ZDM_SBP) with three periodicities and for a horizon validity of six years as shown in Figure 7.20. We kept the horizon long because once storage bucket profile gets used, we cannot modify it. Also, this duration will suffice for data storage requirements for demand planning.

The transaction code or menu path for creating storage bucket profile is as follows.

Transaction Code: /SAPAPO/TR32

Menu Path: SAP MENU • ADVANCED PLANNING AND OPTIMIZATION • DEMAND PLANNING • ENVIRONMENT • CURRENT SETTINGS • PERIODICITIES FOR PLANNING AREA

The IMG path for this configuration in the SCM system is:

SAP – IMPLEMENTATION GUIDE • ADVANCED PLANNING AND OPTIMIZATION • SUPPLY CHAIN PLAN-
NING • DEMAND PLANNING (DP) • BASIC SETTINGS • DEFINE STORAGE BUCKETS PROFILE

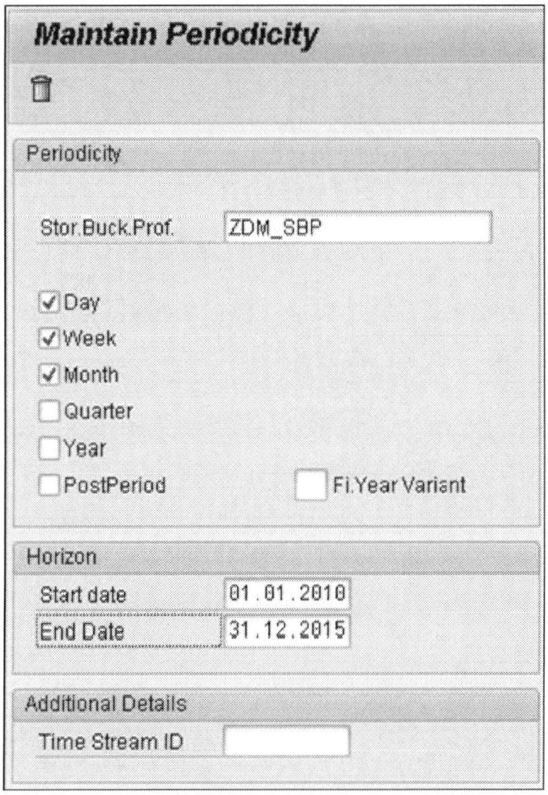

Figure 7.20: Maintenance of the storage bucket profile

We make entries and flag options as shown in Figure 7.20 and save.

Next, we define the planning bucket profile.

7.5.2 Planning bucket profile

The *planning bucket profile* (also called the *time bucket profile*) determines the past or future time horizon for planning. It incorporates the time buckets that are used for planning,
number of periods for each time bucket, and the sequence in which the time buckets are
displayed in the planning table. For all purposes, the time bucket periodicity is the subset of
periodicities defined for the storage bucket profile associated with the relevant planning
area. We can define multiple planning bucket profiles for a planning book depending on the
number of data views. We associate planning bucket profiles with specific data views.
Therefore, data can be displayed using different periodicities and different horizons for the
same planning run. We described the planning book and data views in detail in Sections
7.8.1 and 7.8.2 respectively in this chapter.

You will find the reference to this section as 'Planning Bucket Profile Creation' in the block 'Design in APO DP' in the APO DP process flow depicted in Figure 4.2.

For our business scenario at DM Consumer Appliances, we maintain two planning bucket profiles: *Demo Time Bucket Profile-H* (ZDM_TBP_H) for the history horizon and *Demo Time Bucket Profile-F* (ZDM_TBP_F) for the future horizon. However, the periodicity for both the planning bucket profiles is kept on a monthly basis for ease of transferring the data to ERP. We can choose to maintain an additional data view with different time bucket profile to display and use multiple periodicity data for the same planning run.

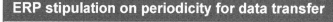

ERP stipulation on periodicity for data transfer

 ERP does not allow for a combination of periodicities for planning the data transfer from SCM to ERP.

The number of periods for both the HISTORY and the FUTURE PLANNING BUCKET PROFILES are kept at 24 MONTHS for display as shown in Figures 7.21 and 7.22 respectively.

The transaction code or menu path for maintaining the time bucket profile in SCM system is as follows:

Transaction Code: /SAPAPO/TR30

Menu Path: SAP MENU • ADVANCED PLANNING AND OPTIMIZATION • DEMAND PLANNING • ENVIRONMENT • CURRENT SETTINGS • MAINTAIN TIME BUCKETS PROFILE FOR DEMAND

The IMG path for configuration in SCM is:

SAP – IMPLEMENTATION GUIDE • ADVANCED PLANNING AND OPTIMIZATION • SUPPLY CHAIN PLANNING • DEMAND PLANNING (DP) • BASIC SETTINGS • DEFINE PLANNING BUCKETS PROFILE

We make entries as shown in Figure 7.21 for the time bucket profile for HISTORY for DM Consumer Appliances, Inc. and click SAVE.

Maintain Time Buckets Profile DP/SNP

Period list ⑦

| Time buckets prfl ID | ZDM_TBP_H |
| Short text | Demo Time Bucket Profile-H |

Time Buckets Prof. Details

Number	Basic periodicity	FYV 2	Display periodicity	FYV 1
24	M		M	
	M			

Figure 7.21: Maintenance of time bucket profile for history

Once we have clicked SAVE, we get this message:

☑ The time buckets profile ZDM_TBP_H has been saved

We make entries as shown in Figure 7.22 for the TIME BUCKET PROFILE for FUTURE for DM Consumer Appliances, Inc. and then SAVE.

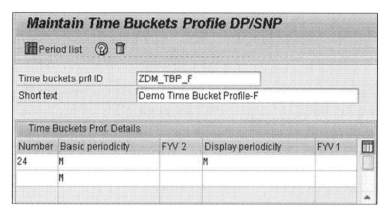

Figure 7.22: Maintenance of time bucket profile for forecast

Once we click SAVE, we get the following message:

☑ The time buckets profile ZDM_TBP_F has been saved

Next, we will look at the planning area and its design.

7.6 Planning area design

The *planning area* is the central edifice for carrying out demand planning and can safely be called the engine for demand planning. The planning area consolidates and centralizes all of the planning objects and parameters that define the boundary of planning. It also controls the way data gets processed and stored in the LiveCache. We covered the LiveCache in Section 2.2.6.

The planning area utilizes the following major parameters for planning purposes:

▶ Key figures with multiple features
▶ Planning characteristics through the master planning object structure
▶ Storage bucket profile
▶ Unit of measure
▶ Currency
▶ Exchange rate types
▶ Aggregation and disaggregation methods
▶ Forecast settings
▶ Locking logic

It makes sense to have different planning areas if different kinds of business exist that are exclusive to one another. Multiple planning areas will help in management and scalability.

Planning area based on business division

One business division frequently uses a particular type of unit of measure that is different from the unit of measure that another business division uses. In such a case, the two divisions can have their respective planning areas and in the process they can avoid the unit conversions.

The planning data typically resides in the planning area LiveCache, but we access it through the planning book and can view it through multiple data views. We can have multiple sets of planning books and data views for a single planning area. We will look at the planning book and data views in detail in Section 7.8.

You will find the reference to this section as 'Planning Area Creation' in the block 'Design in APO DP' in the APO DP process flow depicted in Figure 4.2.

Before we explain the design of the planning area, it is important to know what the major building blocks of the planning area are, along with the key concepts. Let's take a closer look at the major building blocks and key planning area concepts.

7.6.1 Key figures

Key figures constitute one of the main building blocks for the planning area as demand planning revolves around them. *Key figures* represent the parameters that have numerical values.

Examples of key figures

Examples of key figures are: sales history, sales forecast, revenue, etc.

Number values for key figures are called key figure values.

There are three types of key figures:

▶ Quantity: Used for physical quantities
▶ Amount: Used for monetary purposes
▶ Number: Numbers that do not have any currency, or unit of measures (e.g., factors)

We will explain a few of the key figures below that we use in our business scenario.

Historical input

The value for the historical input key figure is used for forecasting. This key figure is mentioned in the *Read Historical Data* section of the *univariate forecast profile*. For our business scenario this key figure is *history* (9AVHISTORY).

Corrected history

This is the key figure that stores values after correcting the historical input value through the system, or manually.

Forecasting based on corrected history

 Set the indicator *Read Corr. History Data from Planning Version* in the univariate forecast profile settings for the system to use the corrected history data for calculating the forecast, in spite of maintaining the historical input key figure in the univariate forecast profile.

The corrected history references the actual history and then corrects it based on: values entered in the *Days in period* field in the univariate forecast profile, or the *outliers (exceptions) correction* field in the univariate forecast profile.

For our business scenario this key figure is called *corrected history* (9AVCORHIST).

Original forecast or baseline forecast

This key figure stores the original forecasting output. It is maintained in the master forecast profile. The existing phase-in/phase-out profile is also applied to this forecast. For our business scenario this key figure is called *forecast* (9ADFCST).

Corrected forecast

This key figure stores the forecast that is obtained after correcting the original, or baseline forecast, based on the actual number of workdays in a period. Workdays in a period is maintained as *Days in period* in the univariate forecast profile. For our business scenario this key figure is called the *corrected forecast* (9AVCORFCST).

Promotion

This key figure stores the promotion value as an absolute number. If a promotion is maintained in percentages, then the system will convert that to an absolute number before storing it in the promotion key figure. For our business scenario, this key figure is called *promotion 1* (9APROM1).

Manual correction

We introduce this key figure to store values that would adjust for any inputs from several departments/stakeholders and thereby reflect consensus planning. We also adjust the values in this key figure to correct any alerts. For our business scenario this key figure is called the *manual correction* (9AMANUP).

Total forecast

We introduce this key figure to store the total forecast value after suitably adding values stored in the key figures: *corrected forecast* (9AVCORFCST), *manual correction* (9AMANUP), and *promotion 1* (9APROM1).

Total forecast = corrected forecast + manual correction + promotion 1

For our business scenario this key figure is called the *total forecast* (9ATOTFC).

Ex-post forecast

Ex-post forecast is the forecast that we calculate in the past considering past history. This we do with the intention of comparing the ex-post forecast with the actual history values so as to measure the forecast accuracy for any particular forecast model. The ex-post forecast does not apply for *forecast strategies 13, 14, 60, 70, 80* and *90*. Typically, we divide the history data into two groups and use the first group of history data (❶) for INITIALIZATION and we use second group of history data (❷) for calculating EX-POST FORECAST VALUES (❸) as depicted in Figure 7.23. Ex-post forecast values helps us to identify the appropriate forecast model and settings by studying the fitment between ex-post forecast values and history values. Once we are convinced that the forecast model and settings are correct, we generate the ACTUAL FORECAST (❹) based on the entire history.

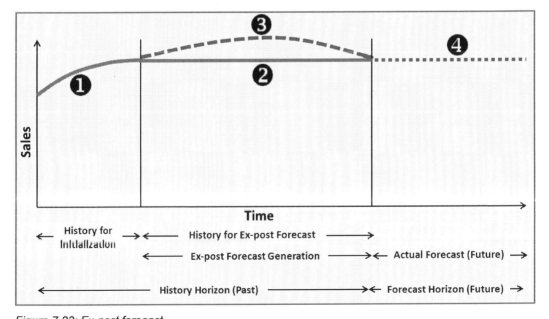

Figure 7.23: Ex-post forecast

For our business scenario we calculate and store the ex-post forecast values in the key figure *expost forecast* (9AVEXPOST).

Proportional Factor

This key figure stores the proportion that controls the disaggregation of the demand plan from the aggregate level. We generate proportional factors from the historical data and save that internally in the key figure APODPDANT.

Manual proportional factors maintenance

Maintain proportional factors manually in the planning book if we do not have any past data to calculate proportional factors automatically. We can bring up the proportional factor key figure in the planning book for manual maintenance, if we maintain the settings for *manual proportion mainte-nance* in the planning book.

For our business scenario, we keep the option of bringing up the proportional factor key figure APODPDANT in the planning book.

For our business scenario, we will keep two spare key figures, i.e., *Additional Field 1* (9AADDKF1) and *Additional Field 2* (9AADDKF2) for any potential use in our planning area.

7.6.2 Characteristics and attributes

Characteristics and attributes form part of the planning area through the master planning object structure.

Characteristics

Characteristics represent selection, sorting, or classifying parameters and are used as reference objects for key figures. Characteristic values are the level of detail at which key figure values are stored. Characteristic values happen to be the discrete names or numbers.

Examples of characteristics and its values

Characteristics are: location, product group, sales organization, material numbers, etc.

While location is a characteristic, its values may be names like Atlanta, Frankfort, Philadelphia, etc.

Characteristics will be used to create the master planning object structure as detailed in Section 7.3. Next, for the group of characteristics pertaining to the master planning object structure we maintain the characteristics value combination as explained in Section 7.4 in order to proceed with planning.

Attributes

An *attribute* is a characteristic that we assign and subordinate to another characteristic. Navigational attributes balance between a method of planning multiple objects, vis-à-vis ensuring appropriate system performance.

> **Inclusion of necessary key figures and characteristics**
>
> Include all possible key figures and characteristics in planning area design keeping future business expansion in mind. Nevertheless, it is all the more important that we do not try to be too safe and increase the number of key figures and characteristics. This is because more key figures and characteristics impact system performance.

7.6.3 Storage bucket profile

We explained the storage bucket profile in detail in Section 7.5.1.

7.6.4 Unit of measure

In order to execute seamless planning it is essential to define a base unit of measure in the planning area. We define additional units of measures in the product master with appropriate conversions. For our business scenario, we use the Unit of Measure *EA* and maintain the Unit of Measure conversion with *PC* in a 1:1 ratio.

7.6.5 Currency

This specifies the currency in which data is planned in the planning area. For our business scenario we maintain the currency in *USD*. This is an optional field.

7.6.6 Exchange rate type

We maintain the exchange rate type in the planning area to view planning data in multiple currencies. This is an optional field. For our business scenario we maintain this as the *current exchange rate* (100 I).

7.6.7   Aggregation and disaggregation

One of the key concepts in the planning area is aggregation and disaggregation. The planning area makes use of its associated master planning object structure for multiple characteristics, which determines the planning level. Typically, we store data at a lower detailed planning level in time buckets with no reference to orders. However, we do store data at a higher or aggregate level in order to improve planning performance, if aggregates exist. Using aggregation is optional.

Aggregation adds up the demand planning key figure values at a detailed level at runtime and displays or plans them at the aggregated level. Let us say that we have three products belonging to a single product group and we did the forecasting for three products. Then, in the interactive planning book we see the forecast at the product group level as an aggregation, which is the summation of the individual product's forecasts.

Disaggregation is the immediate distribution of the forecast at the aggregate level to the detail level of the individual constituents of the aggregate.

Disaggregation of regional forecast example

Forecast at the regional level gets distributed to all the distribution channels, product groups, products.

The aggregation and disaggregation mechanism is a company-oriented prerogative that helps with consistent planning.

The aggregation and disaggregation consist of two types: 'structural aggregation and disaggregation' and 'time-based aggregation and disaggregation'. Structural aggregation and disaggregation relates to aggregation and disaggregation at different planning levels. Time-based aggregation and disaggregation explains the way data gets aggregated and disaggregated over time. Data gets stored over time bucket based on the storage bucket profile. If we maintain *monthly* as well as *weekly* buckets in the storage bucket profile, then the data would get stored in weekly buckets.

Disaggregation of forecast: region and quarter

Structural disaggregation. Planning entry numbers entered at region level get disaggregated to the lower level of the county level.

Time-based disaggregation: Planning entry numbers entered for the quarter get disaggregated to the month level or week or day level.

Options for the structural disaggregation are as follows

S (Pro-rata): This option means that planning data for the members determines the ratio for disaggregation and if there is no data at the lower level, then the numbers are equally distributed to the lower level.

P (Based on another Key Figure): This option means that data is disaggregated to lower levels in the proportion/ratio that is derived from another key figure for example APOD-PDANT (a key figure that represents the proportional factor calculated based on the history).

I (Mix of S & P above): In this option, the initial proportion is based on another key figure (*P* above), but later it is based on the planning data (*S* above).

A (Average of key figures): This option leads to the disaggregation of a number which is the same for all the lower level members and represents average, for example prices or times.

D (Average based on the lowest level): This option is similar to *A*, but the average here is derived based on the lowest planning level; hence the number could be different from *A* above.

N (No Disaggregation): This option means that there is no disaggregation to the lower levels.

E (Average of all details that do not equal zero): This option is similar to *A*, except that it does not consider the initial values.

F (Average of lowest detail level not equal to 0; disaggregation pro rata): This option is similar to *D* except that it does not consider the initial values.

Options for time-based disaggregation are as follows:

P (Proportional Distribution): In this option, the key figure value gets distributed to the smallest storage bucket according to the time-based proportion of the value in the aggregated period.

E (Equal Distribution): In this option, the key figure value gets equally distributed to each of the time buckets.

N (No time-based disaggregation): This option means that the number from the planning bucket is copied to the storage bucket.

I (Proportional distribution; in the case of initial disaggregation, according to another key figure): This option is similar to *P*, except that in this case if a time bucket does not have a value, then the data distribution happens based on another key figure.

K (Based on another key figure): In this option, the values are distributed to a storage bucket in the same proportion that can be derived from the values of another key figure.

7.6.8 Locking logic

This is to prevent other users from changing the planning data when one user is changing the planning data. Locking logic helps avoid potential data inconsistencies. Multiple locking options exist including LiveCache lock, key figure-specific lock, and detailed lock. For our business scenario, we go with the default *LiveCache lock*.

7.6.9 Forecast settings

Through this setting in the planning area we decide which particular key figures should correspond to different demand planning forecasting functions. Refer to Figure 7.27. For our business scenario, we have set up the key figures 9ADFCST, 9AVCORHIST, 9AVCORFCST, and 9AVEXPOST for the FORECAST key figure, CORRECTED HISTORY, CORRECTED FORECAST, and EX-POST FORECAST respectively.

We mentioned in the beginning of Section 7.6 that the planning area is the central edifice for planning. Therefore, we carry out the design with all present and future business requirements, as it is not a best practice to change planning areas often.

For our business scenario, we will maintain planning area, *Demo Planning Area* (ZDM_DPPA), for DM Consumer Appliances, Inc. We will make use of the *Demo Planning Object Structure* (ZDM_MPOS) for its planning characteristics, *Storage Bucket Profile* ZDM_SBP, key figures mentioned as building blocks in Section 7.6.1 and other settings mentioned in this section. We will create the planning area called *Demo Planning Area* (ZDM_DPPA) for DM Consumer Appliances, Inc. as explained below.

The transaction code or menu path for creating planning area in the APO system is as follows:

Transaction Code: /SAPAPO/MSDP_ADMIN

Menu Path: SAP MENU • ADVANCED PLANNING AND OPTIMIZATION • DEMAND PLANNING • ENVIRONMENT • ADMINISTRATION OF DEMAND PLANNING AND SUPPLY NETWORK PLANNING

The IMG path for this configuration in the SCM system is this:

SAP – IMPLEMENTATION GUIDE • ADVANCED PLANNING AND OPTIMIZATION • SUPPLY CHAIN PLANNING • DEMAND PLANNING (DP) • BASIC SETTINGS • S&DP ADMINISTRATION

Refer to Figure 7.24 for instructions on how to create a *Demo Planning Area* (ZDM_DPPA). Once we are on the transaction mentioned above, click to pull down the option of planning area as shown in ❶ and click on that. It takes us to the screen listing the existing planning areas. Right click and click CREATE PLANNING AREA (❷). Next, it takes us to the screen PLANNING AREA CREATE and we make entries as shown in ❸. Click ENTER ✅ (❹) and it takes us to the screen with the GENERAL SETTING DETAILS (❺). Next, click the KEY FIGS tab. Using the REMOVE KEY FIGURES ▶ (❻), remove the key figures that are not required and use ADD KEY FIGURES ◀ (❼) to shift all the key figures that are required. We do need to ensure that we have the list of key figures as shown in ❽. Next, click on DETAILS (❾). This constitutes the Part 1 of 'Planning area design'.

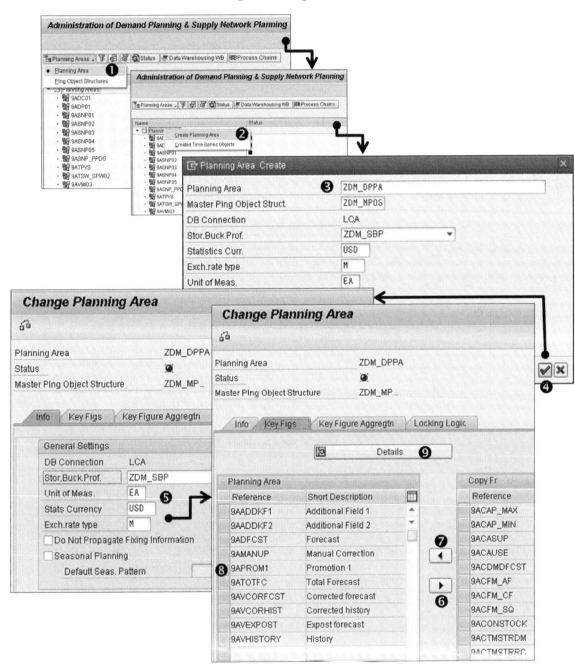

Figure 7.24: Planning area design: Part 1

Let's continue on to Part 2 of 'Planning area design', as shown in Figure 7.25. We need to go to the detailed key figures view of the screen. For each of the key figures we allocate a SEMANTIC (❶) so that the particular key figures have a meaning. This allocation is necessary if the system has to search the particular key figure. For our business scenario, we have chosen the semantic 001 (TS: QUANTITY). We scroll to the right to figure out additional parameters, if any. For our business scenario, we flag ZERO ALLOWED for two of the key figures, i.e., MANUAL CORRECTION and the CORRECTED FORECAST as shown in (❷) in Figure 7.25. We continue to scroll to the right for other settings as shown in (❸). Next, click on the KEY FIGURE AGGREGATION tab (❹). This completes the Part 2 of the 'Planning area design'.

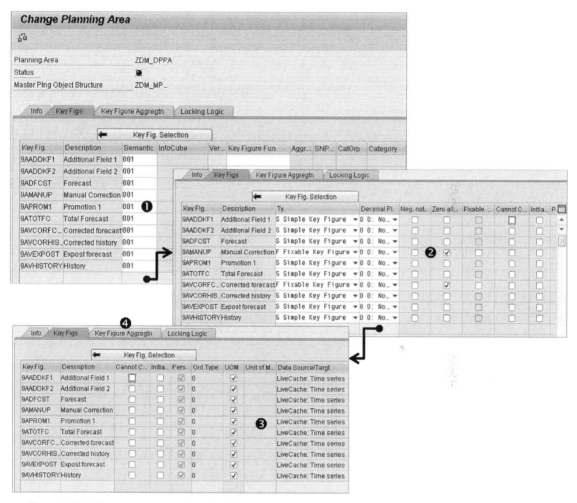

Figure 7.25: Planning area design: Part 2

Let's continue with Part 3 of 'Planning area design', as shown in Figure 7.26. We go to the KEY FIGURE AGGREGATION view of the screen. Here, for each of the key figures we need to assign a CALCULATN TYPE for structural aggregation/ disaggregation. Refer to Section 7.6.7 of this chapter for an explanation of structural aggregation/disaggregation types.

For our business scenario, we select the CALCULATN TYPE S (PRO RATA) (❶) for all of the key figures except for the FORECAST (9ADFCST) and CORRECTED FORECAST (9AVCORFCST) key figures. For the key figures FORECAST and CORRECTED FORECAST we select the CALCULATN TYPE P as shown in ❷ and ❸. *Calculation type P implies based on a different key figure.* We select the proportionate factor key figure APODPDANT as shown in ❹ and ❺ as the key figure on which disaggregation will be based, for the FORECAST (9ADFCST) and CORRECTED FORECAST (9AVCORFCST).

Next, we click on the tab LOCKING LOGIC (❻) and it takes us to the screen with view LOCK-ING LOGIC. We keep the default flag ACTIVATE LIVECACHE LOCK (❼). We retain this for our business scenario. Next, we do a consistency check for the planning area design by clicking on 🔧 (❽). This completes Part 3 of 'Planning area design'.

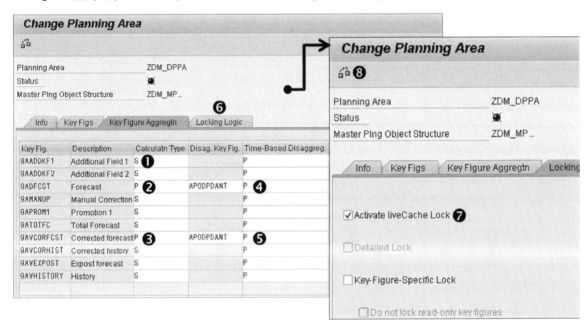

Figure 7.26: Planning area design: Part 3

We will continue on with Part 4 of 'Planning area design' as shown in Figure 7.27. We go to the EXTRAS-FORECAST SETTINGS (❶). Click to go to the screen ASSIGN FORECAST KEY FIG-URES. Select the particular key figures for our business scenario for the FORECAST KEY FIG-URE, CORRECTED HISTORY, CORRECTED FORECAST and the EX-POST FORECAST as shown in (❷).

This setting will populate values for each of these key figures in the planning book on statistical forecasting. This will be evident when we carry out the forecast execution.

After we have assigned the key figures for our business scenario, click on ADOPT (❸) and the key figures get populated as shown in (❹). Go to the screen CHANGE PLANNING AREA and click SAVE 💾 (❺). With this step, we have created planning area ZDM_DPPA for our business scenario.

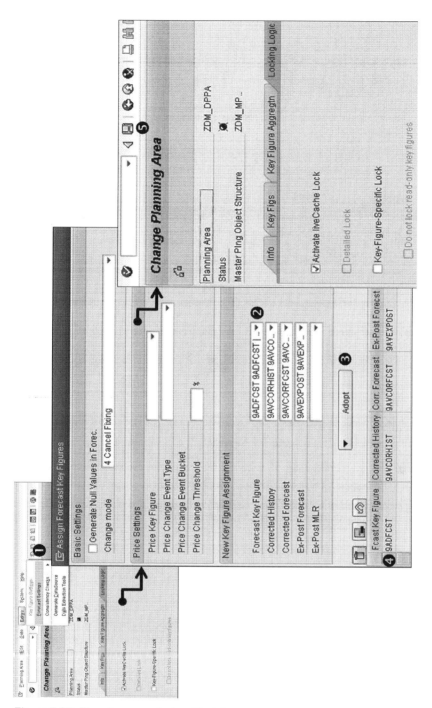

Figure 7.27: Planning area design: Part 4

We created the planning area, but the design is still not complete as this planning will not be available for use, i.e., we cannot work and view the planning book for demand planning based on this planning area. To make the planning area useful we have to generate a network of characteristics and key figures in the LiveCache. We do this by creating time series objects for the planning area. This process is also called initialization of the planning area.

Planning area initialization

The planning area can be initialized for a particular planning version and for certain time duration

We already explained the planning version in Section 7.2.1. Also, we can initialize a different time horizon for different key figures.

Past and future horizon initialization

We can initialize a past horizon for the history key figure and a future horizon for the forecast key figure.

Performance improvement through reinitialization and time series deletion

We can keep changing the horizons and reinitialize the planning area to maintain a rolling horizon. Furthermore, we can delete the time series if it is not required. In all these ways, we can improve the performance of the system.

You will find reference to planning area initialization as 'Initialization (Time Series Generation)' in the block 'Design in APO DP' in the APO DP process flow depicted in Figure 4.2.

Let's now look at the initialization process for the planning area ZDM_DPPA for our business scenario. Refer to Figure 7.28 for instructions.

The transaction code or menu path for planning area design is as follows:

Transaction Code: /SAPAPO/MSDP_ADMIN

Menu Path: SAP MENU • ADVANCED PLANNING AND OPTIMIZATION • DEMAND PLANNING • ENVIRONMENT • ADMINISTRATION OF DEMAND PLANNING AND SUPPLY NETWORK PLANNING

The IMG path for this configuration in the SCM system is as follows:

SAP – IMPLEMENTATION GUIDE • ADVANCED PLANNING AND OPTIMIZATION • SUPPLY CHAIN PLANNING • DEMAND PLANNING (DP) • BASIC SETTINGS • S&DP ADMINISTRATION

Once we are in the screen ADMINISTRATION OF DEMAND PLANNING & SUPPLY NETWORK PLANNING, we place cursor on the planning area ZDM_DPPA and right click to choose the option CREATE TIME SERIES OBJECTS (❶). Click on that to bring up the screen CREATE TIME SERIES

OBJECTS. Make entries for planning version 000 (❷) and time period (❸) as shown. Click on KEY FIGURE VIEW (❹) and it takes us to the screen KEY-FIGURE-SPECIFIC SETTINGS. For our business scenario, we retain the default settings as shown (❺). Click on EXECUTE ⬇ (❻) and it takes us back to the CREATE TIME SERIES OBJECTS screen. Click on EXECUTE ⬇ (❼). With this step, the time series objects get generated for planning area ZDM_DPPA and the status of the planning area turns green (❽).

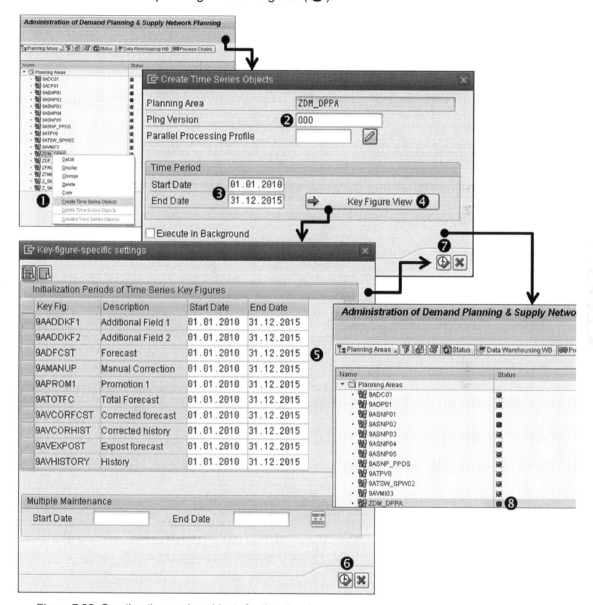

Figure 7.28: Creating time series objects for the planning area

With this step, we have completed the planning area design. In the next section, we will discuss the data structure realignment and copying functionality.

7.7 Data structure realignment and copy functionality

In business, changes happen constantly.

Changes need to be incorporated to demand planning as well. However, it would be a cumbersome process if we had to incorporate these changes manually in the demand planning system. Therefore, SAP introduced two automatic methods: data realignment and data copy.

The transaction code or menu path for data realignment in the SCM system is as follows:

Transaction Code: /SAPAPO/RLGCOPY

Menu Path: SAP MENU • ADVANCED PLANNING AND OPTIMIZATION • DEMAND PLANNING • ENVIRONMENT • DATA ADMINISTRATION • DATA REALIGNMENT

7.7.1 Data realignment

In the *data realignment* method, new CVCs are created based on the selected values of existing CVCs. Next, key figure data in all planning areas for the master planning object structure copies data from existing CVCs to the target CVCs. We can optionally delete the old CVCs along with their data. This method is typically adopted when we want to automatically create CVCs, as well as copy data. This option is limited to the level of master planning object structure.

Refer to Figure 7.29. In order to carry out realignment, go to the transaction mentioned above and choose the option REALIGNMENT (❶). Next, select the planning object structure ZDM_MPOS (❷). In order to carry out the realignment, we have to first create a realignment table by clicking on CREATE/CHANGE TABLE (❸). The realignment table is used to maintain the realignment steps using the option shown in ❹ after creating the realignment table as shown in Figure 7.30. As shown in Figure 7.29, we can do realignment for all of the key figures, or we can choose select set of KEY FIGURES (❺). We can also run realignment for the INFOCUBE (❻), provided it has a structure similar to the master planning object structure.

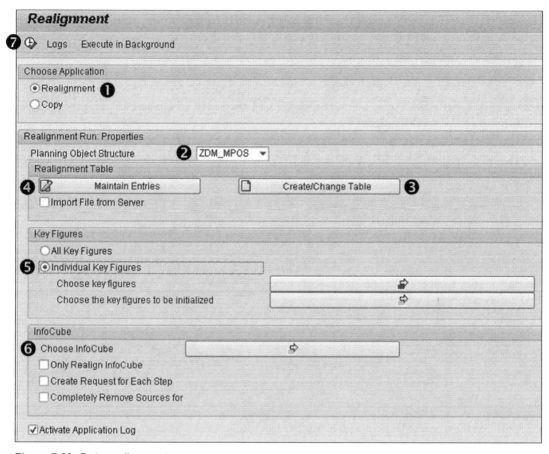

Figure 7.29: Data realignment

When we click on 🖉 [Maintain Entries] as shown in Figure 7.29, it takes us to the screen OVERVIEW OF REALIGNMENT TABLE (❶) as shown in Figure 7.30. We click on CREATE 🗋 (❷) and it takes us to the screen MAINTAIN REALIGNMENT STEP (❸). We choose COPY LOGIC M (OVERWRITE) or A (Add) as shown in ❹. We make entries as shown in ❺. Once all of the entries are made, we can save the realignment step by clicking on SAVE 🖫 (❻). Likewise, we can maintain multiple steps. Once the realignment steps are maintained, we can go back to the REALIGNMENT screen shown in Figure 7.29.

Next, we can run realignment in the foreground by clicking on EXECUTE ⊕ (❼) as shown in Figure 7.29.

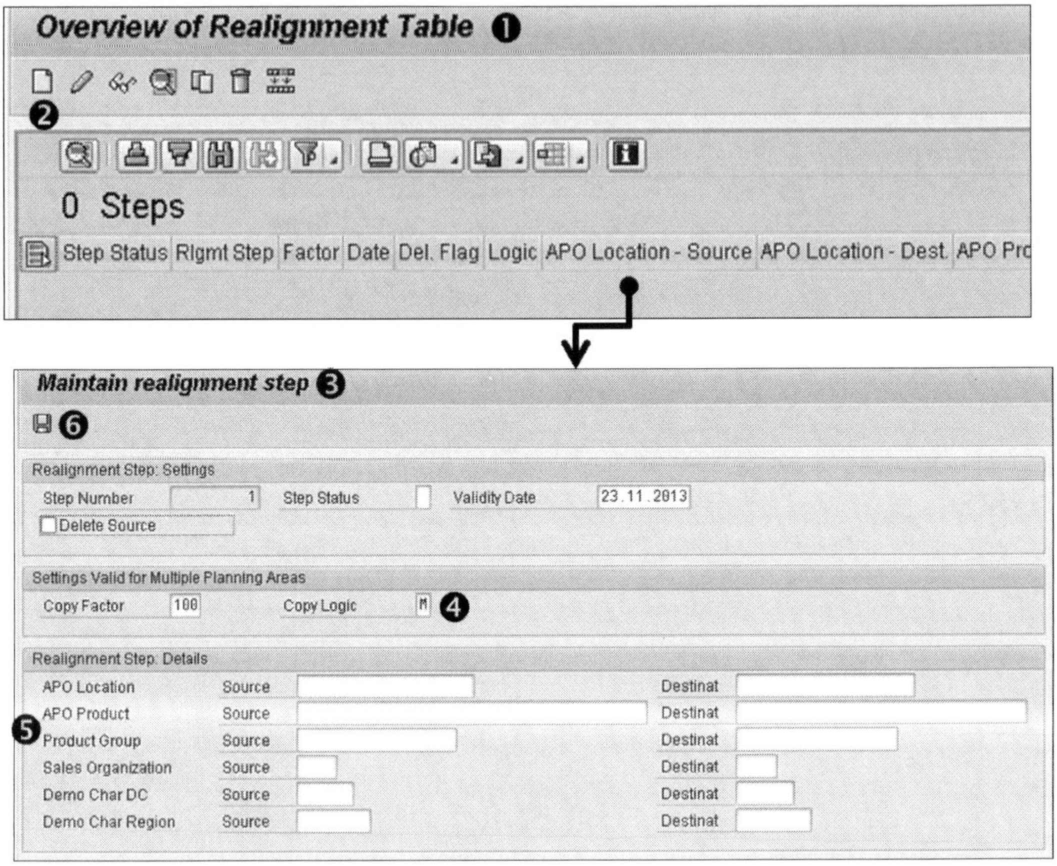

Figure 7.30: Data realignment steps

7.7.2 Data copy

We know that data exists at the planning area level. The *data copy* method is adopted at the planning area level wherein CVCs already exist and we want to copy data from one CVC to another CVC. We adopt this method only when we want to copy data and not create any CVCs. We can copy data for the following:

- ▶ From one planning version to another planning version
- ▶ Restricted key figures
- ▶ Restricted period

Refer to Figure 7.31. In order to carry out the data copy, we need to use the transaction mentioned above and choose the option COPY (❶). Next, we select the planning area ZDM_DPPA (❷). In order to copy, we first have to create a copy table by clicking on CREATE/CHANGE TABLE (❸). We maintain the copy steps using the copy table by following the option shown in ❹ after creating the copy table. After clicking on ❹, we go to the screen shown in Figure 7.32. The copy can be done for all planning versions, or select individual planning versions. As shown in Figure 7.31, we can choose to copy ALL PLANNING VERSIONS (❺). Also, we can restrict the PERIOD OF COPY (❻). Copying can be done for all of the key figures, or we can choose a select set of KEY FIGURES (**7**). We can also run copy for the INFOCUBE (**8**).

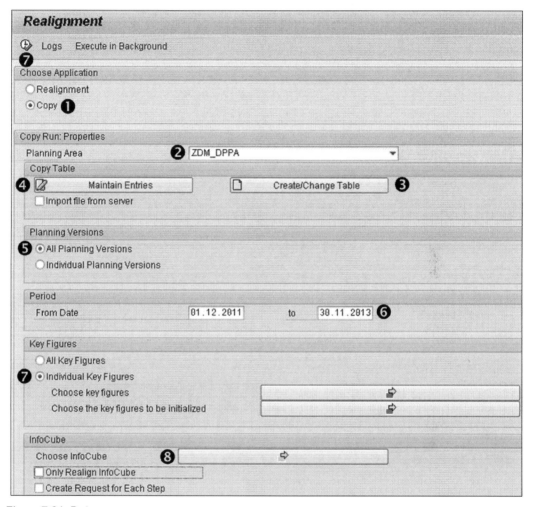

Figure 7.31: Data copy

By clicking ☑ Maintain Entries as shown in Figure 7.31, it takes us to the screen OVERVIEW OF COPY TABLE (**1**) as shown in Figure 7.32. When we click on CREATE ☐ (**2**) it takes us to the screen MAINTAIN COPY STEP (**3**). We select copy logic M (OVER-WRITE) or A (Add) as shown in **4**. We make entries as shown in **5**. Once all the entries are made, the copy step can be saved by clicking SAVE 🖫 (**6**). Likewise, multiple steps can be maintained. Once we maintain the copy step, we go back to the REALIGNMENT screen for copying shown in Figure 7.31.

Next, we can run realignment in the foreground by clicking on EXECUTE ⊕ (**7**) as shown in Figure 7.31.

Overview of Copy Table ❶

❷

0 Steps

Step Status	Copy Step	Factor	Date	Logic	APO Location - Source	APO Location - Dest.	APO Product - Source	APO Product - Dest.	Product

Maintain copy step ❸

❻

Copy Step: Settings

Step Number	1	Step Status		Validity Date	23.11.2013

Settings Valid for Multiple Planning Areas

Copy Factor	100	Copy Logic	M ❹

Copy Step: Details

❺

APO Location	Source		Destinat	
APO Product	Source		Destinat	
Product Group	Source		Destinat	
Sales Organization	Source		Destinat	
Demo Char DC	Source		Destinat	
Demo Char Region	Source		Destinat	

Figure 7.32: Data copy steps

Restricted depiction of data realignment or data copy

All of the steps and screenshots are not depicted for data realignment or data copy. This is because for our business scenario at DM Consumer Appliances, Inc. and for the new product launch, we don't copy data from existing data combinations. Instead, we generate the forecast using new product lifecycle planning. Nevertheless, data realignment and data copy is an important functionality that meets real business scenarios.

In the next section, we will look at the planning settings that we will use in our business scenario.

7.8 Planning book, data view, and selections

The planning book, data view, and selections determine the extent to which the planning data is available for viewing and planning. We will explain each of these elements and the way we use it for our business scenario

7.8.1 Planning book

The *planning book* is a planning tool that makes controlled use of the planning area to determine the data content and planning layout for carrying out interactive planning. In this context, the planning book is a subset of the planning area. The planning book, like the planning area, uses select functions, key figures, characteristics, and multiple data views in its design. We explained data views in Section 7.8.2. Furthermore, macros for establishing key figure values based on calculations can also be assigned to the planning book. The preconfigured planning book design depends on what function we choose for it to have. The different functions that a planning book offers are:

▶ *Univariate forecasting* that does time series-based forecasting
▶ Promotional functionality that allows for *promotions planning*
▶ *Multiple Linear Regression* (MLR) functionality that is based on causal analysis where demand planning is based on several independent variables
▶ *Composite forecasting* functionality that combines both univariate forecasting and MLR functionality

---

Planning books based on roles/departmental needs

 Planning books are designed based on particular roles/ departmental needs and accordingly, users are associated. Meaning, certain users belonging to certain roles/departments can only have certain visibility into demand planning and can only perform certain types of activities. Therefore, for a single company there can be multiple planning books each with an exclusive set of functionality, key figures, characteristics, and data views.

You will find reference to this section as 'Planning Book Creation' in the block 'Design in APO DP' in the APO DP process flow depicted in Figure 4.2.

For our business scenario we maintain one planning book *Demo Planning Book-1* (ZDM_DPPB-1) based on the planning area ZDM_DPPA for both demand planning and promotion planning. We create the planning book *Demo Planning Book-1* (ZDM_DPPB-1) for DM Consumer Appliances, Inc. as explained below.

The transaction code or menu path for defining the planning book in the SCM system is as follows:

Transaction Code: /SAPAPO/SDP8B

Menu Path: SAP MENU • ADVANCED PLANNING AND OPTIMIZATION • DEMAND PLANNING • ENVIRONMENT • CURRENT SETTINGS • DEFINE PLANNING BOOK

The IMG path for this configuration in the SCM system is:

SAP – IMPLEMENTATION GUIDE • ADVANCED PLANNING AND OPTIMIZATION • SUPPLY CHAIN PLANNING • DEMAND PLANNING (DP) • BASIC SETTINGS • DEFINE PLANNING BOOK

Refer to Figure 7.33 for instructions on how to create the *Demo Planning Book-1* (ZDM_DPPB-1). Once we are on the screen for the transaction code mentioned above, we choose to make an entry for the *planning book* ZDM_DPPB-1 (❶) and click on ☐ Create (❷). This takes us to the PLANNING BOOK WIZARD. Select planning area ZDM_DPPA (❸) and make an entry for planning book text (❹). Next, we flag MANUAL PROPORTION MAINTENANCE (❺) to bring up the PROPORTIONAL FACTOR key figure in the planning book. Flag the planning book for PROMOTION and UNIVARIATE FORECAST (❻), as we intend to do promotion planning and univariate forecasting only for DM Consumer Appliances, Inc. Next, click on ☐ Continue (❼). It takes us to the screen listing all the key figures (❽) for the planning area ZDM_DPPA. Next, select the required key figures and click ☐ (❾) to add them to the planning book ZDM_DPPB-1. This completes Part 1 of 'Creating the Demo Planning Book-1'.

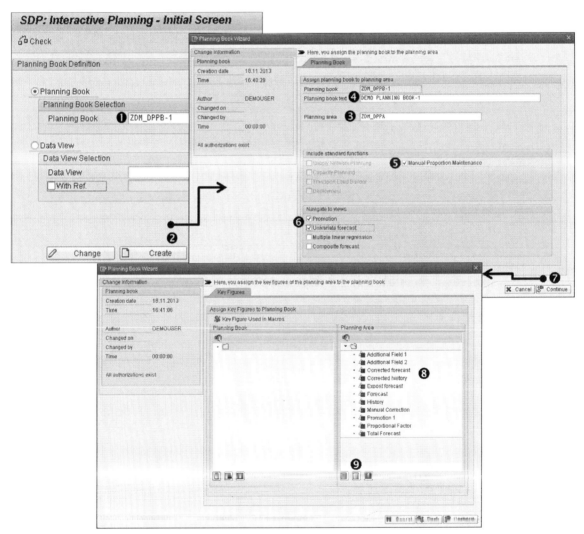

Figure 7.33: Creating the Demo Planning Book-1: Part 1

Let's continue on to Part 2 of 'Creating the Demo Planning Book-1', as shown in Figure 7.34. Once we have added all of the required key figures, as explained in Part 1, it appears as shown in ❶. Next we click on 🔲 Continue (❷) and it takes us to the screen listing all the CHARACTERISTICS (❸) for the planning area ZDM_DPPA. For our business scenario, select all the characteristics by clicking ADD ALL CHARACTERISTICS 🔲 (❹) and add them to the planning book ZDM_DPPB-1 as shown in ❺. Next, click on 🔲 Continue (❻) and it takes us to the screen for creating the data views for DEMO PLANNING BOOK-1. This completes Part 2 of 'Creating the Demo Planning Book-1' for DM Consumer Appliances, Inc.

Figure 7.34: Creating the Demo Planning Book-1: Part 2

155

Planning book: minimum of one data view

The planning book needs to have at least one data view and therefore, the design for the planning book will get completed only when we complete the design for at least one data view.

For our business scenario, we will create two data views. We continue with the design of the data views for our business scenario, as shown in Figures 7.35 through 7.38. However, before we continue with the design of the data views for DM Consumer Appliances, Inc. we will explain the concept of data views in Section 7.8.2.

7.8.2 Data view

Data view is a planning tool that makes controlled usage of the planning book to determine the data content and planning layout for carrying out interactive planning. In this context, data view is a subset of the planning book with additional restrictions like past and future time horizon, select characteristics, select key figures, etc. Therefore, data views help view and plan only restricted data content for the planning area data. This also makes sense as a different data set is required for different activities and all of the data available in the planning area is not always necessary.

Data view: optimum number of key figures and characteristics

The data view references the planning book and uses select key figures and characteristics for its design. It is essential that we create data views only with the minimal key figures and characteristics. If we don't, unnecessary processing of additional key figures will impact performance.

Macros preference: data view level

Associate only necessary macros to the data view level and not at the planning book level, otherwise, macros will execute for data views when it's not even required, thereby impacting system performance

Data view based on tasks

If we design planning books based on particular roles/departmental needs then we design data views based on a set of tasks associated with particular roles/departmental needs. Meaning, certain users have access to particular data views can only perform the functions desired for them.

You will find the reference to this section as 'Data View Creation' in the block 'Design in APO DP' in the APO DP process flow depicted in Figure 4.2.

For our business scenario we maintain two data views for the planning book *Demo Planning Book-1* (ZDM_DPPB-1) for DM Consumer Appliances, Inc.:

▶ *Demo Data View-1-1* (ZDM_DPDV-1-1) for statistical forecasting, promotion planning, lifecycle planning, and consensus planning

▶ *Demo Data View-1-2* (ZDM_DPDV-1-2) for proportionate factor calculation

We continue from Figure 7.34 and proceed to create the two data views from the DEMO PLANNING BOOK-1. Once, we have clicked on [Continue] (**6**) as shown in Figure 7.34 we go to the DATA VIEW screen as shown in Figure 7.35.

We will refer to Figure 7.35 to create *Demo Data View-1-1* (ZDM_DPDV-1-1) for our business scenario. In the DATA VIEW screen, we make entries as shown in **1** and **2**. Next, we make entries for the TIME BUCKET PROFILE for FUTURE HORIZON (**3**) to restrict the planning data in future. Similarly, we make entries of the TIME BUCKET PROFILE for HISTORY (**4**). We also make an entry of the date from which the data will be visible and will be available for change in **5**. We explained the time bucket profile and design for our business scenario in Section 7.5.2. Next, click on [Continue] (**6**). This completes Part 1 of 'Creating the Demo Data View-1-1'.

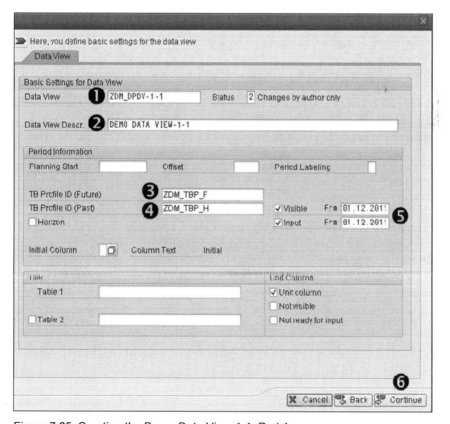

Figure 7.35: Creating the Demo Data View-1-1: Part 1

We continue on with Part 2 of 'Creating the Demo Data View-1-1', as shown in Figure 7.36. Once we click on [🖳 Continue] as mentioned in Part 1, it takes us to the screen listing all of the KEY FIGURES (❶) for the DEMO PLANNING BOOK-1. For DEMO DATA VIEW-1-1, we select the required key figures by clicking ADD SELECTED KEY FIGURE [🖳] (❷) and add them to the DEMO DATA VIEW-1-1 as shown in ❸. Next, click on [↑ Complete] (❹) and a window appears to complete the planning book and data views. Click [Yes] (❺).

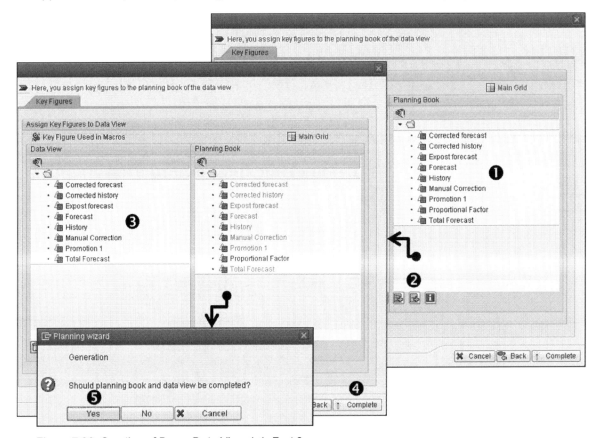

Figure 7.36: Creation of Demo Data View-1-1: Part 2

With this step, we have created the DEMO PLANNING BOOK-1 (ZDM_DPPB-1) and the associated DEMO DATA VIEW-1-1 (ZDM_DPDV-1-1) for our business scenario.

Once this is complete, we created the characteristic APO PLANNING VERSION (❶) automatically for the DEMO PLANNING BOOK-1 (ZDM_DPPB-1) as shown in Figure 7.37.

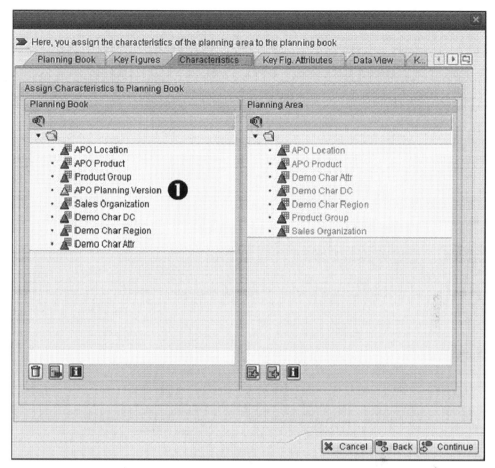

Figure 7.37: Automatic creation of the characteristic APO planning version

Following a similar method, we make an entry for the DEMO DATA VIEW-1-2 (ZDM_DPDV-1-2) (❶) as shown in Figure 7.38. We make entries of the same time bucket profile for both future and history. However, we restrict the number of key figures as shown in ❷. Next, click [Complete] (❸) and create the DEMO DATA VIEW-1-2 (ZDM_DPDV-1-2).

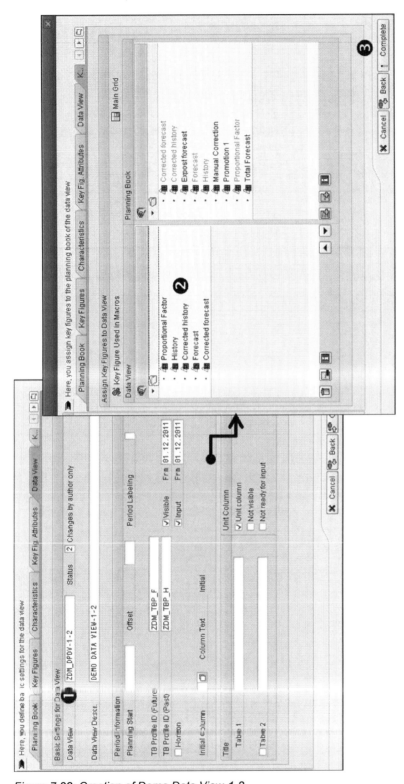

Figure 7.38: Creation of Demo Data View-1-2

With this step, we have completed the design for the *Demo Planning Book-1* and its two data views: *Demo Data View-1-1* and *Demo Data View-1-2*. In the next section, we will discuss how to maintain the selection for carrying out demand planning.

7.8.3 Maintain selection

Selections are a group of planning objects that collectively determine the planning run. Alternatively, they are the select CVCs out of the entire set of CVCs available for the planning area. We uniquely identify *selections* with a *selection ID*, which we can assign to a user profile, for the user to get the choices of *selection IDs* by default.

You will find the reference to this section as 'Selection Maintenance' in the block 'Design in APO DP' in the APO DP process flow depicted in Figure 4.2.

For our business scenario we maintain the following *selection IDs*:

▶ ZDM_DPSEL_SFC: This *selection* is for the product group for *LCD TVs* (ZDM_PG1) in order to do statistical forecasting.

▶ ZDM_DPSEL_NLC: This *selection* is for the newly launched product *40" DM LED 1080p HDTV* (ZDM_FG4) belonging to *LED TVs* product group and corresponding reference product *39" DM LCD 1080p HDTV* (ZDM_FG3) belonging to *LCD TVs* product group in order to do lifecycle planning and to realize the effect of promotion and cannibalization.

▶ ZDM_DPSEL_PROMO: For *selection* of promotion for promotion planning.

▶ ZDM_DPSEL_PG1_PDTS: This *selection* is for all products belonging to product group *LCD TVs* (ZDM_PG1) for consensus planning.

▶ ZDM_DPSEL_REL_SNP: This *selection* is for all products belonging to distribution center and retail stores of DM Consumer Appliances, Inc. for the purpose of releasing the consensus demand plan to APO SNP for supply network planning.

▶ ZDM_DPSEL_TFR_ECC: This *selection* is for all products belonging to the *Atlanta Manufacturing Plant* of DM Consumer Appliances, Inc. for the purpose of transferring the consensus demand plan to execution system ERP for production planning.

The transaction code or menu path for maintaining *selection* in the SCM system is as follows:

Transaction Code: /SAPAPO/MC77

Menu Path: SAP MENU • ADVANCED PLANNING AND OPTIMIZATION • DEMAND PLANNING • ENVIRONMENT • SELECTION ORGANIZATION • MAINTAIN SELECTION ASSIGNMENTS

Refer to Figure 7.39 to maintain selection ZDM_DPSEL_SFC. Once we are on the screen for the transaction code mentioned above and get to the screen MAINTAIN SELECTION PROFILES FOR USERS (❶). Click SELECTION 🔲 (❷) and it brings up the screen OBJECT SELECTION. Select the PRODUCT GROUP (❸). Select the planning version (❹) and product group (❺) and click SAVE 🔲 (❻). Once saved a pop up box appears in which we enter the selection description ZDM_DPSEL_SFC (**7**). Next, we click SAVE 🖫 (**8**) and we get the following message:

☑ Selection successfully saved

Next, click ENTER ☑ (**9**).

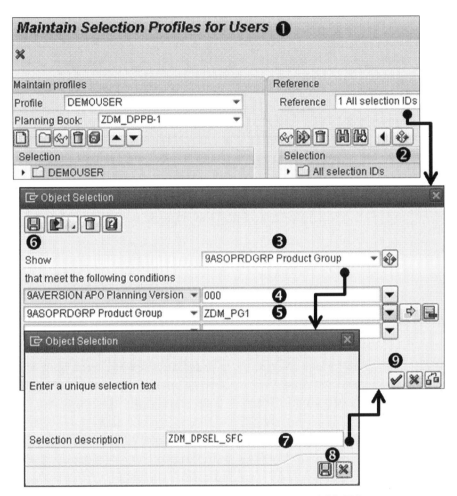

Figure 7.39: Maintenance of selection for the product group LCD TVs

Next, it takes us to the screen as shown in Figure 7.40. You will find the *selection ID* ZDM_DPSEL_SFC as shown in **1**. We place the cursor on ZDM_DPSEL_SFC (**2**) and drag and drop it to the user DEMOUSER as shown in (**3**). Next, click SAVE 🖫 (**4**).

DEMOUSER is a user at DM Consumer Appliances, Inc.

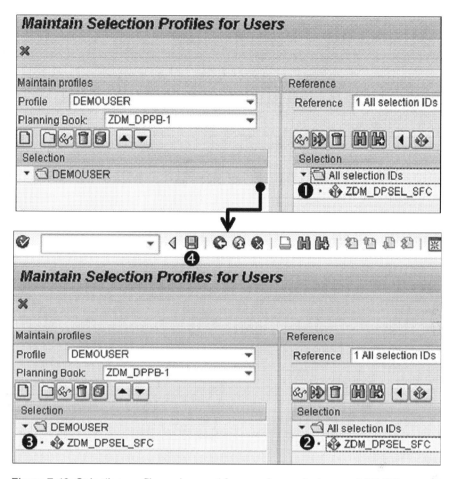

Figure 7.40: Selection profile assignment for user for product group LCD TVs

With this step, we have completed the *selection ID* maintenance for ZDM_DPSEL_SFC, which will be used for the *LCD TVs* (ZDM_PG1) product group in order to do statistical forecasting.

Similarly, we follow the same procedure to maintain the other *selection IDs* required. The selection criteria for each of the *selection IDs* are shown below.

Selection criteria for *selection ID* ZDM_DPSEL_NLC for lifecycle planning is shown in Figure 7.41.

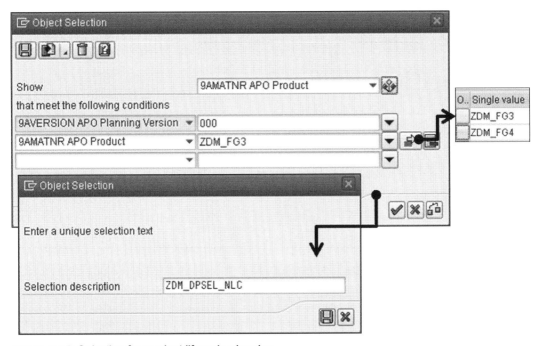

Figure 7.41: Selection for product lifecycle planning

The selection criteria for *selection ID* ZDM_PROMO_LAUNCH for promotions planning is indicated in Figure 7.42.

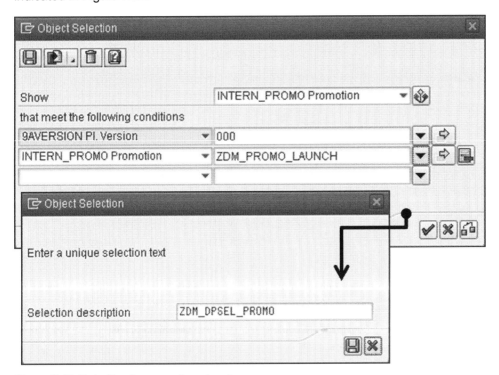

Figure 7.42: Selection for promotion planning

The selection criteria for *selection ID* ZDM_DPSEL_PG1_PDTS for consensus planning is shown in Figure 7.43.

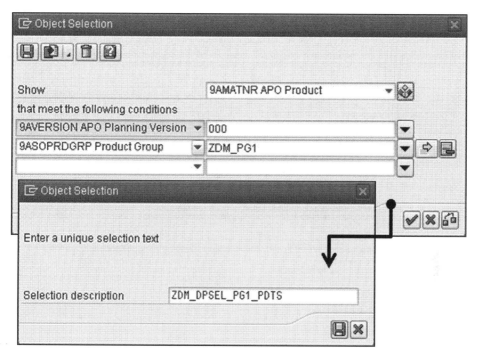

Figure 7.43: Selection for individual products for LCD TVs

The selection criteria for the *selection ID* ZDM_DPSEL_REL_SNP for release of demand to APO SNP for supply network planning is shown in Figure 7.44.

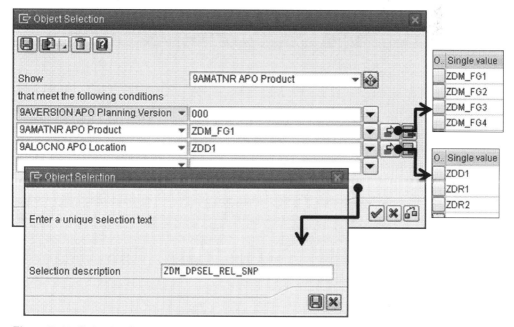

Figure 7.44: Selection for release to SNP

The selection criteria for the *selection ID* ZDM_DPSEL_TFR_ECC for transfer of demand to ERP for production planning is shown in Figure 7.45.

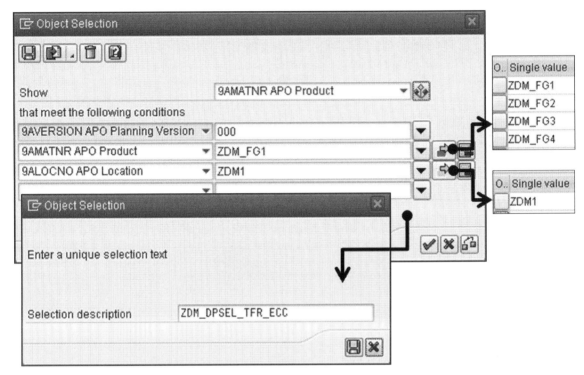

Figure 7.45: Selection for transfer to ERP

We created the *selection IDs*: ZDM_DPSEL_NLC, ZDM_DPSEL_PROMO, ZDM_DPSEL_ PG1_PDTS, ZDM_DPSEL_REL_SNP and ZDM_DPSEL_TFR_ECC as shown in ❶ of Figure 7.46. We select all selection IDs and drag and drop them to DEMOUSER as shown in ❷. Next, we click on SAVE 💾 (❸) and then click ENTER ✅ (❹).

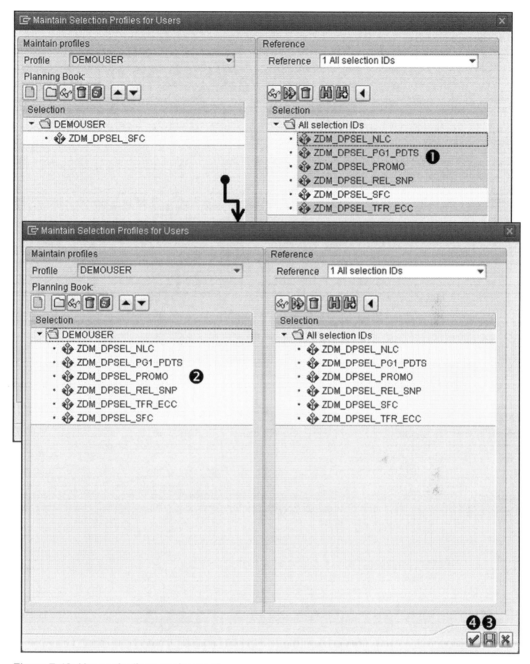

Figure 7.46: User selections assignment

We have now completed the Selection IDs assignment to the user.

7.9 Summary

In this chapter, we introduced the basic design for APO DP including connectivity for configurations, master data, and the basic framework required for demand planning. We explained DP design concepts, how each of the design aspects are linked to the bigger picture of demand planning, and how they can be exemplified through our business scenario.

In Chapter 8, we will continue with advanced design in APO DP, i.e., forecast profile design, design of alerts, and macros. While forecast profile design is indeed a foundational design, yet because of the multiple control parameters, features and complexities in forecast profile itself, we decided to include this in Chapter 8. As for design of macros and design of alerts, those are advance features that take into account intricate business requirements.

8 Advanced design in APO DP

APO DP has many provisions for influencing and aiding higher demand planning effectiveness through various features and functionalities. We consider all of the features and functionalities as advanced design in APO DP. In this chapter, we will introduce the forecasting concepts, factors that influence forecast, forecast profile design, and forecast errors. We will also look at the concepts behind alerts, alert design, and concepts behind macros and macros design.

Advanced design controls various aspects of demand planning. As we progress through the sections in this chapter, we will get into the details of the forecast profile, alert profiles, and macros. Advanced design aids demand management along with demand planning.

8.1 Forecast profile setup: Master forecast profile

The *forecast profile* is the central structure that controls the way forecasting is executed. The forecast profile is setup for a planning area as a master forecast profile. Different control parameters for the master forecast profile are:

- ▶ **Forecast key figure**: The key figure used for executing the forecast and storing the forecast output.
- ▶ **Forecast horizon**: The duration for forecast with a provision for offsetting the duration by certain period, i.e., postponement or preponement.
- ▶ **History horizon**: Duration for history of a forecast with a provision for offsetting the duration by certain period, i.e., postponement or preponement.
- ▶ **Period indicator**: The periodicity of the forecasts by period, e.g., months, years, etc.
- ▶ **Provision for lifecycle planning**: An indicator that helps enable provision for lifecycle planning.
- ▶ **Fiscal year variant**: Determines the fiscal year.
- ▶ **Type of forecast profiles**: There are three types of forecast profiles: univariate forecast profile, multiple linear regression profile, and composite forecast profile. We describe each of these profiles in Sections 8.1.1, 8.1.2 and 8.1.3 respectively.

The master forecast profile control parameters are depicted in the MAINTAIN FORECAST PROFILE screen in Figure 8.2.

The number of master forecast profiles depends on the number of forecasting key figures, the number of different forecasting models, and the planning level. A master profile is particularly distinguished by the type of forecast profile, i.e., univariate forecast profile, multiple linear regression profile, and composite profile. One master forecast profile can have one or more types of forecast profiles.

Of all the types of forecast profiles, the univariate forecast profile is most popular. We will explain the univariate forecast profile in detail in Section 8.1.1.

8.1.1   Univariate forecast profile

The *univariate forecast profile* is fundamentally based on the premise that the future replicates the past. To elaborate, the univariate forecast profile analyzes the past sales history and identifies a pattern as constant, trend, or seasonal and generates the forecast with or without any errors. The method of using historical data to forecast future demand is called the *time series method.* The univariate forecast profile contains a host of design and control parameters that constitute the way univariate forecasting is executed.

Before we get into the details of the univariate forecast profile design, let's review a few of the key concepts that are important to understand first.

Time series

Time series is a series of data gathered over a period of time at intervals.

Time series example

Monthly sales revenue, daily orders, and annual income.

Time series patterns

The following list includes the different types of time series patterns, also depicted in Figure 8.1, that are handled in the univariate forecast profile.

- ▶ **Constant demand**: Demand deviates very little from the mean and can be assumed to be constant over time.
- ▶ **Trend demand**: Demand either increases or decreases continuously over time and can be assumed to be a trend with a constant rate of increase or decrease in demand.
- ▶ **Seasonal demand**: Demand varies with the seasons and is therefore cyclical. Peak season demand and off season demand vary significantly from the mean demand.
- ▶ **Seasonal trend demand**: A combination of seasonal demand and trend demand. Demand varies with the seasons and is cyclical with peak season demand and off season demand varying significantly from the mean demand. Mean demand itself increases or decreases continuously.
- ▶ **Intermittent demand, lumpy demand, or sporadic demand**: Demand varies randomly.

▶ **No changes in demand from the previous year**: Demand is the copy of the actual history from the previous year. Therefore, no forecasting is executed.

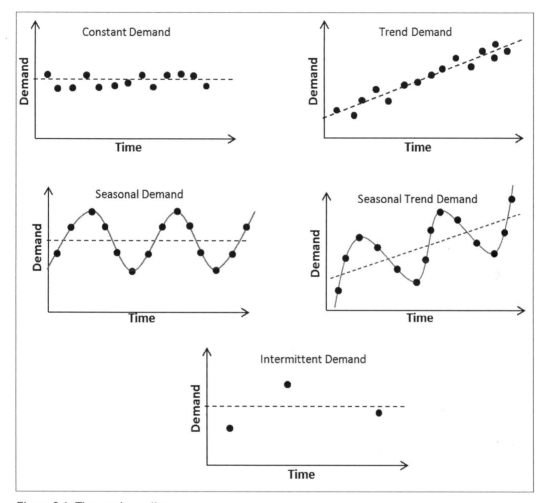

Figure 8.1: Time series pattern

Smoothing

The *smoothing method* averages out or smooths out the trend emerging from irregular components of the time series. Common smoothing methods include:

▶ **Moving averages:** In this method, the average of the raw time series with equal weightage is used for forecasting for the next period. It will smooth out sudden fluctuations.

▶ **Weighted moving average**s: In this method, the raw time series average is based on different weights to different data sets in the period. Preferably, recent data sets are given more weight. This method is generally used when a trend is present in the data sets. It will smooth sudden fluctuations.

▶ **Centered moving averages:** In this method, the average of the raw time series for multiple periods is associated with the mid-point of the period. The centered moving average is useful in calculating seasonal indexes.

▶ **Exponential smoothing:** In this method average of the raw time series is assigned exponentially decreasing weights over time with highest weights to the most recent data points. This method is also called exponentially weighted moving average. Smoothing is ensured by smoothing factors including:

  ▶ *Alpha (α)* represents the smoothing factor for a *basic value (G)*.
  ▶ *Beta (β)* represents the smoothing factor for a *trend value (T)*.
  ▶ *Gamma (γ)* represents the smoothing factor for *seasonal indices (S)*.

Basic value (G) is a measure of the vertical placement of sales value and gets calculated based on actual history, trend, and length of the season. Basic value depends on the forecast model.

Trend value (T) is the measure of leaning or direction of the sales values and it gets calculated based on actual history and length of the season.

Seasonal indices (S) represents the seasonal behavior of the sales and also happens to be the measure of the divergence from the basic value.

Value of alpha, beta, or gamma varies from *0* to *1*. A higher value implies more importance to recent values. These smoothing factors will give a higher weight to the recent values in the time series which implies that the recent values will have more impact on forecasting compared to the past values. If smoothing is done once, it is called first order exponential smoothing. However, this may not work best if there are trend patterns or seasonal variations in the data points. In such cases, smoothing is done again and it is called second order exponential smoothing. Second order exponential smoothing ensures a more appropriate and closer simulation to the actual time series values.

Model initialization
(Source: SAP Help Documentation)

Model initialization is the mechanism of establishing the first model parameters for a forecast model type. Different model parameters are basic value (G), seasonal indices (S), trend value (T), and mean absolute deviation (MAD). *Mean absolute deviation* is the average of the absolute deviation of the sales values from the mean. Values for *model parameters* vary from model type to model type as follows.

a) Model Type: Constant

Model Parameters:

Basic Value $=$ Hist(1) wherein Hist(i) is the ith historical value,

Trend Value $-$ 0,

Seasonal Indices $= 1$,

$MAD = 0$

b) Model Type: Trend

Model Parameters:

$$\text{Trend Value} = \frac{\{\text{Hist}(3) - \text{Hist}(1)\}}{2}$$

$$\text{Basic Value} = \frac{\{\text{Hist}(1) + \text{Hist}(2) + \text{Hist}(3)\}}{3} + \text{Trend}$$

Seasonal Indices $= 1$

$$\text{MAD} = \sum_{i=1}^{3} \frac{|\{\text{Basic Value} - \text{Hist}(i)\}|}{3}$$

c) Model Type: Seasonal

Model Parameters:

Basic Value = Mean of the historical values of the first historical season

Trend Value $= 0$,

Seasonal Index for a period $=$ Historical value for that period divided by the basic value

$MAD = 0$

d) Model Type: Seasonal Trend

Model Parameters for model type 'Seasonal Trend':

$$\text{Trend Value} - \frac{\{\text{Hist}(1 + \text{SL}) + \text{Hist}(2 + \text{SL}) + \text{Hist}(3 + \text{SL}) - \text{Hist}(1) - \text{Hist}(2) - \text{Hist}(3)\}}{(3 * \text{SL})}$$

Where, $\text{Hist}(i)$ is the ith Historical Value and SL is the length of the season i.e. season length

$$\text{Basic Value} = \sum_{i=4}^{SL+3} \frac{\{Hist(i)\}}{SL} + \frac{\{Trend*(SL-1)\}}{2}$$

$$\text{Seasonal Index for a period} = S\,(i+3) = \frac{Hist\,(i+3)}{\{Basic\,Value - Trend * (SL - i)\}}$$

Where, S (i) is the ith seasonal index

$$MAD = \sum_{i=1}^{SL} \frac{|[\{Basic\,Value - (SL-i)*Trend\}*S(i) - Hist(i+3)]|}{SL}$$

Model initialization is based on a fixed number of historical values and it depends on the model type as follows:

- ▶ Number of historical values for constant model type: 1
- ▶ Number of historical values for trend model type: 3
- ▶ Number of historical values for seasonal model type: 1 season
- ▶ Number of historical values for seasonal trend model Type: 3 + 1 season
- ▶ Number of historical values for second order exponential smoothing model type: 3

Ex-post forecast

Ex-post forecast is the forecast that is calculated in the past considering past history. We explained the ex-post forecast in Section 7.6.1.

Forecast calculations

Forecasting is done using complex statistical formulas and is based on the historical values, its behavior in terms of distribution, patterns, etc. and the forecast model. To bring pattern and accuracy to the forecast output we need to make use of the different *smoothening techniques* as explained. *Smoothing factors* determine how quickly the forecast reacts to the change in time series data.

Smoothing factor influence on time series

 If we choose the smoothing factor Alpha (α) as '0', then forecasting gives more weight to the old values and the new average will be equal to the old one. In contrast, if we choose Alpha (α) as '1' then the new average will be equal to the last value in the time series

The most common values for *Alpha (α)* lie between 0.1 and 0.5.

Let's take a closer look at the two formulas in following situations.

a) First order exponential smoothing
(Source: SAP Help Documentation)

Two main principles form the foundation of *first order exponential smoothing* — the older the time series data, the lower the impact on forecasting and current forecast errors are taken into consideration in subsequent forecasts.

The formula for first order exponential smoothing for trend and seasonal models is as shown below.

Forecasting for the period $(t+i)$:

$$P(t + i) = (G(t) + i * T(t)) * S(t - L + i)$$

Basic Value:

$$G(t) = G(t - 1) + T(t\text{-}1) + \alpha\{\frac{V(t)}{S(t)} - G(t - 1) - T(t - 1)\}$$

Trend Value:

$$T(t) = T(t - 1) + \beta[G(t) - \{G(t\text{-}1) - T(t\text{-}1)\}]$$

Seasonal Index:

$$S(t + L) = S(t) + \gamma\{\frac{V(t)}{G(t)} - S(t)\}$$

The general formula above can be made specific by adopting the following:

For Constant Model:

$$T(t) = 0, \beta = 0, S(t) = 1, \gamma = 0$$

For Trend Model:

$$S(t) = 1, \gamma = 0$$

For Seasonal Model:

$$T(t) = 0, \beta = 0$$

The explanation of the formula components is as follows:

- ▶ $P(t + i)$ is the forecast calculated for the period $(t + i)$ in the current period (t)
- ▶ 'i' is the forecast horizon
- ▶ $G(t)$ is the current basic value for the current period (t)
- ▶ $G(t\text{-}1)$ is the previous basic value from the previous period
- ▶ L is the period length

- ▶ $V(t)$ is the actual demand (history) for the current period (t)
- ▶ $T(t)$ is the current trend value calculated for the current period
- ▶ $T(t-1)$ is the previous trend value from the previous period
- ▶ $S(t)$ is the seasonal index for the period (t)
- ▶ $S(t-L)$ is the previous seasonal index for the period (t)
- ▶ Alpha (α) is the smoothing factor for the basic value 'G' where $0 < \alpha < 1$
- ▶ Beta (β) is the smoothing factor for the trend value 'T' where $0 < \beta < 1$
- ▶ Gamma (γ) is the smoothing factor for the seasonal indices 'S' where $0 < \gamma < 1$

b) Second order exponential smoothing
(Source: SAP Help Documentation)

Second order exponential smoothing is based on a linear trend and basically has two equations, wherein the first equation corresponds to the first order exponential smoothing and second equation uses the first order exponential smoothing outcome as its inputs.

The formula for second order exponential smoothing is as shown below.

Seasonal Index:

$$G^1(t) = \alpha V(t-1) + (1-\alpha)\, G^1(t-1)$$

$$G^2(t) = \alpha G^1(t) + (1-\alpha)\, G^2(t-1)$$

We explain the formula components as follows:

- ▶ $G^1(t)$ is the current simply smoothed basic value for the current period (t)
- ▶ $G^1(t-1)$ is the previous simply smoothed basic value from the previous period
- ▶ $G^2(t)$ is the current doubly smoothed basic value for the current period (t)
- ▶ $G^2(t-1)$ is the previous doubly smoothed basic value from the previous period
- ▶ $V(t-1)$ is the actual demand history from the previous period
- ▶ Alpha (α) is the smoothing factor for the basic value 'G' where $0 < \alpha < 1$

Univariate forecast profile design depends on several settings as shown in Figure 8.2. The settings as follows:

Read historical data

The key figure mentioned in READ HISTORICAL DATA is used for calculating forecast. If we set the indicator READ CORR. HISTORY DATA FROM PLANNING VERSION, then the system uses CORRECTED HISTORY DATA for calculating the forecast, in spite of maintaining HISTORICAL INPUT KEY FIGURE in the univariate forecast profile.

Univariate forecasting model types, forecast strategies, and model parameters

FORECASTING MODEL TYPES are a broad categorization of forecast models which follow a uniform method for forecasting. FORECASTING STRATEGIES are even more specific forecasting techniques belonging to a particular forecasting model types.

We mention the forecasting strategies in the univariate forecasting profile design.

There are multiple **Forecasting Model Types** with corresponding forecasting strategies which are used for forecasting as follows.

(Source: SAP Help Documentation)

Constant

Forecasting Strategy	Strategy Number	Properties
Constant Model	10	▶ Makes use of first-order exponential smoothing of time series data. ▶ Used when demand varies marginally from the average. ▶ Applicable for time series data with no seasonality/trend.
First-order exponential smoothing	11	▶ Smoothing factor is chosen by the planner. ▶ Makes use of first-order exponential smoothing of time series data. ▶ Applicable for time series data with no seasonality/trend. ▶ Suitable for short-term planning, i.e., less than 3 months.
Constant Model with Automatic Alpha Adaptation (1st Order)	12	▶ Makes use of first-order exponential smoothing of time series data. ▶ Alpha factor gets adapted automatically with every ex-post forecast based on ex-post forecast deviation (error total and mean absolute deviation). ▶ Applicable for time series data with no seasonality/trend.

Moving Average

Forecasting Strategy	Strategy Number	Properties
Moving average	13	▶ All past data is weighted equally. ▶ Ex-post forecast is not possible. ▶ Applicable for time series data with no seasonality/trend.
Weighted Moving Average	14	▶ All past data is weighted differently through weighting factor based on diagnosis group design. ▶ Recent data are weighed more. ▶ Ex-post forecast is not possible. ▶ Applicable for time series data with no seasonality/trend.

Trend

Forecasting Strategy	Strategy Number	Properties
Forecast with Trend Model	20	▶ Data neither has seasonality, nor is constant. ▶ Makes use of first-order exponential smoothing of time series data.
Holt's method	21	▶ Makes use of first-order exponential smoothing of time series data. ▶ Allows forecasting of data with trends, but not for seasonal data. ▶ Better accuracy for short duration forecast (i.e., < 3 months).
Second-Order Exponential Smoothing	22	▶ Makes use of second-order exponential smoothing of time series data.
Trend Model with Automatic Alpha Adaptation (2nd Order)	23	▶ Same as forecast strategy 22 except that alpha value is adapted automatically by the system. ▶ Alpha factor adaptation is based on mean absolute deviation and error total.

Seasonal

Forecasting Strategy	Strategy Number	Properties
Forecast with Seasonal Models	30	▶ Makes use of first-order exponential smoothing of time series data. ▶ Takes into account seasonal variation and trend value of the time series data. ▶ Alpha and Gamma factors are considered.
Seasonal Model Based on Winters' Method	31	▶ Makes use of first-order exponential smoothing of time series data. ▶ Takes into account seasonal variation and trend value of the time series data. ▶ Alpha and Gamma factors are considered.
Seasonal Linear Regression	35	▶ Linear regression is done after calculating the seasonal indexes and after removing the seasonal impacts. ▶ Once linear regression is complete, the seasonal indexes are applied to bring up the seasonal flavor. ▶ This method is not applicable if there are strong trends in the time series. ▶ Use this method if there are many zeroes, or small values in the time series.

Median Method

Forecasting Strategy	Strategy Number	Properties
Median Method	36	► This method establishes the median of basic, trend, and seasonal indexes. ► Outlier correction and initialization is not necessary. ► This method needs to be avoided for time series values that is either in steps, or for a long duration.

Seasonal Trend

Forecasting Strategy	Strategy Number	Properties
Forecast with Seasonal Trend Models	40	► Makes use of first-order exponential smoothing of time series data. ► Alpha, Beta, and Gamma values are used.
Holt and Winters' Exponential Smoothing	41	► Same as forecast strategy 40.

Automatic Model Selection

Forecasting Strategy	Strategy Number	Properties
Forecast with Automatic Model Selection 1	50	► System adopts this strategy when no clear time series pattern emerges. ► Forecast execution tests all patterns, i.e., constant, seasonal, trend, and their combinations. ► System adopts the pattern that it senses as the closest. ► If the system is not able to sense any pattern then it adopts 'constant' strategy. ► System reads the smoothing factors (Alpha, Beta and Gamma) from the univariate profile. However, it adopts the smoothing factors from planning table if there is a difference. In case no value exists, then the system adopts a default value of 0.3 for all smoothing factors. ► This strategy works faster, albeit less precisely, than forecast strategy 56.

Forecasting Strategy	Strategy Number	Properties
Test for trend	51	▶ We use this strategy when we think there is a trend in the time series pattern. ▶ The system carries out regression analysis for trend pattern. However, if it does not sense any such pattern then it defaults to constant pattern. ▶ Smoothing factors, i.e., Alpha, Beta, and Gamma are also calculated. ▶ Execution is faster than forecast strategy 50 or 56 as a fewer number of tests are carried out.
Test for season	52	▶ We use this strategy when we think there is a seasonal pattern in the time series. ▶ The system removes any trend patterns it identifies. Next, it carries out autocorrelation test for seasonal pattern. However, if it does not sense any such seasonal pattern then it defaults to constant pattern. ▶ Smoothing factors, i.e., Alpha, Beta, and Gamma are also calculated. ▶ Execution is faster than Forecast strategy 50 or 56 as less number of tests are carried out
Test for trend and season	53	▶ We use this strategy when we think there is a seasonal and/or trend pattern in the time series. ▶ The system carries out regression analysis to identify any trend pattern in the time series. ▶ Next, the system removes any trend patterns and carries out autocorrelation test for seasonal pattern. ▶ If a seasonal and/or trend pattern is detected, then the system uses a seasonal model or trend model or a combined model for these two. ▶ However, if it does not sense any such seasonal and/or trend pattern, then it defaults to a constant pattern. ▶ Smoothing factors i.e. Alpha, Beta and Gamma are also calculated ▶ Execution is faster than forecast strategy 50 or 56 as a fewer number of tests are carried out.
Seasonal model and test for trend	54	▶ We use this strategy when we think there is a trend pattern in the time series and we already know that there is a seasonal pattern. ▶ The system carries out regression analysis to identify any trend pattern in the time series. ▶ If the trend pattern gets identified then we use the seasonal trend model; otherwise only a seasonal model is used. ▶ Smoothing factors, i.e., Alpha, Beta, and Gamma are also calculated.

Forecasting Strategy	Strategy Number	Properties
Trend model and test for seasonal pattern	55	▶ We use this strategy when we think there is a seasonal pattern in the time series and we already know that there is a trend pattern. ▶ Next, the system removes trend patterns and carries out an autocorrelation test for a seasonal pattern. ▶ If a seasonal pattern is detected, then the system uses a seasonal trend model, otherwise it only uses a trend model. ▶ Smoothing factors, i.e., Alpha, Beta, and Gamma are also calculated.
Forecast with Automatic Model Selection 2	56	▶ We use this strategy when we want to do detailed testing for constant, trend, seasonal, and seasonal trend patterns. ▶ We use this strategy when we do not have knowledge of the pattern of time series. ▶ This testing is done for varying values of smoothing factors, i.e., Alpha, Beta, and Gamma. ▶ Next, the system calculates the mean absolute deviation for each of the possible combinations. ▶ The system then chooses the strategy that gives the minimum mean absolute deviation. ▶ Execution of this strategy takes longer because of exhaustive testing. However, this forecast strategy gives most precise results. ▶ This strategy is not recommended for mass execution.

Historical Data Model

Forecasting Strategy	Strategy Number	Properties
Historical data adopted	60	▶ Suitable for situations where demand does not change compared to history. ▶ We do not do any forecasting. Instead history data is copied for the future. ▶ Ex-post forecast is not possible.

Manual forecasting

Forecasting Strategy	Strategy Number	Properties
Manual forecast	70	▶ Suitable for manual execution of forecast in the foreground. ▶ Planner manually specifies the Basic Value (Alpha), Trend Value (Beta), Trend Dampening Profile, and Seasonal Indices (Gamma). ▶ Ex-post forecast is not possible.

Sporadic Demand

Forecasting Strategy	Strategy Number	Properties
Croston's model	80	▶ We use Croston's model when there is sporadic or intermittent demand. ▶ This strategy is carried out by first generating an exponential smoothing estimate out of the average size of the demand. ▶ Next, we figure out the intervals between demands and execute a forecast using a constant model. Thereby, the system generates only a single forecast value. ▶ The forecast depends on the spread of data, i.e., whether data is clustered at some time horizon, or is distributed over a period of time.

Linear Regression

Forecasting Strategy	Strategy Number	Properties
Linear regression	94	▶ Used for forecasting trends. ▶ Line is derived from the complete datasets using best fit least square methods. ▶ Method is similar to multiple linear regression with only one independent variable with which the dependent variable has a linear relationship. ▶ Forecast accuracy depends on number of data points. ▶ Forecasting does not depend on smoothing parameters. However, it uses a trend dampening profile. ▶ Initialization is not carried out. ▶ Mostly used from medium term horizon, i.e., > 3 months but </ = 24 months.

No Forecast

Forecasting Strategy	Strategy Number	Properties
No forecast	98	▶ We do not generate forecast if we chose this option.

External Forecast

Forecasting Strategy	Strategy Number	Properties
External forecast	99	▶ Forecasting is done using custom development (ABAP) to develop a forecast model that is not available in standard SAP. ▶ SAP specified user exits are available for use, if any.

Table 8.1: Forecasting model types and forecast strategies

MODEL PARAMETERS like ALPHA (α), BETA (β), and GAMMA (γ) are explained in the section above on smoothing. SIGMA FACTOR (σ) is used for correcting outliers (i.e., exceptions) in historical values. ALPHA 2 is the Alpha factor for second order exponential smoothing.

Weighting profile

The WEIGHTING PROFILE consists of weights in the form of percentages that are used for distributing weights to historical values for executing weighted moving average forecasts (*forecasting strategy 14*).

Historical value markings

Historical value marking is used is to mark the historical values for its consideration in time series for outlier correction. If the HISTORICAL VALUE MARKING field is not used in the univariate forecast profile, then all of the historical values will be considered for outlier correction.

Diagnosis group

DIAGNOSIS GROUP specifies the upper limit for each of the forecast errors. On forecast execution, the system generates alerts if the UPPER LIMITS of forecast errors are exceeded.

Model reinitialization settings

MODEL REINITIALIZATION SETTINGS in the univariate forecast profile controls the way forecast values are readjusted in the event of a structural disruption, or a major change in the trend in the history values. Recalculation of basic value, trend value, and seasonal indices happen through reinitialization. We can choose the options as shown in section MODEL REINITIALIZATION SETTINGS in Figure 8.2.

Trend dampening settings

We specify multiple control parameters in TREND DAMPENING SETTINGS to streamline strong upward trends that would otherwise create a very optimistic forecast. Trend dampening is applicable for forecast models with a trend component. We can choose the options as shown in section on TREND DAMPENING SETTINGS in Figure 8.2. This includes the option of using a TREND DAMPENING PROFILE, setting UPPER LIMIT OF TREND VALUE, setting UPPER LIMIT OF FORECAST DEVIATION FROM BASIC VALUE, PHI PARAMETERS, etc.

The PHI PARAMETER is used to dampen trend value more efficiently. The smaller the value is, the more effective the dampening is. The Phi parameter value ranges from 0 to 1. A Phi parameter value of 1 signifies no trend dampening.

Control parameters

You will find CONTROL PARAMETERS in the section on control parameters in Figure 8.2. These parameters effectively control the history and forecast output. OUTLIER CORRECTION and DAYS IN PERIOD are two control parameters.

Outlier correction:

Outliers are exceptional historical values that lie outside of the permissible limits. Outliers get in the way of accurate forecasting and therefore, warrant correction. If the OUTLIER CORRECTION option is flagged in the univariate forecast profile, then the system generates a tolerance lane. Any values falling outside of the tolerance lane are identified as outliers and are subject to correction. There are two methods for outlier correction.

> ▶ **Ex-post method for outlier correction**
> *(Source:SAP Help documentation)*
> In the EX-POST METHOD FOR OUTLIER CORRECTION, the system generates a tolerance lane based on the ex-post method, forecast error 'MAD' and Sigma Factor (σ). Tolerance lane = Ex-post Forecast +/- (σ * MAD).
>
> ▶ **Median method for outlier correction**
> *(Source:SAP Help documentation)*
> In the MEDIAN METHOD FOR OUTLIER CORRECTION method, the system generates a tolerance lane based on the expected value for each historical period and Sigma Factor (σ). Wherein, the expected value is based on the median values of: basic value, trend value and seasonal index generated through median method of the ex-post forecast.
> Tolerance lane = σ * Expected Value

For both of the methods mentioned above, ex-post forecasting is done twice. First to correct the outliers and second, to generate the ex-post forecast based on the corrected outliers. Based on the outlier correction, the revised history gets stored in the corrected history key figure automatically.

Days in period

We specify the actual number of workdays per period and not calendar days. Based on that, the history values get recalculated and stored in the corrected history key figure if the option of READ CORRECTED HISTORY FROM PLANNING VERSION is not selected in the univariate forecast profile. Similarly, based on the DAYS IN PERIOD values, forecasts too get recalculated and saved in the corrected forecast key figure.

Forecast errors

Forecast error is the deviation of the actual demand values from the forecasted demand values. Forecast errors typically indicate two aspects: the magnitude of the forecast errors and the direction of the forecast errors. A minimal forecast error implies high forecast accuracy. Therefore, *forecast accuracy* is the opposite of forecast errors. In effect, forecast errors reflect how far-fetched the forecasts are from the actual business results. Forecast errors can be calculated both retroactively, as well as predictively.

In the univariate forecast profile, the following forecast error measurement options are available for ex-post forecast to decide on the suitability of any particular forecast model and its parameters. These options can be seen in the section FORECAST ERRORS in Figure 8.2. Forecast errors that we flag in the univariate forecast, will get calculated and appear in the FORECAST ERRORS tab in the INTERACTIVE PLANNING screen.

The following section explains each of the types of forecast errors:

(Source: SAP Help documentation)

a) Mean absolute deviation (MAD)

The *mean absolute deviation* is the average of the absolute difference between the ex-post forecasted values and the historical values. Positive and negative errors do not nullify each other. MAD forecast error is calculated as follows:

$$MAD(t) = (1-\delta)*MAD(t-1) + \delta*|V(t) - P(t)|$$

- ▶ $V(t)$ is Actual history values
- ▶ $P(t)$ is the ex-post forecast values
- ▶ $\delta = 0.3$

b) Mean absolute percentage error (MAPE)

Mean absolute percentage error is the measure of average absolute deviation as percentage of the actual historical values. Deviation is between the ex-post forecast values and the actual historical values. MAPE forecast error is calculated as follows:

$$MAPE = \frac{1}{n}\sum_{t=1}^{n} |PE(t)|$$

$$PE(t) = \left\{\frac{e(t)}{V(t)}\right\} * 100$$

$$e(t) = V(t) - P(t)$$

▶ $V(t)$ is Actual history values

▶ $P(t)$ is the ex-post forecast values

▶ 'n' is the number of ex-post periods

c) Mean square error (MSE)

Mean square error is the measure of the average of the sum of the squares of forecast errors, or error variance wherein the error is the difference between each ex-post forecast values and actual historical values. The MSE method goes by the premise that large errors are more expensive than small errors. MSE forecast error is calculated as follows:

$$MSE = \frac{1}{n}\sum_{t=1}^{n} e(t)^2$$

$$e(t) = V(t) - P(t)$$

▶ $V(t)$ is actual history values

▶ $P(t)$ is the ex-post forecast values

▶ 'n' is the number of ex-post periods

d) Mean percentage error (MPE)

Mean percentage error is the measure of average deviation as percentage of the actual historical values. Deviation is between ex-post forecast values and the actual historical values. MPE forecast error is calculated as follows:

$$MPE = \frac{1}{n}\sum_{t=1}^{n} PE(t)$$

$$PE(t) = \left\{\frac{e(t)}{V(t)}\right\} * 100$$

$$e(t) = V(t) - P(t)$$

▶ $V(t)$ is actual history values

▶ $P(t)$ is the ex-post forecast values

▶ 'n' is the number of ex-post periods

e) Root mean square error (RMSE)

Root mean square error is the measure of the square root of the average of the sum of the squares of forecast errors or error variance wherein the error is the difference between each ex-post forecast values and actual historical values. RMSE method goes by the premise that large errors are more expensive than small errors. RMSE forecast error is calculated as follows:

$$RMSE = \sqrt{\frac{1}{n} \sum_{t=1}^{n} e(t)^2}$$

$$e(t) = V(t) - P(t)$$

▶ $V(t)$ is actual history values

▶ $P(t)$ is the ex-post forecast values

▶ 'n' is the number of ex-post periods

f) Error total (ET)

Error total is the measure of the total sum of the differences between actual historical values and ex-post forecast values. The negative and positive errors cancel one another out. ET forecast error is calculated as follows:

$$ET = \sum_{t=1}^{n} \{V(t) - P(t)\}$$

▶ $V(t)$ is actual history values

▶ $P(t)$ is the ex-post forecast values

▶ 'n' is the number of ex-post periods

Promotion

In the PROMOTION field in the univariate forecast profile, we specify the key figure in which the past promotions are stored. We use the promotion key figure values in combination with any of the two options SELECT or CHANGE VALS to correct history by flagging them. For our business scenario, we keep the option open. Hence, we choose the PROMOTION key figure, but do not flag the option SELECT or CHANGE VALS as we plan to make a decision on correcting history in near future.

We explained the major concepts behind the forecast profile and the different choices that exist. We shall now design a forecast profile for our business scenario.

You will find the reference to this section as 'Forecast Profile Maintenance (Master Profile-Univariate)' in the block 'Design in APO DP' in the APO DP process flow diagram depicted in Figure 4.2.

For our business scenario DM Consumer Appliances, Inc., we maintain a master profile called *Demo Forecast Profile* (ZDM_MASTER_FCST_PF) and its corresponding univariate forecast profile *Demo Univar Fcst Profile* (ZDM_UNI_FCST_PF), as explained below. Let's look at two alternative designs for *Demo Univar Fcst Profile* for the same *Demo Forecast Profile*.

Alternative: Forecast profile based on *Croston's Model*

Alternative: Forecast profile based on *Automatic Model Selection 1*.

We will use each of these designs one by one for forecast execution at DM Consumer Appliances, Inc. On execution, we will examine the forecast errors and results and will finally adopt only one of the alternatives for the forecast profile based on model that best fits our business scenario.

The transaction code or menu path for maintaining forecast profiles in the SCM system is as follows:

Transaction Code: /SAPAPO/MC96B

Menu Path: SAP MENU • ADVANCED PLANNING AND OPTIMIZATION • DEMAND PLANNING • ENVIRONMENT • MAINTAIN FORECAST PROFILES

Alternative: Forecast profile based on *Croston's Model*.

We go to the mentioned transaction code for maintaining the forecast profile. We refer to Figure 8.2 to create the master profile by clicking on the tab MASTER PRFL. (❶).

Select the planning area ZDM_DPPA and make an entry for DEMO FORECAST PROFILE (ZDM_MASTER_FCST_PF) as shown in (❷). We select the forecast key figure 9ADFCST as the key figure in which forecast values will get stored and displayed. As we intend to launch new products for DM Consumer Appliances, Inc. and will use the SAP Lifecycle Planning functionality, we flag LIFECYCLE PLANNING as ACTIVE (❸). We will carry out the forecast for DM Consumer Appliances, Inc. on a monthly basis, so we select the PERIOD M (❹). Next, add entries for HISTORY HORIZON and FORECAST HORIZON of 24 MONTHS (❺)

We proceed to create the univariate forecast profile by clicking on the tab UNIVARIATE PRO-FILE as shown in the Figure 8.2 and make an entry for the univariate forecast profile DEMO UNIVAR FCST PROFILE (ZDM_UNI_FCST_PF) as shown in ❻. We continue to make other entries like descriptive text. Select the key figure 9AVHISTORY and version 000 in READ HISTORY DATA. Values maintained in this particular key figure will be treated as history values for forecasting. Select the forecast strategy 80 (❼), i.e., Croston's Model as first alternative as we consider some element of randomness for history data at DM Consumer Appliances, Inc. Other model parameters including smoothing factors, sigma factors, and periods are maintained in the section called MODEL PARAMETERS in the Figure 8.2. We disable the REINITIALIZATION option. We do not foresee any strong trends and therefore, do not use the TREND DAMPENING settings.

For our business scenario, we do not make entries for the WEIGHTING PROFILE, HISTORY VALUE MARKINGS, and DAYS IN PERIOD. This is because we do not want to weigh the history values. We want all values to be considered for forecast correction and will consider the entire calendar period for forecasting purposes. We adopt the EX-POST METHOD BASED OUTLIER CORRECTION as we intend to have the mean absolute deviation forecast error considered for outlier determination.

At DM Consumer Appliances, Inc., we would like to understand the applicability of the forecast model for the time series through measurement of two types of forecast errors signifying differences between history values and forecast values. One error takes into consideration both positive and negative deviation in totality and thereby give us a complete picture. This is feasible by adopting the forecast *error total* (ET). At the same time, DM Consumer Appliance Inc. would like to judge the forecast model applicability from the perspective of unbiased net standard deviation without the possibility of significant multiplication. This is feasible by adopting the forecast error RMSE. The squaring of the individual deviation nullifies the positive/negative bias and provides the necessary measure of deviation. The subsequent square root of the values standardizes the deviation and reduces the error multiplication effort. We, therefore, flag the ET and RMSE (❽) as forecast error measurement choices for our business scenario in the univariate forecast profile.

We select the key figure PROMOTION (❾) for DM Consumer Appliances, Inc.

For the two forecast error measurement options, we make entries of the upper limits for each of the forecast errors through diagnosis group. We click MAINTAIN DIAGNOSIS GROUP 🖉 (❿) in the DIAGNOSIS GROUP screen.

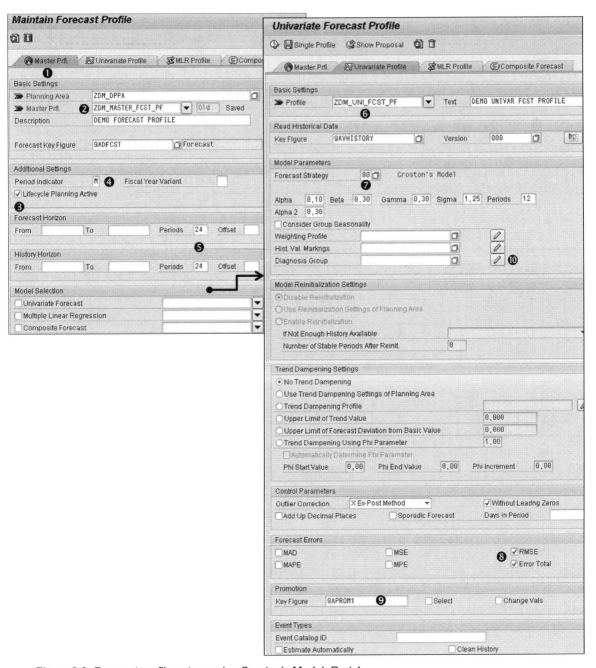

Figure 8.2: Forecast profile set up using Croston's Model: Part 1

This completes the Part 1 of 'Forecast profile set up using Croston's Model'.

Let's continue with Part 2 of 'Forecast profile set up using Croston's Model'. Once we click on MAINTAIN DIAGNOSIS GROUP 🖉 next to DIAGNOSIS GROUP as shown in Figure 8.2 it takes us to the MAINTAIN DIAGNOSIS GROUP screen shown in Figure 8.3. We refer to Figure 8.3 for the remaining process. We make entries for diagnosis group ZDM_DG (❶), ET UPPER LIMIT (❷), and RMSE UPPER LIMIT (❸). Then, click on 🖫 Save Group (❹) and we get the message ☑ Diagnosis Group was saved successfully . Next, click on ADOPT VALUES ⊕ (**⑤**) and it goes back to the UNIVARIATE FORECAST PROFILE screen where we can see the diagnosis group ZDM_DG (**⑥**).

Click ⊞ Single Profile (**⑦**), and we get the message ☑ The single profile has been saved . Next, we click ADOPT ⊕ (**⑧**) and we get the message

☑ The univariate profile was assigned to the master profile .

Next, it takes us to the screen MAINTAIN FORECAST PROFILE. Here, we ensure that the particular univariate forecast profile ZDM_UNI_FCST_PF (**⑨**) is assigned to the master forecast profile called DEMO FORECAST PROFILE (ZDM_MASTER_FCST_PF). We save the master forecast profile by clicking on SAVE ⊞ (**⑩**). We get the following message ☑ Forecast profile has been successfully saved .

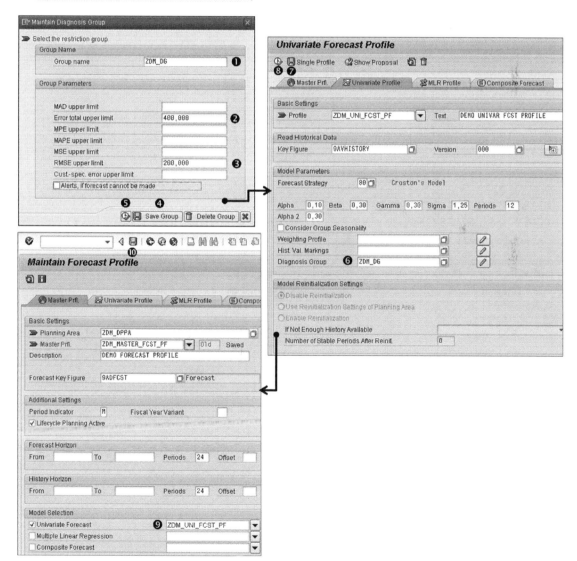

Figure 8.3: Forecast profile set up using Croston's Model: Part 2

This completes the Part 2 of 'Forecast profile set up using Croston's Model' for DM Consumer Appliances, Inc.

With this step, we have completed the design of the master forecast profile called *Demo Forecast Profile* (ZDM_MASTER_FCST_PF) and the univariate forecast profile ZDM_UNI_FCST_PF using *Croston's Model*.

Next, we will explain the alternative forecast profile set up for DM Consumer Appliances, Inc., i.e., forecast profile set up using *Automatic Model Selection 1* as follows.

Alternative: Forecast profile based on *Automatic Model Selection 1*

Creating the forecast profile based on *Automatic Model Selection 1* is not in sequence with the forecast profile set up using *Croston's Model*, rather this is just another alternative. We will elaborate on the additional differences that we would set up for maintaining the forecast profile based on *automatic model selection 1*.

We go to the transaction (Transaction Code: /SAPAPO/MC96B) for maintaining the forecast profile. Refer to Figure 8.4 and create the Master Profile DEMO FORECAST PROFILE (ZDM_MASTER_FCST_PF). Ensure that we have the settings as shown in Figure 8.4. The master profile design is same for both of the alternatives.

We create the univariate forecast profile by clicking on the tab UNIVARIATE PROFILE as shown in Figure 8.4 and make an entry for the univariate forecast profile DEMO UNIVAR FCST PROFILE (ZDM_UNI_FCST_PF) as shown in ❻. Enter a description. Select the key figure 9AVHISTORY and Version 000 in READ HISTORY DATA. Values maintained in this particular key figure will be treated as history values for forecasting. We select the FORECAST STRATEGY 50 (❼), i.e., AUTOMATIC MODEL SELECTION 1 as a second alternative, as we plan for the system to decide and propose the forecast model for the historical data at DM Consumer Appliances, Inc. Other model parameters including smoothing factors, sigma factors, and periods are maintained in the section MODEL PARAMETERS in Figure 8.4. We disable the REINITIALIZATION option. We do not foresee any strong trends; nevertheless, we allow TREND DAMPENING SETTINGS to be inherited from the planning area.

For our business scenario, we do not maintain the WEIGHTING PROFILE, HISTORY VALUE MARKINGS, and DAYS IN PERIOD for the reason similar to the earlier alternative forecast profile set up using CROSTON'S MODEL. We adopt the EX-POST METHOD BASED OUTLIER CORRECTION as we intend to have the mean absolute deviation forecast error considered for outlier determination.

For the alternative forecast profile based on AUTOMATIC MODEL SELECTION 1' as well, we flag the ET and RMSE (❽) as forecast error measurement choices for our business scenario in the univariate forecast profile. The rationale for this Is same as was explained for the alternative forecast profile set up using CROSTON'S MODEL.

Select the key figure for storing PROMOTION (❾) for DM Consumer Appliances, Inc.

For the two forecast error measurement options, we make entries of the upper limits for each of the forecast errors through diagnosis group. We click MAINTAIN DIAGNOSIS GROUP ✎ (❿) next to DIAGNOSIS GROUP.

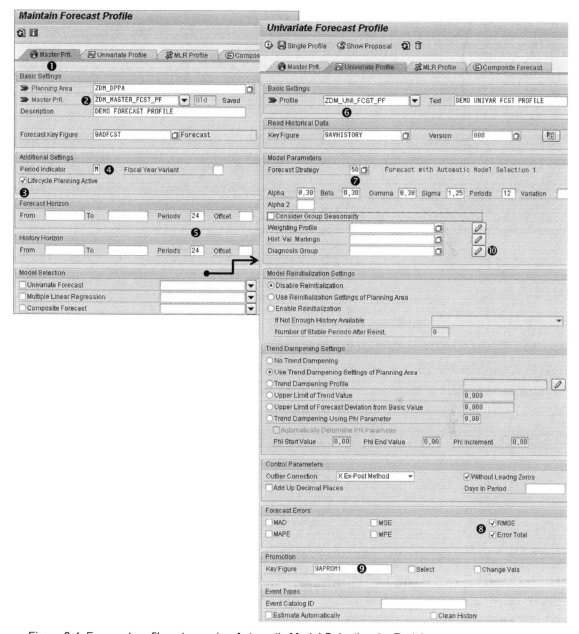

Figure 8.4: Forecast profile set up using Automatic Model Selection 1—Part 1

This completes Part 1 of 'Forecast profile set up using Automatic Model Selection 1'.

We continue on with Part 2 of 'Forecast profile set up using Automatic Model Selection 1' as shown in Figure 8.5. Once we click on MAINTAIN DIAGNOSIS GROUP ✎ next to the DIAGNOSIS GROUP as shown in Figure 8.5 it takes us to the MAINTAIN DIAGNOSIS GROUP screen as shown in Figure 8.5. We refer Figure 8.5 for the remaining portion of the process. We make entries for diagnosis group ZDM_DG (❶), ET UPPER LIMIT (❷), and RMSE UPPER LIMIT (❸) and then click on 🖫 Save Group (❹). Next, click on ADOPT VALUES ⊕ (❺) and it goes back to the UNIVARIATE FORECAST PROFILE screen where we can see the diagnosis group ZDM_DG (❻).

Click 🖫 Single Profile (❼) and then click ADOPT ⊕ (❽). Next, it takes us to the screen MAIN-TAIN FORECAST PROFILE. Here, we ensure that the particular univariate forecast profile ZDM_UNI_FCST_PF (❾) is assigned to the master forecast profile DEMO FORECAST PRO-FILE (ZDM_MASTER_FCST_PF). We save the Master Forecast Profile by clicking on SAVE 🖫 (❿).

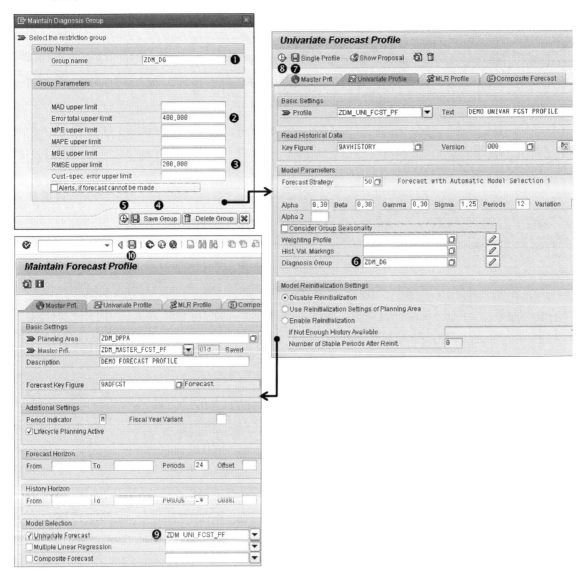

Figure 8.5: Forecast profile set up using Automatic Model Selection 1—Part 2

This completes Part 2 of 'Forecast profile set up using Automatic Model Selection 1' for DM Consumer Appliances, Inc.

With this step, we have completed the design for the master forecast profile DEMO FORECAST PROFILE (ZDM_MASTER_FCST_PF) and the univariate forecast profile ZDM_UNI_FCST_PF using *Automatic Model Selection 1*.

We will use both of these alternatives and evaluate the effect on forecasting. Based on the demand planning outcome and forecast model fitment, we will evaluate which alternative is the best fit for our scenario.

For our business scenario we follow *univariate forecasting* and therefore, we elaborated on all of the design aspects and concepts around univariate forecasting in detail. The other two forecasting methods, i.e., *multiple linear regression* and *composite forecasting* are not being used. Therefore, we will not deal with these two types of forecasting in detail. Nevertheless, we touch upon these two areas in brief in the following two sections.

8.1.2 Multiple linear regression profile

The *multiple linear regression (MLR)* profile makes use of statistical regression analysis, i.e., causal analysis, to determine the forecast for a dependent variable wherein the values for the *dependent variable* are driven by multiple independent variables. Typically, *independent variables values* are known for past and future and are called causal factors. A relationship is established between the dependent variables and the independent variables after applying appropriate weightage to independent variables, keeping the provision of residual errors, etc.

Examples of dependent variable and independent variables

A sales forecast depends on price, the advertising budget, and seasonal factors. Therefore, a sales forecast is a dependent variable and price, advertising budget, and seasonal factors are independent variables.

8.1.3 Composite forecast profile

The *composite forecast profile* is a combination of one or more *univariate forecast profiles* and/or *multiple linear regression profiles*. The forecast based on the composite forecast profile uses both *time series model* and *causal analysis* and thereby, combines multiple forecasts into a single final forecast.

8.2   Alerts design

Alerts help businesses manage exceptions and *alert monitor* informs about the exception situation that occurs in planning. There are three types of alerts:

▶ *Errors* —These alerts are of highest priority and the red color signifies errors.

▶ *Warning* —These alerts are of medium priority and the yellow color signifies a warning.

▶ *Information* —These alerts are of lowest priority and the blue color signifies information.

Demand plan monitoring through alert management

Alert management monitors demand planning for forecast accuracy and successful execution. Planning books and alerts monitors generate alerts and we need to take necessary actions to resolve the alerts, or minimize the adverse impacts.

To generate alerts in the alert monitor or planning book we need to create an alert profile. We create alert profiles in a particular application and save it as an application-specific alert profile. Then, we can assign multiple application specific alert profiles to an overall alert profile.

For demand planning, the following two application specific alert profiles are relevant:

▶ **APO: Forecast Planning** — also referred to as *Forecast Alert Profile*

▶ **APO: Supply & Demand Planning** — also referred to as *SDP Alert Profile* for macro dependent alerts

If the history data does not appropriately align with the forecast strategy chosen, then the system generates forecast alerts. The threshold limit maintained in the diagnosis group for the particular forecast errors forms the basis for alerts generation. Settings maintained in the alert profile category decide alerts.

Dodging alerts

If the upper limit for forecast errors is not maintained in the diagnosis group, then that particular forecast error value is disregarded and alerts are never produced.

There are two types of alerts in supply and demand planning: database alerts and dynamic alerts.

Database alerts

These alerts reflect the planning situation that happened during last planning run, or last macro execution. From a performance standpoint, database alerts are recommended when we deal with huge volumes of data and a large number of alerts. Preferably, background jobs should be run using the appropriate database macros.

Dynamic alerts

These alerts reflect the real time planning situation in the LiveCache and are executed through interactive planning.

Dynamic alerts

 We do not recommend dynamic alerts when we deal with huge volumes of data and a large number of alerts.

Alert monitor is able to distinguish between forecast alerts and macro-dependent alerts.

You will find the reference to this section as 'Alert Profile Creation (FP & SDP)' in the block 'Design in APO DP' in the APO DP process flow diagram depicted in Figure 4.2.

For our business scenario we make entries for one forecast alert profile *Demo Forecast Planning Alert Profile* (ZDM_AP_FP) and one SDP alert profile *Demo Demand Planning Alert Profile* (ZDM_AP_DP). We assign them to the overall alert profile *Demo Overall Alert Profile* (ZDM_AP).

The *Demo Forecast Planning Alert Profile* will help DM Consumer Appliance Inc. generate forecast-related alerts when we test the two forecast strategies described in Section 8.1.1. As for the *Demo Demand Planning Alert Profile*, DM Consumer Appliance Inc. will use the macro driven alert to ensure that the consensus forecast, in the form of the *total forecast*, do not vary significantly from the *corrected forecast*.

We create the *Demo Overall Alert Profile* (ZDM_AP), *Demo Forecast Planning Alert Profile* (ZDM_AP_FP), and *Demo Demand Planning Alert Profile* (ZDM_AP_DP) for DM Consumer Appliances, Inc. as explained below.

The transaction code or menu path for creating the alert monitor profile in the SCM system is as follows:

Transaction Code: /SAPAPO/AMON1

Menu Path: SAP MENU • ADVANCED PLANNING AND OPTIMIZATION • SUPPLY CHAIN MONITORING • ALERT MONITOR • ALERT MONITOR

We refer to Figure 8.6 to create *Demo Overall Alert Profile* (ZDM_AP). Once we are on the screen for the transaction code mentioned above, we click on the ⊞ Alert Profile (❶) and it takes us to the screen ALERT PROFILE MAINTENANCE. We click CREATE PROFILE ▯ (❷) and it takes us to the screen CREATE ALERT MONITOR PROFILE. We choose the OVERALL PROFILE (❸) and make entries for the profile ID ZDM_AP (❹) and its description. Next, click CRE-ATE (❺) and it takes us to the screen ALERT PROFILE MAINTENANCE: CHANGE ZDM_AP and we click SAVE ▤ (❻). We get the message ☑ Profile ZDM_AP saved . Next, we click CREATE PROFILE ▯ (❼) and it takes us to the screen CREATE ALERT MONITOR PROFILE as shown in Figure 8.7.

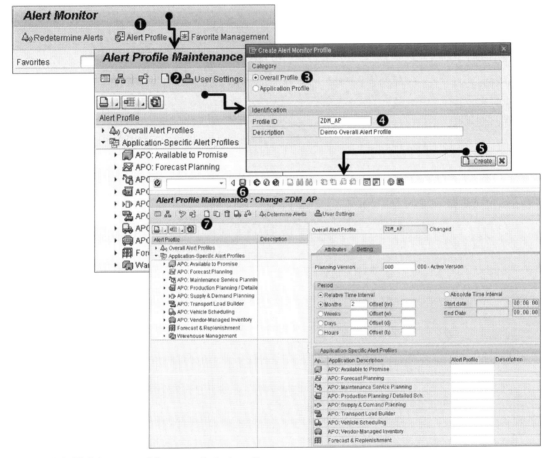

Figure 8.6: Maintenance of the overall alert profile

8.2.1 Forecast planning alert profile

Once we get to the screen CREATE ALERT MONITOR PROFILE as shown in Figure 8.7, we create the forecast planning alert profile. We choose the option APPLICATION PROFILE (❶). Make entries for the profile ID ZDM_AP_FP (❷), description, and select the AMO APPLICA-TION. Next, click CREATE (❸). It takes us to the screen ALERT PROFILE MAINTENANCE: CHANGE ZDM_AP_FP. Make an entry for the planning book ZDM_DPPB-1 (❹). Flag the RMSE UPPER LIMIT EXCEEDED and ERROR TOTAL UPPER LIMIT EXCEEDED options for maintaining forecast alerts threshold values as shown in (❺) and (❻). Click on ⬚ 0,00 ⬚ and make an entry for the threshold values one by one as shown in ❼ and adopt the same by clicking ADOPT (❽). Likewise, make entries for the other threshold values so that it appears like as shown in ❾. Next, click SAVE 💾 (❿).

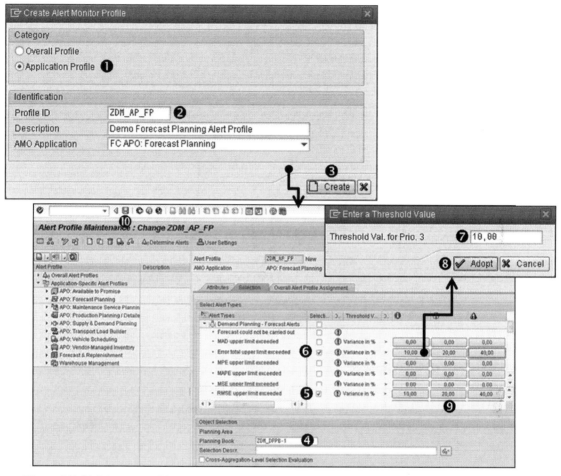

Figure 8.7: Maintenance of forecast planning alert profile

After the FORECAST PLANNING ALERT PROFILE is saved we get the message
✅ Profile ZDM_AP_FP saved .

Next, we go back to the screen ALERT PROFILE MAINTENANCE: CHANGE ZDM_AP as shown in Figure 8.8 in order to assign alert profile ZDM_AP_FP to the overall profile ZDM_AP. Select alert profile ZDM_AP_FP (❶), make the other entries as shown in the diagram and click SAVE 💾 (❷).

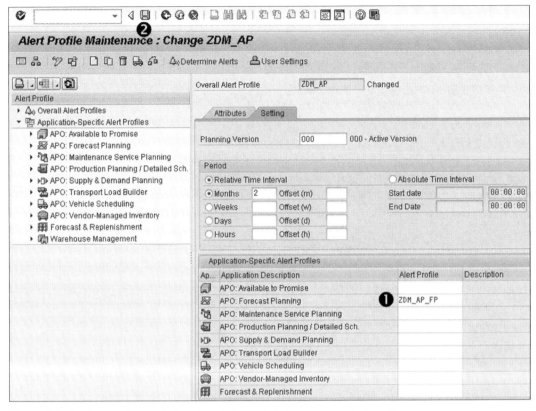

Figure 8.8: Assign the forecast planning alert profile to the overall alert profile

Once saved, we get the message ☑ Profile ZDM_AP saved ;

We assign the overall profile to the user as explained below.

The transaction code or menu path for creating the alert monitor in the SCM system is as follows:

Transaction Code: /SAPAPO/AMON1

Menu Path: SAP MENU • ADVANCED PLANNING AND OPTIMIZATION • SUPPLY CHAIN MONITORING • ALERT MONITOR • ALERT MONITOR

Refer to Figure 8.9. We click on ⊞ Favorite Management (❶) and it takes us to the screen ALERT MONITOR ADMINISTRATION where we see the overall profile ZDM_AP (❷) listed in the worklist of overall profiles. We place the cursor on the overall profile ZDM_AP and drag and drop to the user DEMOUSER as shown in ❸ Next, save it and click ENTER.

The overall profile ZDM_AP appears in the dropdown of FAVORITES as shown in (❹).

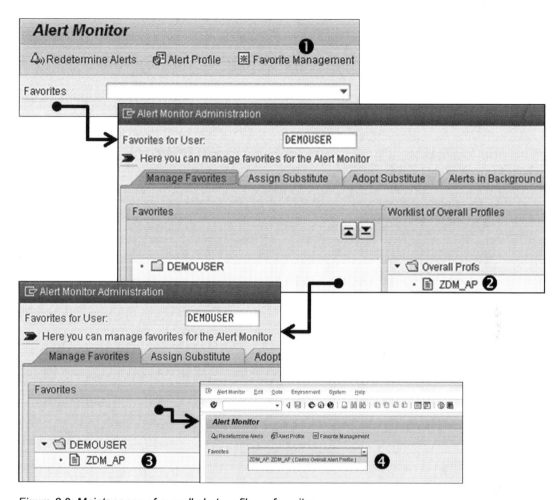

Figure 8.9: Maintenance of overall alert profile as favorites

With this step, we have now completed creating the overall Alert Profile *Demo Overall Alert Profile* (ZDM_AP) and Forecast Alert Profile *Demo Forecast Planning Alert Profile* (ZDM_AP_FP). We also assigned the forecast alert profile to the overall alert profile and also assigned the overall alert profile to the user. In the following section, we will explain how to create and assign the *Demo Demand Planning Alert Profile* (ZDM_AP_DP) for DM Consumer Appliances, Inc.

8.2.2   Demand planning alert profile

Apart from the forecast alert profile, we also make an entry for a macro-driven SDP Alert Profile. We will explain the process and the associated design required to create and assign the SDP Alert Profile *Demo Demand Planning Alert Profile* (ZDM_AP_DP) for DM Consumer Appliances, Inc. as follows:

The initial design is as follows.

We first create the database alert type that would specifically be used to generate an alert when there is a threshold deviation between the *total forecast* and *corrected forecast* for DM Consumer Appliances, Inc.

The IMG path for this configuration in the SCM system is as follows:

SAP – IMPLEMENTATION GUIDE • SCM BASIS • ALERT MONITOR • MAINTAIN DATABASE ALERT TYPES FOR DEMAND PLANNING AND SNP

We refer to screen CHANGE VIEW DATABASE ALERT TYPES FOR DEMAND PLANNING AND SNP as shown in Figure 8.10. We click on New Entries (❶) and it brings up the screen to add new entries for the alert type. We make an entry for alert type 8001 (❷) and make entries as shown in Figure 8.10. Next, we click SAVE 🖫 (❸).

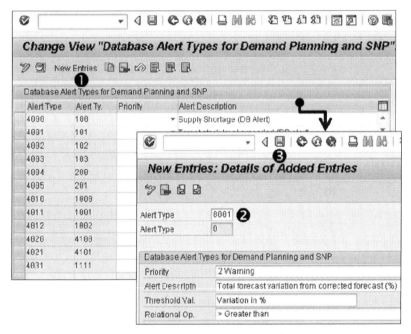

Figure 8.10: Create database alert types for DP and SNP

We make entries for customer-specific settings for outlier correction for DM Consumer Appliances, Inc. as explained below in order to maintain outlier correction for ex-post forecast.

The IMG path for this configuration in SCM system is:

SAP – IMPLEMENTATION GUIDE • ADVANCED PLANNING AND OPTIMIZATION • SUPPLY CHAIN PLANNING • DEMAND PLANNING (DP) • BASIC SETTINGS • MAINTAIN CUSTOMER-SPECIFIC SETTINGS FOR OUTLIER CORRECTION

Refer to the screen CUSTOMIZING FOR OUTLIER CORRECTION in Figure 8.11. We make entries for the NUMBER OF PERIODS IN THE INITIAL PHASE, the NUMBER OF PERIODS WITHOUT OUTLIER, and flag ONLY USE MAD UP TO CURRENT PERIOD for the user as shown in Figure 8.11. Next, we click SAVE 💾.

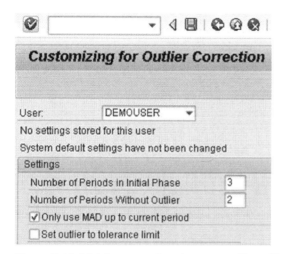

Figure 8.11: Maintenance of customer-specific settings for outlier correction

We will create the *Demo Demand Planning Alert Profile* (ZDM_AP_DP) for DM Consumer Appliances, Inc. as explained below.

The transaction code or menu path for creating the alert profile in SCM system is as follows:

Transaction Code: /SAPAPO/AMON1

Menu Path: SAP MENU • ADVANCED PLANNING AND OPTIMIZATION • SUPPLY CHAIN MONITORING • ALERT MONITOR • ALERT MONITOR

We refer to Figure 8.12 to create *Demo Demand Planning Alert Profile* (ZDM_AP_DP). Once we are on the screen for the transaction code mentioned above, we click on Alert Profile which takes us to the screen ALERT PROFILE MAINTENANCE and click on CREATE PROFILE. That takes us to the screen CREATE ALERT MONITOR PROFILE. We choose the option APPLICATION PROFILE (❶) and make an entry for the profile ID ZDM_AP_DP (❷) and a description. Be sure to select AMO APPLICATION as shown in ❸. Next, click Create (❹) and it takes us to the screen ALERT PROFILE MAINTENANCE: CHANGE ZDM_AP_DP. Make entries for PLANNING BOOK (❺) and DATA VIEW (❻). Flag the appropriate alert type TOTAL FORECAST VARIATION FROM CORRECTED FORECAST (❼) and make entries for the threshold values as shown in (❽). Next, we click SAVE 💾 (❾).

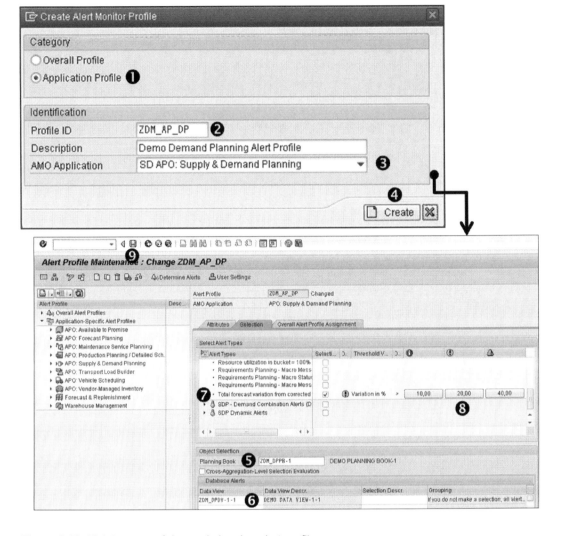

Figure 8.12: Maintenance of demand planning alert profile

When we save, we get the message ☑ Profile ZDM_AP_DP saved .

Next, we go back to the screen ALERT PROFILE MAINTENANCE: CHANGE ZDM_AP as shown in Figure 8.13 in order to assign the alert profile ZDM_AP_DP to the overall profile ZDM_AP. We select the alert profile ZDM_AP_DP (❶), make other entries as shown in the diagram and click SAVE 🖫 (❷).

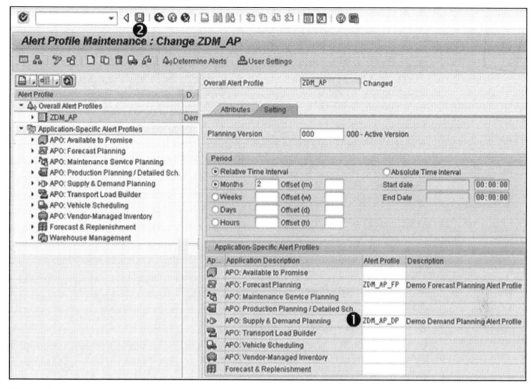

Figure 8.13: Assign the demand planning alert profile to overall profile

Once we save, we get the message ☑ Profile ZDM_AP saved .

With this step, we are done creating and assigning the two application specific alert profiles, i.e., *Demo Forecast Planning Alert Profile* (ZDM_AP_FP) and *Demo Demand Planning Alert Profile* (ZDM_AP_DP) for DM Consumer Appliances, Inc. We also assigned the two application specific alert profiles to the overall alert profile *Demo Overall Alert Profile* (ZDM_AP). Also, we assigned the overall alert profile *Demo Overall Alert Profile* (ZDM_AP) to the DEMOUSER. These alerts will get suitably triggered when we carry out demand planning execution.

In the next section, we explain the two macros that we will create and use for our business scenario.

8.3   Macros design

In this section, we explain macros and how to design the two macros that we use for DM Consumer Appliances, Inc.

Macros are formulas. Macros are similar to the formulas used in a spreadsheet, but macros in demand planning are very flexible and provide comprehensive calculation functionality. Macros typically define key figures calculation using other key figures, operators, and a wide range of functions. It is optional to define macros for demand planning.

Main features of macros:

▶ Consist of multiple *steps*.

▶ *Control instructions* and *conditions* regulate the macro steps processing.

▶ Offers several *functions* and *operators*.

▶ Can trigger an alert on macro execution.

▶ Results can be written in rows, columns, cells, or variables and can be used in next iterations, steps, and macros.

▶ Helps create context specific/user specific planning views.

▶ Helps determine the results of one period based on values from previous period using offsets.

▶ Can restrict execution of macros by periods.

▶ Defines itself either at planning book level, or at data view level.

▶ Can do complex calculations using ABAP code.

▶ User can execute macros manually, or automatically.

▶ Can execute macros in the foreground through interactive planning, and/or in the background.

▶ Can create a macro by copying one macro book to another macro book, where macro books are repository of macros.

▶ Macros can have notes to store important information about the macros.

▶ Can add itself to a *transport request* as *macro books* can transport itself to the target system on release of the request.

▶ Macros can be written through a drag and drop mechanism by making use of macro elements, macro tools, menu functions, mathematical operators, and functions, statistical functions, logical functions, functions for InfoObjects and planning folders, data functions, general and planning table functions, etc.

Macro Workbench and MacroBuilder

We define macros in a *MacroBuilder* that can be launched either from the *macro workbench*, or from the planning book. We described the planning book in Section 7.8.1. We will highlight the different screen areas in the WORKBENCH and MACROBUILDER using rounded rectangles in Figure 8.14.

MACRO WORKBENCH is a repository of MACRO BOOKS (❶) in which we can do the following functions to the macro books: start MacroBuilder, activate, display macros corresponding to the macro book, delete, transport to other systems, export, code display, semantic checks, filter, sort, use 'where used list,' etc. using several available tools and menu functions. Once we display the macros, we can copy, move macros, delete, activate, edit notes, and do a semantic check.

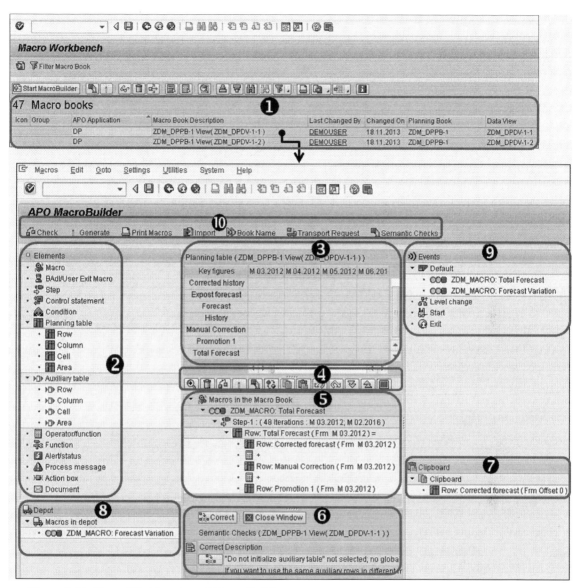

Figure 8.14: Macro Workbench and Macro Builder

We select the MACRO BOOK and click on ⌨ Start MacroBuilder to go to the APO MACROBUILDER screen as shown in Figure 8.14. MACROBUILDER has the following screen areas as shown by rounded rectangles.

Macro elements (❷)

MACRO ELEMENTS as listed in (❷) are used to define or edit the macro in MACRO PROCESSING AREA (❺). We drag and drop the necessary MACRO ELEMENTS to the MACRO PROCESSING AREA to define the macro. The same process can also be done by choosing the right click option. We will demonstrate how to use macro elements when we look at our business scenario in Section 8.3.1.

Planning table (❸)

The PLANNING TABLE as in KEY FIGURES and TIME HORIZON periods appear in the form of a grid for the planning book and data view that corresponds to the macro.

Macro tools (❹)

MACRO TOOLS as listed in (❹) are used to define or edit the macro in the MACRO PROCESSING AREA (❺) by using its functionality as necessary. We will demonstrate how to use MACRO TOOLS when we look at our business scenario in Section 8.3.1.

Macro processing area (❺)

The MACRO PROCESSING AREA is used to define, edit, and generate macros. We will demonstrate the use of the MACRO PROCESSING AREA when we look at our business scenario in Section 8.3.1.

Semantic checks output area (❻)

SEMANTIC CHECKS output get displayed here based on various checks for runtime errors, etc. SEMANTIC CHECK results are typically shown through notes/tips so that the planner can decide whether they want to correct those anomalies or not.

Clipboard (❼)

The CLIPBOARD is a temporary memory area for cut and paste functionality for macros and its elements.

Depot (❽)

DEPOT denotes the parking area for the macros that are not in use for editing. This helps improve performance. We will demonstrate the use of the depot when we look at our business scenario in Section 8.3.1.

Standard macros area (❾)

Macros subjected to automatic execution based on the four types of events below are called standard macros. Standard macros appear in the STANDARD MACROS AREA.

▶ **Default macro**
Demand plan regeneration triggers the DEFAULT macro by pressing Enter or the Tab key, or by opening or saving the demand plan

▶ **Level change macro**
Change in planning level through drill up or down in interactive planning triggers the LEVEL CHANGE macro.

▶ **Start macro**
Planning data load triggers the START macro.

▶ **Exit macro**
Planning data saving triggers the EXIT macro.

Automatic macro execution

 To enable and automate the execution of any macros, we need to drag and drop the particular macro from the macro tree to the desired standard macro category. If we want to confine any particular macro to only automatic run, then we can exclusively ensure that by setting the macro attribute No DIRECT EXECUTION.

We will demonstrate the use of allocating macros to particular events when we look at our business scenario in Section 8.3.1.

Application tool bar (⑩)

Several TOOLS executable at the macro level are placed as shown in ⑩ to carry out functionality like: CONSISTENCY CHECKS, ACTIVATION, PRINTING MACROS, IMPORTING MACROS from other books, TRANSPORT REQUEST, SEMANTIC CHECKS, and the option to change macro BOOK NAMES.

Hierarchical structure of macro definition

We define macros through four levels resembling a hierarchy in the MACRO PROCESSING AREA of MACROBUILDER as shown in Figure 8.15. They are as follows:

▶ **Level I or macro definition level**
LEVEL I is the highest level consisting of different macro names.

▶ **Level II or step level**
LEVEL II contains either STEPS, or CONTROL STRUCTURE. This level contains one or multiple calculations and works in iteration to a predefined period. A minimum of one step is essential to define a macro.

▶ **Level III or result level**
LEVEL III contains macro elements that store interim or final RESULTS of a calculation or operation. This element corresponds to a key figure or auxiliary table element. We also specify control structures, action boxes, documents, process message, and alerts.

▶ **Level IV or argument level**
LEVEL IV contains CALCULATION OPERATIONS and OPERANDS. Conditions are also specified at Level IV if control structures appear in Level III.

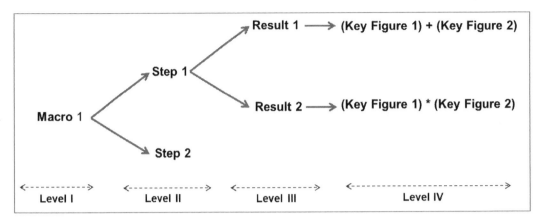

Figure 8.15: Macro definition hierarchical structure

We design the macros for DM Consumer Appliances, Inc. as follows.

You will find the reference to this section as 'Macros (Generation & Assignment)' in the block 'Design in APO DP' in the APO DP process flow depicted in Figure 4.2.

For our business scenario we need to make entries for two macros: *ZDM_MACRO: Total Forecast* and *ZDM_MACRO: Forecast Variation*.

ZDM_MACRO: Total Forecast calculates the consensus forecast for DM Consumer Appliances, Inc. by adding the *corrected forecast*, *manual correction*, and *promotion*. Manual correction is entered as the additional positive or negative sales value that is required to adjust the corrected value. Manual correction is arrived at by taking inputs from different departments. The *ZDM_MACRO: Total Forecast* macro proposes the value in the *total forecast* for further processing.

ZDM_MACRO: Forecast Variation generates the alerts for DM Consumer Appliances, Inc. based on the forecast variation between the *total forecast* and *corrected forecast* to focus attention in the event of substantial variation. We will use these macros for demand planning execution.

We create the two macros *ZDM_MACRO: Total Forecast* and *ZDM_MACRO: Forecast Variation* for DM Consumer Appliances, Inc. as explained below.

The transaction code or menu path for the macro workbench in SCM is as follows:

Transaction Code: / SAPAPO/ADVM

Menu Path: SAP MENU • ADVANCED PLANNING AND OPTIMIZATION • DEMAND PLANNING • ENVIRONMENT • CURRENT SETTINGS • MACRO WORKBENCH

8.3.1 Design of macro for total forecast calculation

For DM Consumer Appliances, Inc. we intend to do consensus forecasting wherein the final forecast will be released for supply planning and production planning. The consensus forecast is the eventual total forecast that takes into account the following:

Total Forecast = Corrected Forecast + Manual Correction + Promotion

As explained earlier, manual correction can be positive or negative values and is based on the inputs received from multiple stakeholders, e.g., marketing, strategy, finance, etc. We do the necessary adjustments and capture them in the key figure *Manual Correction*. Total forecast calculation is addressed with the macro *ZDM_MACRO: Total Forecast*. Let's look at the process of creating the macro *ZDM_MACRO: Total Forecast*.

Figure 8.16 depicts Part 1 of the design of the macro for total forecast calculation. We create the macro for total forecast calculation *ZDM_MACRO: Total Forecast* as follows. Once we are on the screen for the transaction code mentioned above, we go to the MACRO WORKBENCH listing the MACROBOOKS. Click on the MACRO BOOK ZDM_DPPB-1 VIEW (ZDM_DPDV-1-1) as shown in ❶ and then click on Start MacroBuilder (❷). It takes us to the APO MACROBUILDER screen as shown in Figure 8.16.

We place cursor on the MACROS IN THE MACRO BOOK as shown in (❸). Right click to bring up the option ADD MACRO (❹).

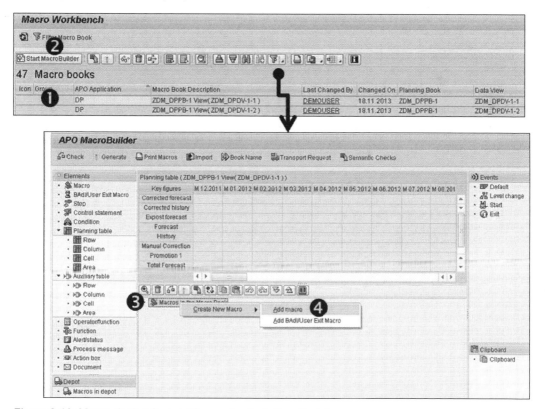

Figure 8.16: Macro design for total forecast calculation: Part 1

Click on ADD MACRO and it takes us to Part 2 of design of macro for total forecast calculation as shown in Figure 8.17.

We make an entry for the descriptive text for ZDM_MACRO: TOTAL FORECAST (❶) to give macro a new name. We make the other entries as shown in Figure 8.17.

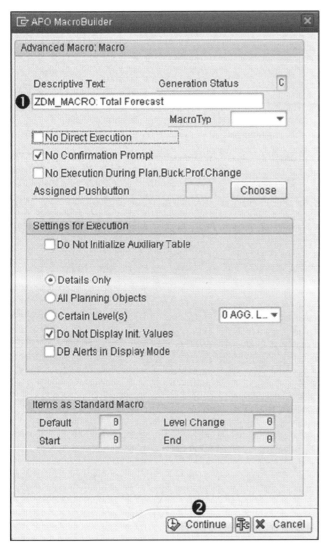

Figure 8.17: Macro design for total forecast calculation: Part 2

Next, we click ⟨🔄 Continue⟩ (❷). It takes us to Part 3 of design of macro for total forecast calculation as shown in Figure 8.18.

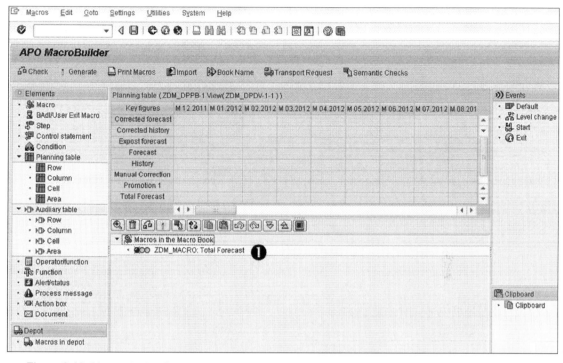

Figure 8.18: Macro design for total forecast calculation: Part 3

We can now see the new macro ZDM_MACRO: TOTAL FORECAST (❶) in the MACRO PROCESSING AREA in Level I. We place the cursor on the MACRO and right click. It takes us to the Part 4 of design of macro for total forecast calculation as shown in Figure 8.19.

Click ADD MACRO ELEMENT • STEP (❶). Click STEP and it takes us to the screen APO MACROBUILDER. Make an entry for the descriptive text for step name STEP 1 (❷). Make entries as shown in the figure and click ⟨🔄 Continue⟩ (❸). The STEP-1 appears in Level II for the macro ZDM_MACRO: TOTAL FORECAST.

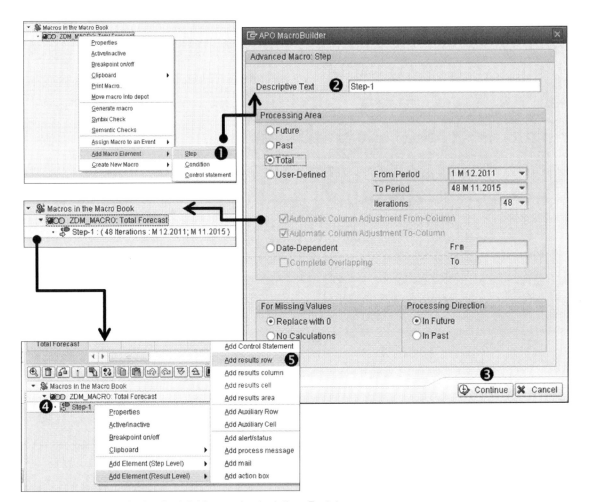

Figure 8.19: Macro design for total forecast calculation: Part 4

Place the cursor on STEP 1 (**4**). Select STEP-1 and right click on the STEP-1 and go to ADD ELEMENT (RESULT LEVEL) • ADD RESULTS ROW (**5**) and click on it. It takes us to the Part 5 of design of macro for total forecast calculation as shown in Figure 8.20.

Select the row TOTAL FORECAST (**1**). Make other entries as shown in the figure and click ☑ Adopt (**2**). It adds the row TOTAL FORECAST (**3**) in Level III in the MACRO PROCESSING AREA.

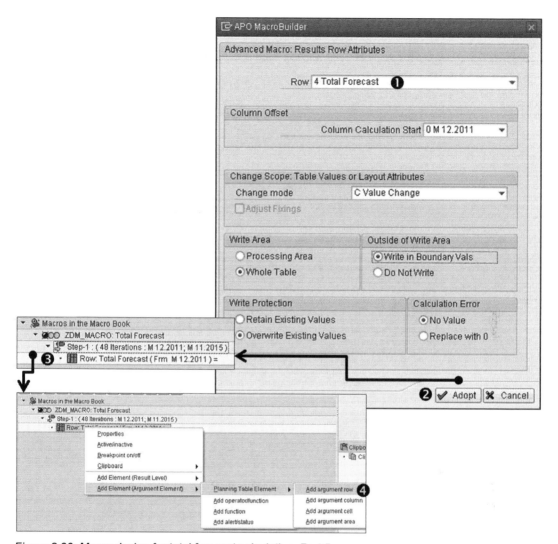

Figure 8.20: Macro design for total forecast calculation: Part 5

Select the row TOTAL FORECAST and right click to bring up options as shown in Figure 8.20. Click on ADD ARGUMENT ROW (❹) and it takes us to Part 6 of design of macro for total forecast calculation as shown in Figure 8.21.

We select the row CORRECTED FORECAST (❶) from the drop down, make the other entries as shown in the figure, and click ⊕ Continue (❷). It takes us to the MACRO PROCESSING screen with the row CORRECTED FORECAST associated with the TOTAL FORECAST row. Place the cursor on ROW: TOTAL FORECAST (❸) and right click to bring up the options as shown in Figure 8.21. Click ADD ARGUMENT ROW (❹). It takes us to the screen ADVANCED MACRO: ARGUMENT ROW ATTRIBUTES. Select the row MANUAL CORRECTION (❺), make other entries as shown in the figure and click ⊕ Continue (❻).

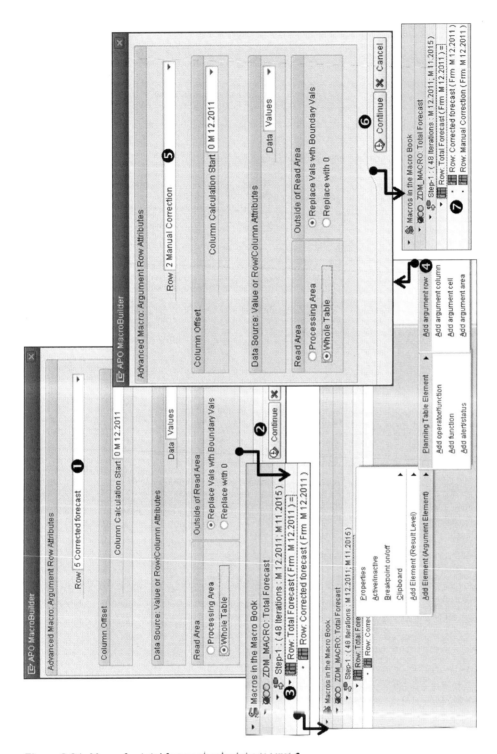

Figure 8.21: Macro for total forecast calculation: Part 6

It takes us to the MACRO PROCESSING screen with the row CORRECTED FORECAST and the row MANUAL CORRECTION associated with the TOTAL FORECAST (❼) row.

We continue on with Part 7 of design of macro for total forecast calculation as shown in Figure 8.22. We place the cursor on the row TOTAL FORECAST and right click to bring up options as shown in Figure 8.22. Click ADD ARGUMENT ROW (❶). It takes us to the screen ADVANCED MACRO: ARGUMENT ROW ATTRIBUTES. Select row PROMOTION 1 (❷) and make other entries as shown in the figure and click ⊕ Continue (❸). It takes us to the MACRO PROCESSING screen with the row CORRECTED FORECAST, row MANUAL CORRECTION, and the row PROMOTION 1 associated with the TOTAL FORECAST (❹) row.

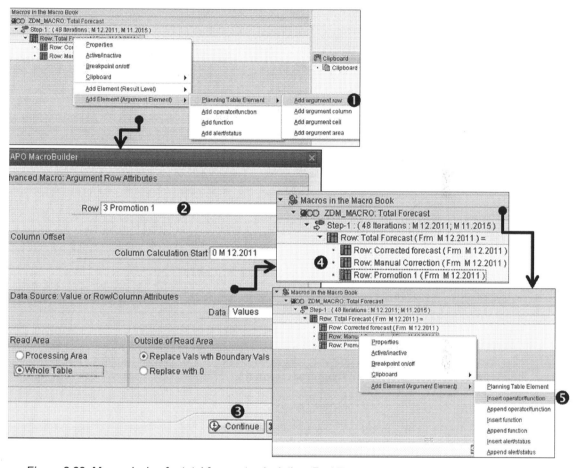

Figure 8.22: Macro design for total forecast calculation: Part 7

Place the cursor on the MANUAL CORRECTION row and right click to bring up options as shown in Figure 8.22. Click INSERT OPERATOR/FUNCTION (❺). It takes us to Part 8 of design of macro for total forecast calculation as shown in Figure 8.23.

We are now on the screen ADVANCED MACRO: OPERATOR/FUNCTION. Make an entry for OPERATOR/FUNCTION AS + (❶), i.e., select + from the COPY FR pull down (it will come as default only, in this case) and click ⊕ Continue (❷). It takes us to the MACRO PROCESSING SCREEN with OPERATOR/FUNCTION + inserted between the row CORRECTED FORECAST and row MANUAL CORRECTION (❸).

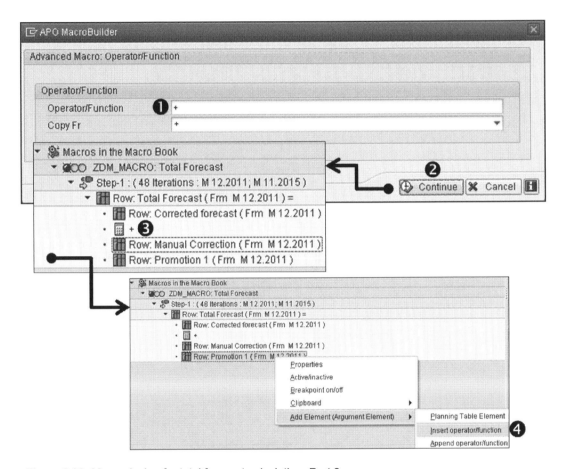

Figure 8.23: Macro design for total forecast calculation: Part 8

Next, place the cursor on the row PROMOTION 1 and right click to bring up options as shown in Figure 8.23. Click INSERT OPERATOR/FUNCTION (❹). It takes us to Part 9 of design of macro for total forecast calculation as shown in Figure 8.24.

It takes us to the screen ADVANCED MACRO: OPERATOR/FUNCTION. Make an entry for OPERATOR/FUNCTION AS + (❶), i.e., select + from the COPY FR pull down (it will come as default only, in this case) and click ⊕ Continue (❷). It takes us to the MACRO PROCESSING screen with OPERATOR/FUNCTION + inserted between the row MANUAL CORRECTION and PROMOTION 1 (❸). Next, we place the cursor on the macro ZDM_MACRO: TOTAL FORECAST (❹) which is not in GENERATED status, i.e., red ⚙OO. We click on GENERATE ⬜ (❺) to generate the macro.

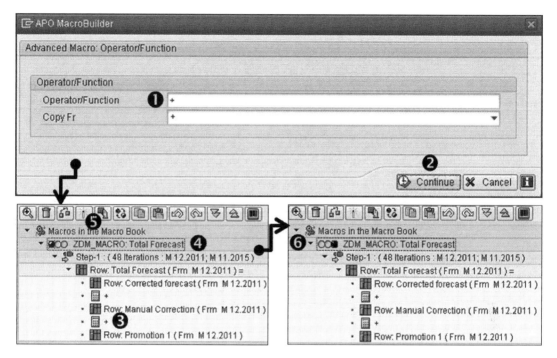

Figure 8.24: Macro design for total forecast calculation: Part 9

Next, the macro ZDM_MACRO: TOTAL FORECAST gets generated and the status changes to green ⊙⊙⊞ (❻). With this step, we have completed creating and generating the macro ZDM_MACRO: TOTAL FORECAST.

We refer Figure 8.25. In order to launch the macro as the default, place the cursor on the macro ZDM_MACRO: TOTAL FORECAST (❶) and drag the macro from the MACRO PROCESSING AREA to the EVENTS section, i.e., the standard macro area and place it onto DEFAULT (❷) as shown in Figure 8.25.

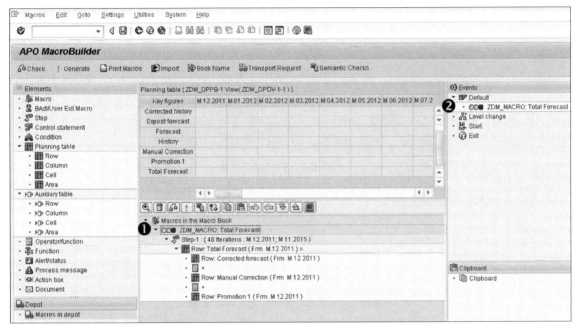

Figure 8.25: Assigning the macro for total forecast calculation to events

Next, we place the cursor on the macro ZDM_MACRO: TOTAL FORECAST (❶) as shown in Figure 8.25. We drag the macro and drop it in the DEPOT area (❶) as shown in Figure 8.26 to free up the MACRO PROCESSING AREA.

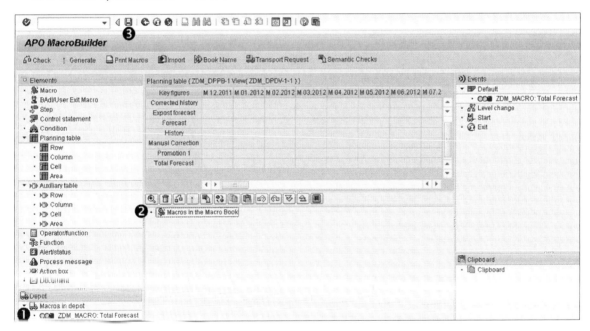

Figure 8.26: Assign the macro for total forecast calculation to depot

After the macro is placed in the depot, the MACRO PROCESSING AREA is empty (❷). We save this arrangement by clicking on SAVE 🖫 (❸). We get the message: ☑ Macros successfully saved .

8.3.2   Design of macro for alerts generation on forecast variation

For DM Consumer Appliances, Inc. we intend to have the system generate alerts if the total forecast exceeds the corrected forecast by a predetermined limit. We will address this requirement with the macro *ZDM_MACRO: Forecast Variation*. We will introduce an alert as we define this macro.

As we already explained the step by step procedure for creating and generating a macro in Section 8.3.1, we will not reproduce a similar process for this macro. Nevertheless, we will touch upon all the significant details of this macro.

Figure 8.27 forms Part 1 of the macro design for alerts generation on forecast variation. We will now create the macro *ZDM_MACRO: Forecast Variation* for alerts generation on forecast variation as explained below.

Transaction Code: / SAPAPO/ADVM

Menu Path: SAP MENU • ADVANCED PLANNING AND OPTIMIZATION • DEMAND PLANNING • ENVIRONMENT • CURRENT SETTINGS • MACRO WORKBENCH

Once we are on the screen for the transaction code mentioned above, we go to the macro workbench listing MacroBooks as shown in Figure 8.27. We click on the macro book ZDM_DPPB-1 VIEW (ZDM_DPDV-1-1) as shown in ❶ and then click on 🔳 Start MacroBuilder (❷). It takes us to the APO MACROBUILDER screen.

We place the cursor on the MACROS IN THE MACRO BOOK as shown in (❸). Right click to bring up the option ADD MACRO (❹).

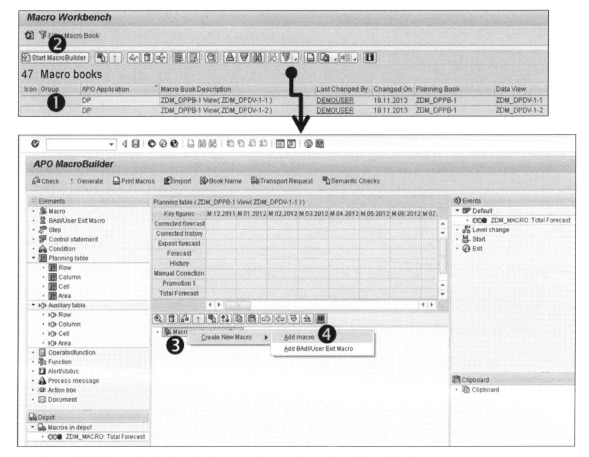

Figure 8.27: Macro design for alerts generation on forecast variation: Part 1

We click on ADD MACRO and it takes us to Part 2 of macro design for alerts generation on forecast variation as shown in Figure 8.28.

Make a descriptive text entry for ZDM_MACRO: FORECAST VARIATION (❶) to give macro a new name. Make the other entries as shown in Figure 8.28.

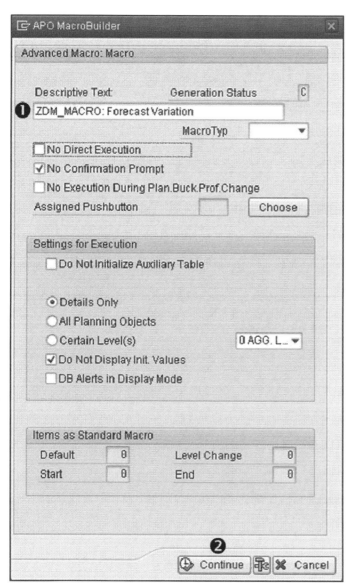

Figure 8.28: Macro design for alerts generation on forecast variation: Part 2

Next, we click ⊕ Continue (❷). It takes us to Part 3 of macro design for alerts generation on forecast variation as shown in Figure 8.29.

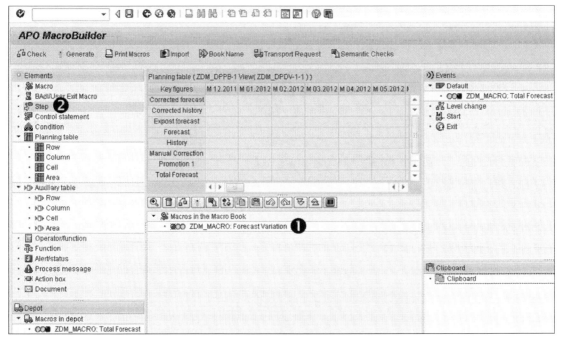

Figure 8.29: Macro design for alerts generation on forecast variation: Part 3

The macro ZDM_MACRO: FORECAST VARIATION appears in the MACRO PROCESSING AREA in Level I (❶). We use STEP (❷) from the elements area to take the process of macro definition forward.

Following a similar process of using the step that we described in Section 8.3.1, we define the step VARIANCE CALCULATION (❶) as shown in Figure 8.30.

Similarly, use the STEP (❷) and other relevant elements from the MACRO ELEMENTS AREA (❸) as shown in Figure 8.30 and define the macro following the process similar to Section 8.3.1.

Once all of the MACRO ELEMENTS, MACRO TOOLS, and INPUTS are used, in compliance with the business requirement, we ensure that we have the macro defined and depicted as in Figure 8.31 for the macro ZDM_MACRO: FORECAST VARIATION.

Referring to Figure 8.31, let's do a consistency check for the macro. Place the cursor on the macro ZDM_MACRO: FORECAST VARIATION (❶) and then click CHECK 📋 (❷).

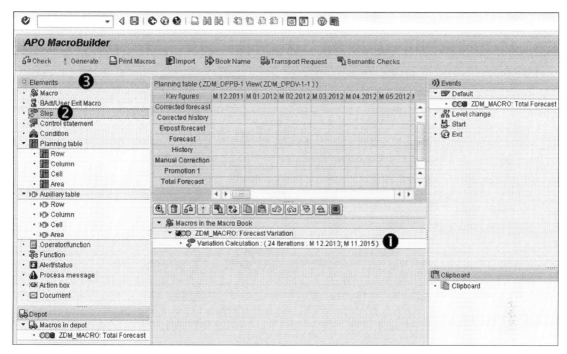

Figure 8.30: Macro design for alerts generation on forecast variation: Part 4

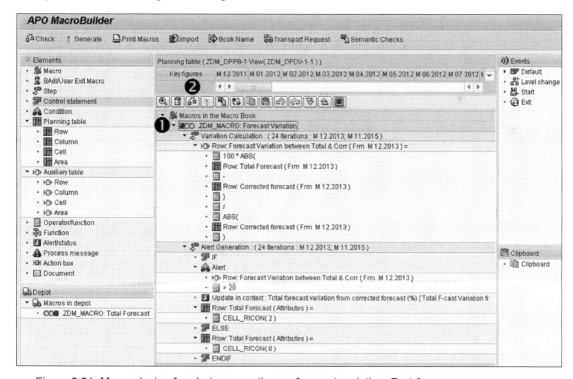

Figure 8.31: Macro design for alerts generation on forecast variation: Part 6

Once the consistency check is complete, we get the message ☑ Check made without errors and the status of the macro changes to yellow as shown in Figure 8.32.

Figure 8.32: Macro design for alerts generation on Forecast Variation: Part 7

Refer to Figure 8.32 for instructions on macro design for alerts generation on forecast variation. We select the macro ZDM_MACRO: FORECAST VARIATION (❶) and click GENERATE [ ] (❷) to generate the macro. Once the macro ZDM_MACRO: FORECAST VARIATION is generated the status turns green ❀❀❀ (❸). With this step, we have created and generated the macro ZDM_MACRO: FORECAST VARIATION.

To launch the macro as default, place the cursor on the macro ZDM_MACRO: FORECAST VARIATION as shown in Figure 8.32 and drag the macro from the MACRO PROCESSING AREA to the EVENTS section (i.e., standard macro area) and place it on DEFAULT (❶) as shown in Figure 8.33. Next, we place the cursor on the macro ZDM_MACRO: FORECAST VARIATION and we drag the macro and drop in in the DEPOT area (❷). After the macro is placed in the DEPOT, the MACRO PROCESSING AREA is empty (❸). We save this arrangement by clicking to SAVE [ ] (❹). We get the message: ☑ Macros successfully saved .

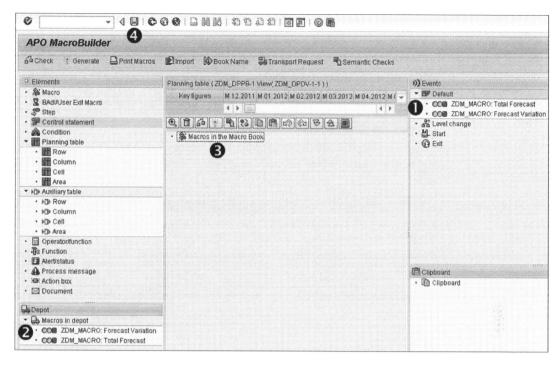

Figure 8.33: Assigning the macro for alerts generation on forecast variation to events and to the depot

All the key figures being used in the macro will have their corresponding icon changed in the DATA VIEW as shown in Figure 8.34.

Click the DATA VIEW tab (❶) and then bring up the screen for the data view ZDM_DPDV-1-1 (❷).

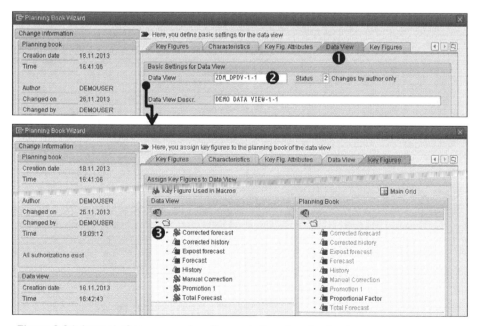

Figure 8.34: Impact of macros on key figures in the planning book

We see that the icons for the key figures like CORRECTED FORECAST, MANUAL CORRECTION, PROMOTION 1, and TOTAL FORECAST changed (❸) implying that those key figures were used in building macros.

With this step, we have completed creating and generating the second macro *ZDM_MACRO: Forecast Variation*. We will use this macro during demand planning execution.

8.4 Summary

In this chapter, we introduced advanced design concepts in APO DP including forecast design concepts, forecast algorithm, forecast model parameters, and strategies, alert design, macro design and alert-based macro design. We also explained advanced DP design concepts with statistical and rational approaches. We also explained how the advanced design aspects are linked to the bigger picture of demand planning by connecting each of the pieces to the overall process flow diagrams and how they can be exemplified through our business scenario.

9 Appendices

9.1   Business scenario data: DM Consumer Appliances, Inc.

We present here all of the data pertaining to connectivity, design, settings, master data, and transactions data that we used for our business scenario at DM Consumer Appliances, Inc. in this book.

Data Type	Data
ERP System ID	ED1
ERP Logical System	ED1CLNT100
APO System ID	SD1
APO Logical System	SD1CLNT100
Integration Model for Locations	ZDM_LOC
Integration Model for Materials	ZDM_MAT
Integration Model for Transactions	ZDM_TR

Table 9.1: System and core interface details

Data Type	Data
Company Name	DM Consumer Appliances, Inc.
Plant	ZDM1 ZDD1 ZDR1 ZDR2
Plant Description	Atlanta Manufacturing Plant (ZDM1) Frankfort Distribution Center (ZDD1) Columbus Retail Store (ZDR1) Philadelphia Retail Store (ZDR2)
Cities	Atlanta, GA (Georgia) for Plant ZDM1 Frankfort, KY (Kentucky) for Plant ZDD1 Columbus, OH (Ohio) for Plant ZDR1 Philadelphia, PA (Pennsylvania) for Plant ZDR2
Storage Location	ZDS1

Data Type	Data
Storage Location Description	Atlanta Stg Loc
Material	ZDM_FG1 ZDM_FG2 ZDM_FG3 ZDM_FG4
Material Description	32" DM LCD 720p HDTV (for material ZDM_FG1) 32" DM LCD 1080p HDTV (for material ZDM_FG2) 39" DM LCD 1080p HDTV (for material ZDM_FG3) 40" DM LED 1080p HDTV (for material ZDM_FG4)
Sales Organization	5001
Sales Organization Description	DM Sales Org USA
Distribution Channel	10 20
Distribution Channel Description	Direct Sales (for Distribution Channel 10) Indirect Sales (for Distribution Channel 20)
MRP Controller	001
MRP Strategy Group	10

Table 9.2: Business scenario data points in ERP

Data Type	Data
Location	Same as 'Plant' as shown in Table 9.2
Product	Same as 'Material' as shown in Table 9.2
Product Group	ZDM_PG1 (for materials ZDM_FG1, ZDM_FG2 and ZDM_FG3) ZDM_PG2 (for materials ZDM_FG4)
Product Group Description	LCD TVs (for Product Group ZDM_PG1) LED TVs (for Product Group ZDM_PG2)
Demo Char Region	USA
MPOS	ZDM_MPOS
MPOS Description	Demo Planning Object Structure
Planning Area	ZDM_DPPA
Time Bucket Profile (History)	ZDM_TBP_H

Data Type	Data
Time Bucket Profile (History) Description	Demo Time Bucket Profile-H
Time Bucket Profile (Future)	ZDM_TBP_F
Time Bucket Profile (Future) Description	Demo Time Bucket Profile-F
Storage Bucket Profile	ZDM_SBP
Planning Book	ZDM_DPPB-1
Planning Book Description	Demo Planning Book-1
Data View	ZDM_DPDV-1-1
Data View Description	Demo Data View-1-1
Data View	ZDM_DPDV-1-2
Data View Description	Demo Data View-1-2
Selection-Stat. Forecasting	ZDM_DPSEL_SFC
Selection-Release to SNP	ZDM_DPSEL_REL_SNP
Selection-Transfer to ECC	ZDM_DPSEL_TFR_ECC
Selection-Promotion	ZDM_DPSEL_PROMO
Selection-New Lifecycle	ZDM_DPSEL_NLC
Selection-Products	ZDM_DPSEL_PG1_PDTS
Master Profile/ Forecast Profile	ZDM_MASTER_FCST_PF
Master Profile Description	Demo Forecast Profile
Univariate Profile	ZDM_UNI_FCST_PF
Univariate Profile Description	Demo Univar Fcst Profile
Diagnosis Group name	ZDM_DG
Overall Alert Profile	ZDM_AP
Overall Alert Profile Description	Demo Overall Alert Profile
Application-Specific Alert Profile	ZDM_AP_FP
Application-Specific Alert Profile Description	Demo Forecast Planning Alert Profile
Application-Specific Alert Profile	ZDM_AP_DP

Data Type	Data
Application-Specific Alert Profile Description	Demo Demand Planning Alert Profile
Macro	ZDM_MACRO: Total Forecast
Macro	ZDM_MACRO: Forecast Variation

Table 9.3: Business scenario data points in APO DP

Data Type	Data
Source System	ZDM_SS
Source System Description	Demo Source System
Infoarea	ZDM_INFOAREA
Infoarea Description	Demo Infoarea
Characteristic (InfoObject)	ZDM_REG
Characteristic (InfoObject) Description	Demo Char Region
Attribute for Char	ZDM_ATB
Attribute for Char Description	Demo Char Attr
Characteristic (InfoObject)	ZDM_DC
Characteristic (InfoObject) Description	Demo Char DC
Key Fig (InfoObject)	ZDM_QTY01
Key Fig (InfoObject) Description	Demo Key Fig Qty-1
Key Fig (InfoObject)	ZDM_QTY02
Key Fig (InfoObject) Description	Demo Key Fig Qty-2
Application Component	ZDM_AC
Application Component Description	Demo Appln Comp
Data Source	ZDM_DS
Data Source Description	Demo Data Source
InfoSource	ZDM_IS
InfoSource Description	Demo Infosource

Data Type	Data
InfoPackage	ZDM_IP
InfoPackage Description	Demo InfoPackage
DSO	ZDM_DSO
DSO Description	Demo DSO
Infocube	ZDM_IC
Infocube Description	Demo Infocube

Table 9.4: Business scenario data points in APO BW

Location	Location Code	Product Group	Product Group Code	Product	Product Code	City	Sales Organization Code	Region	Distribution Channel Code
Atlanta Manufacturing Plant	ZDM1	LCD TVs	ZDM_PG1	32" DM LCD 720p HDTV	ZDM_FG1	Atlanta, GA	5001	USA	10 & 20
Atlanta Manufacturing Plant	ZDM1	LCD TVs	ZDM_PG1	32" DM LCD 1080p HDTV	ZDM_FG2	Atlanta, GA	5001	USA	10 & 20
Atlanta Manufacturing Plant	ZDM1	LCD TVs	ZDM_PG1	39" DM LCD 1080p HDTV	ZDM_FG3	Atlanta, GA	5001	USA	10 & 20
Atlanta Manufacturing Plant	ZDM1	LED TVs	ZDM_PG2	40" DM LED 1080p HDTV	ZDM_FG4	Atlanta, GA	5001	USA	10 & 20
Frankfort Distribution Center	ZDD1	LCD TVs	ZDM_PG1	32" DM LCD 720p HDTV	ZDM_FG1	Frankfort, KY	5001	USA	10 & 20
Frankfort Distribution Center	ZDD1	LCD TVs	ZDM_PG1	32" DM LCD 1080p HDTV	ZDM_FG2	Frankfort, KY	5001	USA	10 & 20
Frankfort Distribution Center	ZDD1	LCD TVs	ZDM_PG1	39" DM LCD 1080p HDTV	ZDM_FG3	Frankfort, KY	5001	USA	10 & 20
Frankfort Distribution Center	ZDD1	LED TVs	ZDM_PG2	40" DM LED 1080p HDTV	ZDM_FG4	Frankfort, KY	5001	USA	10 & 20
Columbus Retail Store	ZDR1	LCD TVs	ZDM_PG1	32" DM LCD 720p HDTV	ZDM_FG1	Columbus, OH	5001	USA	10 & 20
Columbus Retail Store	ZDR1	LCD TVs	ZDM_PG1	32" DM LCD 1080p HDTV	ZDM_FG2	Columbus, OH	5001	USA	10 & 20
Columbus Retail Store	ZDR1	LCD TVs	ZDM_PG1	39" DM LCD 1080p HDTV	ZDM_FG3	Columbus, OH	5001	USA	10 & 20
Columbus Retail Store	ZDR1	LED TVs	ZDM_PG2	40" DM LED 1080p HDTV	ZDM_FG4	Columbus, OH	5001	USA	10 & 20
Philadelphia Retail Store	ZDR2	LCD TVs	ZDM_PG1	32" DM LCD 720p HDTV	ZDM_FG1	Philadelphia, PA	5001	USA	10 & 20
Philadelphia Retail Store	ZDR2	LCD TVs	ZDM_PG1	32" DM LCD 1080p HDTV	ZDM_FG2	Philadelphia, PA	5001	USA	10 & 20
Philadelphia Retail Store	ZDR2	LCD TVs	ZDM_PG1	39" DM LCD 1080p HDTV	ZDM_FG3	Philadelphia, PA	5001	USA	10 & 20
Philadelphia Retail Store	ZDR2	LED TVs	ZDM_PG2	40" DM LED 1080p HDTV	ZDM_FG4	Philadelphia, PA	5001	USA	10 & 20

Table 9.5: List of demand planning level entities at DM Consumer Appliances, Inc.

9.2 Important transaction codes

The important transaction codes in ERP as well as APO that are relevant for demand planning are noted in Table 9.6.

Transaction Code	Transaction Description
CFG1	Display CIF Application Log
CFG3	Find in Application Log
CFGD	Delete Application Log Entries
CFM1	Create Integration Model
CFM2	Manually Activate Integration Models
CFM3	Activate Integration Models (Background)

Transaction Code	Transaction Description
CFM4	Display Integration Models
CFM5	Integration Model Object Search
CFQ1	Display qRFC Monitor
MD04	Display Stock/Requirements Situation
MD07	Current Material Overview
MD61	Create Planned Independent Requirements
MD62	Change Planned Independent Requirements
MD63	Display Planned Independent Requirements
MD70	Copy Total Forecast
MD73	Display Total Independent Requirements
MM01	Create Material
MM02	Change Material
MM03	Display Material
MS64	Create Simulation Version
SLG1	Application Log: Display Logs
SM36	Schedule Background Job
SM37	Overview of job selection
SMQ1	qRFC Monitor (Outbound Queue)
SMQ2	qRFC Monitor (Inbound Queue)
SP01	Output Controller

Table 9.6: Important transaction codes in ERP ECC

Transaction Code	Transaction Description
/SAPAPO/AC05	Time Series
/SAPAPO/ADVM	Macro Workbench
/SAPAPO/AMON_REORG	Delete Database Alerts
/SAPAPO/AMON1	Alert Monitor
/SAPAPO/AMON3	Alert Monitor – Alert Overview
/SAPAPO/C3	Display Application Log

Transaction Code	Transaction Description
/SAPAPO/C6	Delete Application Log
/SAPAPO/CALENDAR	Calendar
/SAPAPO/CC	Core Interface Cockpit
/SAPAPO/CCR	CIF—Comparison/Reconciliation of Transaction Data
/SAPAPO/CONSCHK	Model Consistency Check
/SAPAPO/CPP	CIF Post-processing
/SAPAPO/CQ	SCM Queue Manager
/SAPAPO/DFCT	Maintain Distribution Function
/SAPAPO/DMP2	Generate Planned Independent Requirements
/SAPAPO/LCOUT	Release from SNP ⇨ DP
/SAPAPO/LOC_DEL_LOG	Location: Delete Application Log
/SAPAPO/LOC_DISP_LOG	Location: Display Application Log
/SAPAPO/LOC3	Master Data: Locations
/SAPAPO/MAT1	Product
/SAPAPO/MC62	Maintain Characteristic Values
/SAPAPO/MC77	Change Selection
/SAPAPO/MC8D	Mass Processing: Create Planning
/SAPAPO/MC8E	Mass Processing: Change Planning
/SAPAPO/MC8F	Delete Planning Job
/SAPAPO/MC8G	Schedule Mass Processing
/SAPAPO/MC8I	Mass Processing: Check Planning
/SAPAPO/MC8J	Copy Mass Processing Jobs
/SAPAPO/MC8K	Logs
/SAPAPO/MC8S	Transfer Profiles
/SAPAPO/MC8T	Activity
/SAPAPO/MC8U	Maintain Release Profile
/SAPAPO/MC8V	Calculate Proportional Factors
/SAPAPO/MC90	Release to Supply Network Planning
/SAPAPO/MC96B	Maintain Forecast Profile

Transaction Code	Transaction Description
/SAPAPO/MD74	Reorganization: Adapt Independent Requirements
/SAPAPO/MP31	Maintain Promotion Attribute Types
/SAPAPO/MP32	Maintain Cannibalization Group
/SAPAPO/MP33	Maintain Promotion Key Figures
/SAPAPO/MP34	Supply & Demand Planner: Initial Screen
/SAPAPO/MP40	Maintain Promotion Bases
/SAPAPO/MP42	Promotion Management
/SAPAPO/MSDP_ADMIN	Administration of DP and SNP
/SAPAPO/MSDP_FCST1	Lifecycle Settings
/SAPAPO/MSDP_FCST2	Assign Forecast Profiles
/SAPAPO/MVM	Model/Planning version
/SAPAPO/PERFMON	APO Application Monitor
/SAPAPO/PSTRUCONS	Planning Object Structure Consistency Check
/SAPAPO/RLCDEL	Delete Orders from LiveCache
/SAPAPO/RLGCOPY	Realignment
/SAPAPO/RRP3	Product View
/SAPAPO/SCC07	Supply Chain Engineer
/SAPAPO/SDP8B	Define Planning Book
/SAPAPO/SDP94	Interactive Demand Planning
/SAPAPO/SDPALPR	Assign Planners to Alert Profiles
/SAPAPO/SDPPLBK	Assign User to Planning Book
/SAPAPO/SDPUSET	SDP User Settings
/SAPAPO/SNP94	SNP: Interactive Planning
/SAPAPO/SNPFCST	Release SNP Forecast
/SAPAPO/TR30	Maintain DP/SNP Time Buckets Profile
/SAPAPO/TR32	Periodicities for Planning Area
/SAPAPO/TSCONS	Time Ser. Network Consistency Check
/SAPAPO/TSCOPY	Copy/Version Management
/SAPAPO/TSCUBE	Load Planning Area Version

Transaction Code	Transaction Description
/SAPAPO/TSINIT	Initialize Planning Area
/SAPAPO/TSINIT_KF	Initialize Time Series Key Figures
/SAPAPO/TSKEYFMAIN	Mass Maintenance. for Time Series Key Fig
/SAPAPO/TSLCREORG	Check LC Time Series Master Data
/SAPAPO/VERCOP	Copy Version
RSA1	Modeling – DW Workbench
RSMO	Data Load Monitor
RSPC	Process Chain Maintenance
SLG1	Application Log: Display Logs
SLG2	Application Log: Delete logs
SM37	Overview of job selection
SMQ1	qRFC Monitor (Outbound Queue)
SMQ2	qRFC Monitor (Inbound Queue)
SP01	Output Controller

Table 9.7: Important transaction codes in APO DP

9.3   Important tables

The important tables in ERP, as well as in APO, that are relevant for demand planning are noted in Table 9.8.

Table Name	Table Description
CIF_IMMARD	Integration Model Reference Table for Storage Location Stock
CIF_IMMAT	Integration Model Reference Table for Material
CIF_IMMSKA	Integration Model Reference Table for Sales Order Stock
CIF_IMOD	Basis Table of Integration Model for APO Interface
CIF_IMPIR	IMod Reference Table for Planned Independent Requirement
CIF_IMPLT	Integration Model Reference Table for Plants
MAKT	Material Descriptions

Table Name	Table Description
MARA	General Material Data
MARC	Plant Data for Material
MVKE	Sales Data for Material
PBED	Independent requirements data
PBHI	Independent requirements history
PBIM	Independent requirements for material
TRFCQIN	tRFC Queue Description (Inbound Queue)
TRFCQOUT	tRFC Queue Description (Outbound Queue)

Table 9.8: Important tables in ERP ECC

Table Name	Table Description
/SAPAPO/ADMAKRO	Advanced Macros
/SAPAPO/ADVM	Advanced Macros: Definition Views
/SAPAPO/AGGLEVEL	InfoCube: Aggregation Level
/SAPAPO/APO01	APO Planning Version
/SAPAPO/CBGPBODY	Contents of the Cannibalization Group
/SAPAPO/CBGPHEAD	Header Table for Cannibalization Group
/SAPAPO/CBPRF	Detail of Cannibalization Profile
/SAPAPO/CBPRFHD	Header Table of cannibalization Profile
/SAPAPO/CBPRFT	Text Table of Cannibalization Profile
/SAPAPO/DP_ACCUR	Profiles for Forecast Accuracy
/SAPAPO/DP_HEAD	Demand Planning Header
/SAPAPO/DP_SCHED	Demand Planning Schedule Line
/SAPAPO/DP440G	Master Forecast Profile
/SAPAPO/DP440P	Univariate Forecast Profile
/SAPAPO/FCST_VS	Number of Creatable Forecast Versions
/SAPAPO/FCSTACCU	Parameters for Forecast Accuracy
/SAPAPO/FCSTCHAR	Graphical Settings for Forecast
/SAPAPO/FCSTHEAD	Header Table for Forecast Results

Table Name	Table Description
/SAPAPO/FCSTOUTL	Outlier Correction Settings
/SAPAPO/FCSTPARA	Forecast Parameters
/SAPAPO/FCSTVALU	Forecast Results
/SAPAPO/FUN_RES	Results of Macro Steps and Conditions Within the Step
/SAPAPO/FUN_STEP	Macro steps
/SAPAPO/LISUP	Release Profile: Demand Planning to SNP
/SAPAPO/LOC	Locations
/SAPAPO/MATKEY	Product Master
/SAPAPO/MATLOC	Location product Master
/SAPAPO/MATMAP	Mapping Table for Products
/SAPAPO/MATMOD	Model assignment of location product
/SAPAPO/MF_HEAD	Header Table for Manual Forecast
/SAPAPO/MF_VALUE	Values Table for Manual Forecast
/SAPAPO/MODEL	Model
/SAPAPO/PAT	Alert types in an Alert Monitor profile
/SAPAPO/PBKEYHDR	Storage of Key Figures (Header Information)
/SAPAPO/PBKEYSTP	Storage of Key Figures, Periods
/SAPAPO/PBKEYVAL	Storage of Key Figures (Value Series)
/SAPAPO/PBMADVM	Defined Macros in Planning Book
/SAPAPO/PBMLCHA	Planning Book Worklist (Characteristics)
/SAPAPO/PBMLKEY	Planning Book Worklist (Key Figures)
/SAPAPO/PBMLKEYT	Text Table for Key Figures of a Planning Book
/SAPAPO/PBMSELID	Assigned Selections ⇨ Planning Book (Data View)
/SAPAPO/PBMVW	Existing Planning Books
/SAPAPO/PBMVWOBJ	Standard Objects for Planning Book
/SAPAPO/PHINPRF	Phase – In Profile
/SAPAPO/PHOUTPRF	Phase – Out Profile
/SAPAPO/PHPA	Assignment Planning Areas for Profile

Table Name	Table Description
/SAPAPO/PHVALUE	Value Table for Phase–In and Phase–Out Profiles
/SAPAPO/PROFTEXT	Forecast Profile Texts
/SAPAPO/PROMATTR	Attributes of Promotion
/SAPAPO/PROMAVAL	Attribute Values of Promotion Attributes
/SAPAPO/PROMBASE	Table for Promotion Bases
/SAPAPO/PROMBODY	Detail of Promotion
/SAPAPO/PROMHEAD	Promotion Plan
/SAPAPO/PROMKEYF	Key Figures for Promotion
/SAPAPO/PROMPOS	Value of Promotion
/SAPAPO/PROMTION	Table for Promotion
/SAPAPO/SDP_DB	Views + Selections for SDP Alert Profile (Database Alerts)
/SAPAPO/SDP_DYN	Views + Selections for SDP Alert Profile (Dynamic Alerts)
/SAPAPO/SDP_PROF	SDP Alert Profile
/SAPAPO/SDP_USER	Settings for Interactive Planning
/SAPAPO/SDPALERT	Assign Planner to Alert Profile in SDP
/SAPAPO/SDPSETKO	Header Information for User Settings
/SAPAPO/SDPTB	Table for Time Bucket Profile SNP/DP
/SAPAPO/SDPTSTR	Time Streams for SNP/DP
/SAPAPO/SHSDPUSR	User Settings for SDP Shuffler
/SAPAPO/T445PLBK	Planning Book Assignments – Users in Interactive Planning
/SAPAPO/TIMESERI	Time Series in Forecast
/SAPAPO/TSUPR3	Transfer Profile: Demand Planning to R/3
/SAPAPO/TSUPREL	Release Profile: Demand Planning to SNP
/SAPAPO/TSVERSIO	Planning Versions for Planning Area
/SAPAPO/V_ATSDP	Dynamic Alert Types for Demand Planning and SNP

Table 9.9: Important tables in APO DP

9.4 Important user exits and BADI functionality

The important user exits and BADIs in APO that are relevant for demand planning are noted in Table 9.10.

User Exit/ BADI Name	User Exit/ BADI Description	Type
/SAPAPO/ADVX	Use this BADI for complex calculations in Planning book	BADI
/SAPAPO/SCM_FCSTMAN	Manual Forecast	BADI
/SAPAPO/SCM_FCSTPARA	Forecast Parameters	BADI
/SAPAPO/SDP_AUTH_CHK	SDP: Authorization Check	BADI
/SAPAPO/SDP_BATCH	Enhancements for DP Background Jobs	BADI
/SAPAPO/SDP_CALC_PRP	Enhancements for Proportion Calculation	BADI
/SAPAPO/SDP_COLWIDTH	Planning Period Column Width Default	BADI
/SAPAPO/SDP_FCST	Enhancement for the forecast	BADI
/SAPAPO/SDP_FCST_EXT	External Forecast	BADI
/SAPAPO/SDP_FCST2	Extension forecast 2	BADI
/SAPAPO/SDP_FCST3	Enhancement for the forecast	BADI
/SAPAPO/SDP_FCST4	Save Forecast Versions in Background	BADI
/SAPAPO/SDP_FCST5	Forecast Selection Enhancements	BADI
/SAPAPO/SDP_FCSTAUTH	Customer–Specific Authorization Check for Forecasting	BADI
/SAPAPO/SDP_FCSTCURV	Forecast Graphic	BADI
/SAPAPO/SDP_FCSTERR	Forecast Errors	BADI
/SAPAPO/SDP_FIXWIDTH	Set Column Width for InfoObjects	BADI
/SAPAPO/SDP_IC_LOAD	Load Data from the InfoCube	BADI
/SAPAPO/SDP_INTERACT	SDP: Interactive Planning	BADI
/SAPAPO/SDP_IODJNM	SDP: InfoObjects	BADI
/SAPAPO/SDP_MASTER	Enhance Characteristic Value Combinations	BADI
/SAPAPO/SDP_NOTE	Notes Enhancement	BADI
/SAPAPO/SDP_REL_SNP	Data Modification During Release from SNP to DP	BADI

User Exit/ BADI Name	User Exit/ BADI Description	Type
/SAPAPO/SDP_RELDATA	Modification of Data During Release from DP to SNP – Orders	BADI
/SAPAPO/SDP_RLGCOPY	SDP: Realignment and Copy	BADI
/SAPAPO/SDP_SAVE	Data Save Operation Check	BADI
/SAPAPO/SDP_SELECTOR	Selection Check	BADI
EXIT_/SAPAPO/SAPLCIF_LOC_001	APO CIF Inbound – Location	User Exit
EXIT_/SAPAPO/SAPLCIF_PROD_001	APO CIF Inbound – Product	User Exit
EXIT_/SAPAPO/SAPLMCPF_003	User Exit for outlier check	User Exit
EXIT_SAPLCLOC_004	R/3 CIF Outbound – Location	User Exit
EXIT_SAPLCMAT_001	R/3 CIF Outbound – Material	User Exit

Table 9.10: Important user exits and BADIs in APO DP

9.5 Important SAP Notes

The important SAP Notes relevant for demand planning are covered in Table 9.11.

SAP Notes	Notes Description
16083	Standard jobs, reorganization jobs
153909	Demand Planning: Performance – Consulting
187455	Generation and activation of integration models in batch
195157	Application log: Deletion of logs
327725	Advice: Example of how to import external promotions
333243	Analysis of faulty definition and execution of macros
335771	Improvement of Program RAPOKZFX
350065	Consultation: User parameters in forecast
350381	Promotion: Report for updating active promotions
357789	Consulting: Horizons forecast and planning folder
359761	Demand Planning: loading performance data

SAP Notes	Notes Description
369007	qRFC: Configuration for the QIN Scheduler
372939	APO consulting: Compare forecast in interactive & batch mode
373756	Data extraction from a planning area
375566	Many entries in tRFC and qRFC tables
375965	APO Consulting: Alerts in forecast
378903	Queue status in SMQ1, SMQ2 and table ARFCRSTATE
386735	DP: Extract data to an IC with delta update
388260	APO Consulting forecast: Automatic model selection
390592	qRFC Monitoring (with documentation attached)
393763	Help for troubleshooting during R/3 – APO integration
394076	Consulting: USER-EXITS and BAdIs in the forecast
400330	Outbound Scheduler/qOUT Scheduler
403050	Consulting Note: Release from DP to SNP
410680	Unexpected Disaggregation Result
412429	Definition of jobs with macros
416475	APO CIF: Customizing for inbound queues
418801	Creating a User Exit Macro
420927	Data extraction of selected key figures
425825	Consistency checks, /sapapo/om17, /sapapo/cif_deltareport
426806	Memory/performance problems during data extraction
428102	Performance: Loading planning area version
434750	RAPOKZFX performance program
441269	Setting up tRFC/qRFC monitoring in the alert monitor (RZ20)
454644	Consultancy: Lock logic in promotion planning
482494	Loading data from liveCache: Performance optimization
492399	Realignment Consulting
495027	Changing delivered APO InfoObjects (9A*)
495166	Tips and Tricks for Handling Alert Monitor
500063	Overview of performance notes for the Alert Monitor

SAP Notes	Notes Description
503363	Use & management of fixed aggregates in Demand Planning
504620	Deletion of R/3 data that are no longer required in APO
506393	Conversion exits when creating characteristics combinations
512184	Background processing: Periodically delete job log
515120	Performance of extraction of InfoCube–based key figures
515523	Unexpected numerical results in Demand Planning
519014	Handling Planning Version Management
520876	Inconsistencies in time series objects
521639	Generation of DB Alerts in Background
527481	tRFC or qRFC calls are not processed
533755	Description of the delta logic or the program RIMODINI
539797	Collective consulting note on macros
539848	Collective consulting note on background processing in DP
540282	Collective consulting note on promotion planning
540571	Collective consulting note on data extraction in DP
540926	Collective consulting note on planning object structures
541189	Collective consulting note on selections in Demand Planning
541252	Collective consulting note for planning book maintenance
541618	Collective consulting note on BW and InfoObjects in DP
541633	Collective consulting note on interactive planning
541703	Collective consulting note on technical subjects in DP
546079	FAQ: Background jobs in Demand Planning
549184	FAQ: What is important for extraction
558995	Advice on consistency report for forecast profiles
563806	FAQ: APO CIF
568506	Collective consulting note on consumption of forecasts
568669	Collective consulting note on release DP – SNP
570397	Consulting: Workaround – Copying Planning Object Structures
571629	How does the note management work?

SAP Notes	Notes Description
572003	SCM operating concept
573127	Creating several char. combinations: /SAPAPO/MC62
576015	Collective Consulting Note for Demand Planning
593413	Termination of initial data transfer if errors occur
602484	Restrictions with CIF error handling/post-processing (CA)
758618	Disaggregation and rounding in DP
786446	Setting up qRFC queue names for CIF
830673	AMON: Some consulting issues when handling alert monitor
844456	AMON: Writing Alerts in background
848109	/SAPAPO/TS_PAREA_DE_INITIALIZE: Performance
864950	Performance problems in DP mass processing
884334	Alert monitor: Performance when you determine alerts
890623	Performance improvement with Lifecycle planning
892940	MC62 and generation of CVCs: performance improvement
897887	Performance improvement lifecycle planning
993572	Correction for Planning Area Initialization in background considering Key figure horizon
1068603	Handling of initial key figure values using macros
1385616	Do not execute programs RAPOKZFX and RCIFIMAX in parallel
1405656	Implementation recommendations for APO 7.0 DP
1614525	Consulting Note: Macro FIX_CALC()

Table 9.11: Important SAP Notes in APO DP

You have finished the book.

A   About the Authors

Avijit Dutta

Avijit is a senior Supply Chain Management (SCM) professional with experience in SAP Centers of Excellence, delivery management, business development, consultancy, engineering, and operations management. He has hands-on experience working on implementations, rollouts, support and transformational projects in SAP technology for multiple global customers.

Currently, he leads the SAP SCM Center of Excellence with a global leader in IT services, consulting, and business solutions where he is responsible for providing solutions and roadmaps to customers.

Avijit worked with public sector, private sector, and multinational companies. He has worked with Fortune 500 customers from a variety of industries. Avijit has extensive experience working with one of the world's largest steel manufacturing companies which has helped him relate his SCM technology prowess to business realities.

Avijit has been awarded and recognized for SCM expertise by his company and customers alike. He maintains a strong interest in business transformation through SCM technology solutions that continues to innovate and make a difference to business and life.

You can reach Avijit at *avijit1111@yahoo.com*

Shreekant Shiralkar

Shreekant is a senior management professional with extensive experience leading and managing business functions, as well as technology consulting.

Shreekant played critical part in multiple transformation programs for Bharat Petroleum Corporation Ltd. including designing their supply chain strategy. He developed SAP Technology business for Tata Consultancy Services Ltd. by winning strategic clients in new & existing geographies, creating innovative service offerings, and playing a key role in organizational restructuring and formation of Industry Solution Unit.

Shreekant has established, developed, and diversified businesses, both within India and globally for fortune 500 firms. He established the public service business in India for Accenture, launched and developed the Shell Gas business in India for a JV of Shell.

Shreekant is author of best seller books & white papers on technology and holds patents for innovations.

You can reach Shreekant at *S_Shiralkar@yahoo.com*

B Index

C Disclaimer

This publication contains references to the products of SAP SE.

SAP, R/3, SAP NetWeaver, Duet, PartnerEdge, ByDesign, SAP BusinessObjects Explorer, StreamWork, and other SAP products and services mentioned herein as well as their respective logos are trademarks or registered trademarks of SAP SE in Germany and other countries.

Business Objects and the Business Objects logo, BusinessObjects, Crystal Reports, Crystal Decisions, Web Intelligence, Xcelsius, and other Business Objects products and services mentioned herein as well as their respective logos are trademarks or registered trademarks of Business Objects Software Ltd. Business Objects is an SAP company.

Sybase and Adaptive Server, iAnywhere, Sybase 365, SQL Anywhere, and other Sybase products and services mentioned herein as well as their respective logos are trademarks or registered trademarks of Sybase, Inc. Sybase is an SAP company.

SAP SE is neither the author nor the publisher of this publication and is not responsible for its content. SAP Group shall not be liable for errors or omissions with respect to the materials. The only warranties for SAP Group products and services are those that are set forth in the express warranty statements accompanying such products and services, if any. Nothing herein should be construed as constituting an additional warranty.

More Espresso Tutorials Books

Claudia Jost:

First Steps in the SAP® Purchasing Processes (MM)

- ▶ Compact manual for the SAP procurement processes
- ▶ Comprehensive example with numerous illustrations
- ▶ Master data, purchase requirements and goods receipt in context

http://5016.espresso-tutorials.com/

Matthew Johnson:

SAP® Material Master — A Practical Guide

- ▶ Understand SAP Master concepts
- ▶ Maximize your value stream through SAP Materials Management (MM)
- ▶ Walk through practical implementation examples

http://5028.espresso-tutorials.com

Björn Weber:

First Steps in the SAP® Production Processes (PP)

- ▶ Compact manual for discrete production in SAP
- ▶ Comprehensive example with numerous illustrations
- ▶ Master data, resource planning and production orders in context

http://5027.espresso-tutorials.com/

Stephen Birchall:

Invoice Verification for SAP®

- ▶ Learn everything you need for invoice verification and its role in FI and MM
- ▶ Keep user input to a minimum and automate the process
- ▶ Discover best practices to configure and maximize the use of this function

http://5073.espresso-tutorials.com

Uwe Goehring:

SAP® Capacity Planning

▶ Deep dive into capacity planning functionality in SAP ERP

▶ Options for capacity scheduling in SAP ERP

▶ Automatic resource and material scheduling with SAP APO

▶ Tips for incorporating capacity management into your operations strategy

http://5080.espresso-tutorials.com/

Tobias Götz, Anette Götz:

Transportation Management with SAP®

▶ Supported business processes

▶ Best practices

▶ Integration aspects and architecture

▶ Comparison and differentiation to similar SAP components

http://5082.espresso-tutorials.com/

Kevin Riddell, Rajen Iyver:

Practical Guide to SAP® GTS

▶ Compliance Management

▶ Legal Control — Export and Import

▶ Customs and Risk Management

▶ System Administration

http:/5100.espresso-tutorials.com/

Avijit Dutta, Shreekant Shiralkar:

Demand Planning with SAP® APO—Execution

▶ Step-by-Step Explanations and Easy to Follow Instructions

▶ Combination of Theory, Business Relevance and 'How to' Approach

▶ APO DP Execution Explained using a Business Scenario

▶ Centralized Process Flow Diagram to Illustrate Integration

http://5106.espresso-tutorials.com

Made in the USA
Lexington, KY
01 April 2015